MESTIZAJE

STUDIES IN LATINO/A CATHOLICISM

A series sponsored by the
Center for the Study of Latino/a Catholicism
University of San Diego

Previously published

Orlando O. Espín and Miguel H. Díaz, editors, *From the Heart of Our People: Latino/a Explorations in Catholic Systematic Theology*

Raúl Gómez-Ruíz, *Mozarabs, Hispanics, and the Cross*

Orlando O. Espín and Gary Macy, editors, *Futuring Our Past: Explorations in the Theology of Tradition*

María Pilar Aquino and Maria José Rosado-Nunes, editors, *Feminist Intercultural Theology: Latina Explorations for a Just World*

Studies in Latino/a Catholicism Series

MESTIZAJE

(RE)MAPPING RACE, CULTURE, AND FAITH IN LATINA/O CATHOLICISM

NÉSTOR MEDINA

ORBIS BOOKS

Maryknoll, New York 10545

Founded in 1970, Orbis Books endeavors to publish works that enlighten the mind, nourish the spirit, and challenge the conscience. The publishing arm of the Maryknoll Fathers and Brothers, Orbis seeks to explore the global dimensions of the Christian faith and mission, to invite dialogue with diverse cultures and religious traditions, and to serve the cause of reconciliation and peace. The books published reflect the views of their authors and do not represent the official position of the Maryknoll Society. To learn more about Maryknoll and Orbis Books, please visit our website at www.maryknollsociety.org.

Published by Orbis Books, Maryknoll, NY 10545–0308.

Manufactured in the United States of America
Manuscript editing and typesetting by Joan Weber Laflamme.

Library of Congress Cataloging-in-Publication Data

Medina, Néstor.
    Mestizaje : (re)mapping race, culture, and faith in latina/o catholicism / Néstor Medina.
       p. cm. — (Studies in latino/a catholicism series)
       Includes bibliographical references and index.
       ISBN 978-1-57075-834-8 (pbk.)
    1. Hispanic American theology. 2. Mestizaje—Religious aspects—Christianity. 3. Catholic Church—Doctrines. I. Title.
       BT83.575.M43 2009
       230.089'68073—dc22
                                2009009509

Contents

Acknowledgments

Words are insufficient to describe my gratitude for my life partner, Samia Saad, my best friend and colleague. Thank you for your untiring support all these years. Your keen eye and perceptive critique continue to challenge me to remain authentic in my academic work and my commitment to justice. I look forward to what the future has in store for us.

I am especially grateful to the University of San Diego's Center for the Study of Latina/o Catholicism for sponsoring the publication of this book as part of its series with Orbis Books. I am also indebted to the Hispanic Theological Initiative for its support and for creating the space for interacting with Latina/o colleagues and friends. I thank Joanne Rodríguez, the director of the HTI, for her friendship and encouragement throughout these years.

I thank Professor Orlando Espín for his wisdom as my mentor and friend. When I was truly alone, he came and believed in me, for which I thank him heartily. Finally, I am grateful to Professor Lee Cormie for his accompaniment throughout the process of writing this volume. His wisdom, encouragement, and dedication challenged me often to remain grounded and not to lose my voice amid the tumultuous world of scholarly work.

Introduction

U.S. Latina/o theologians are at a crossroads. The rapid changes in the social and political context of the United States and the increasing difficulty of speaking about the U.S. Latina/o population because of its ethnic and cultural reconfiguration present serious challenges to U.S. Latina/o theologians conjecturing the future course of U.S. Latina/o theology. This makes it increasingly necessary to review and interrogate earlier U.S. Latina/o theological articulations of ethnic and cultural identity, particularly their use of the category of *mestizaje*.

Contextualizing their reflections on the U.S. Latina/o population experiences of faith in God, and deeply indebted to Latin American liberation theology, U.S. Latina/o theologians understood theology as "the critical reflection on the praxis" of the people, a praxis that thanks to their different sociopolitical, cultural, and historical contexts, Goizueta reminds us, would need to reflect "explicitly and systematically on the praxis of the U.S. Latino/a [communities]." These communities are not homogeneous. Their wide range of ethnic, cultural, and religious traditions contribute to the richness and complexity of U.S. Latina/o theology.

Consistent with their liberation heritage, U.S. Latina/o scholars put the people at the center of the theological task. The people's reality of oppression, marginalization, and praxis of resistance served as the privileged center of theological reflection. These theologians challenged traditional approaches to theology by emphasizing that religious symbols, traditions, and faith expressions of the people are at the center of their theological articulations. People's concrete expressions of their faith in God are also known as popular religion.

Such faith expressions are by definition also cultural expressions, with culture being the avenue through which these people resist in their everyday activities the assimilationist power of the U.S. dominant Anglo culture. It is in these privileged spaces, say the theologians, that the divine is encountered in refreshingly new ways and where people find in God a source of strength to resist oppressive forces. For U.S. Latina/o theologians, ethnic and cultural identity is therefore central for theological inquiry.

Ethnic and cultural identity is a source of great creativity for U.S. Latina/o theologians because of their connection to their communities, their histories, and their experience as marginalized peoples in the United States. By highlighting their ethnic and cultural identity, U.S. Latina/o theologians have reclaimed their own histories and asserted the theological import of their distinct faith experiences. Yet, ethnocultural identity is presently a great source of tension among U.S. Latina/o scholars and communities; what should or can be included in the concept of U.S. Latina/o identity? Part of the difficulty relates to the use of the labels *Latina/o* and *Hispanic*, which conceal the rich diversity of peoples subsumed under these classifications.

U.S. Latina/o does not refer to Latin Americans or Latin American immigrants in the United States. There are certainly Latin American immigrants among Latinas/os in the United States, but they do not form the bulk of the Latina/o population. Most Latinas/os have regional roots that go far back before the independence of the United States or the Mexico–United States war in 1848. And many sectors of the population that identify with Puerto Rico, Cuba, and other Latin American countries are represented by second, third, and even fourth generations born in the United States. Therefore, *Latina/o theology* refers specifically to theology done by U.S. scholars, most of whom were born in the United States and who ethnically and culturally self-identify as U.S. Latinas/os. Although they have had and continue to have deep historical connections with Latin America, they do not understand themselves to be under the umbrella designation Latin American.

The tensions among the diverse communities represented by U.S. Latina/o theology are also reflected in the various other names U.S. Latina/o scholars use to identify women and their theological contributions. Ada María Isasi-Díaz, for example, proposed the term *mujerista* to distinguish her work from Anglo U.S. feminist theology. María Pilar Aquino suggests the use of the term *feminista*, to establish bridges with the work of other scholars in Latin America. Loida Martell-Otero uses the term *mujeres evangélicas* to highlight Protestant women's experiences and voices among U.S. Latina/o theologians. These continuing contributions show an ongoing concern among U.S. Latina/o scholars.

Among U.S. Latina/o theologians, the centrality of their culture to their identity has also provoked a systematic rereading of the biblical text and of the various theological traditions these scholars have inherited. According to Justo González, the U.S. Latina/o theological project does not represent issues pertinent only to the U.S. Latina/o communities. It also represents a reconfiguration of the theological task, methods, and sources, a rethinking of the traditions they inherited. This means, he writes, that "every point of theology, doctrine, and biblical interpretation is open to reinspection and rereading."

This rereading of theology and the Bible includes questions of class, gender, culture, and "race," pointing to the manner in which traditional forms of theology and biblical interpretation have contributed to the present condition of marginalization of the U.S. Latinas/os. Moreover, by reclaiming their own history as one characterized by sociocultural marginalization, U.S. Latina/o theologians found in the biblical text a message of hope and liberation from their condition of oppression. As a result, they have articulated systematically, in depth, creatively, and with sophistication their communities' faith experiences and religious expressions.

By reclaiming their history, U.S. Latina/o theologians have also reclaimed their historical experience of biological and cultural intermixture commonly known as *mestizaje*. Originally used to describe the children born from the mixture of indigenous and Spanish and Portuguese peoples in Latin America, today *mestizaje* is used more broadly around the world to describe similar experiences of biological and cultural intermixture. The adoption of *mestizaje* by U.S. Latina/o theologians was not accidental. The initial consideration for adopting *mestizaje* was that the U.S. Latina/o population shared with Latin America the experience of the Spanish invasion and conquest that resulted in the original intermixture with the indigenous peoples. It is for this reason that in this study I keep the context and realities of Latin America and the U.S. Latinas/os closely connected as I deal with issues related to the discourse of *mestizaje*.

U.S. Latina/o theologians' adoption and appropriation of *mestizaje* involved a complex, painful, and creative process of identity formation to name themselves in contrast to the dominant U.S. Anglo culture. A term that was originally used in derogatory ways they redeemed as a term by which to reclaim their ethnic and cultural dignity as a people. Adopting *mestizaje* gave them a way in which to speak theologically about U.S. Latina/o culture, identity, experience of marginalization and oppression, and the people's religious expressions. By adopting *mestizaje*, these scholars not only named themselves but also resisted the U.S. government's attempt to erase their cultural heritage—as well as taking a prophetic posture unmasking their reality of social marginalization and exploitation.

As U.S. Latina/o theologians engaged and developed *mestizaje* discourse, they broadened its meaning and applicability. But in asserting their distinctiveness from the sociocultural and theological context of Latin America, these scholars failed to pay attention to the Latin American context and hegemonic expressions of *mestizaje*. Seeking to establish parallels between the original experience of discrimination of the *mestizo/a* children by their indigenous and Spanish ancestors during the colonial times in Latin America and their own experience of marginalization in the United States, Latina/o theologians, I suggest, uncritically adopted *mestizaje*.

How did this come about? Paying little attention to the historical and sociocultural developments taking place in Latin America, U.S. Latina/o theologians adopted a romantic and idealized understanding of *mestizaje*. In attempting to articulate *mestizaje* as a reconciling force, for example, Mexican American Virgilio Elizondo turned the children of the "original" *mestizaje* into the "reconciling result and alternative" to the violence of the conquest. It is an alternative expressed concretely in the symbol of Our Lady of Guadalupe; Elizondo claims Guadalupe as the *mestizo/a* symbol par excellence, but tellingly says very little about the uneven power relations and dynamics in which Guadalupe became such an important religious symbol for the *mestizo/a* and indigenous peoples of Mexico. Likewise, María Pilar Aquino argues that dealing with *mestizaje* "is a historical fact that still opens up *old* wounds" (emphasis added). But is the history of violence and discrimination that accompanied the birth of the *mestizo/a* people only something of the past? Recent scholarship emerging from Latin America suggests it is very much part of the present! In the Latin American context, the dominant notion of *mestizaje* hides the violence perpetrated against the indigenous and African peoples and is often used to justify constructing a *mestizo/a* society.

This book elucidates the tensions and contradictions in the theological use of *mestizaje* by U.S. Latina/o theologians. I suggest that in promoting the construction of a more inclusive society, these theologians uncritically adopted and appropriated a reified notion of a dual *mestizaje* as a single continuous process by which intermixture-*mestizaje* meant the inclusion of diverse cultural groups and represented the removal of racist tendencies. Without paying attention to the internal tensions within the U.S. Latina/o population due to ethnocultural diversity, and by uncritically adopting the term without examining its larger debates in Latin America, these theologians unwittingly reinscribed notions of exclusion, homogenization, and marginalization of the indigenous and African peoples and voices from other ethnic and cultural traditions. By presenting a homogeneous *mestizo/a* U.S. Latina/o community, U.S. Latina/o theologians occluded the internal tensions and different types of racism within the U.S. Latina/o populations. Such representations of a homogeneous population, I claim, deny different cultural groups within the Latina/o communities a social and discursive space outside of the dominant notions of *mestizaje*.

I make this claim in four ways. First, I show how U.S. Latina/o theologians used *mestizaje* to articulate the sociocultural and political experience of marginalization, to resist the dominant assimilatory culture of the United States, and to give voice to the religious expressions of the U.S. Latina/o communities. Second, in more detail, I examine some of the affirmations that prominent

U.S. Latina/o theologians and Chicano/a scholars make about *mestizaje*, which leave them open to the criticism of adopting romantic reified notions of *mestizaje* when compared to the Latin American context and the present U.S. Latina/o social context. Third, I demonstrate how U.S. Latina/o theologians are confronting the challenges and tensions in the theological use of *mestizaje* in light of the rapidly changing social and political context of the United States. For example, I attend to recent criticisms of *mestizaje* emerging from Latin American women and from the indigenous and African communities. And fourth, I discuss some of the implications of these critiques of *mestizaje* as they pertain to future developments of U.S. Latina/o theology. My goal is to problematize the notion that there is one finished, albeit double, *mestizaje* and to suggest instead that *mestizaje* be spoken of in the plural and in light of the historical context out of which it emerges. In so doing I affirm the need for U.S. Latina/o theologians to engage in interreligious and intercultural conversations, taking the rich, different ethnic and cultural traditions of the population as conversation partners in the struggle to building a more inclusive society.

The first chapter of this work traces briefly some of the historical circumstances that facilitated the irruption of U.S. Latina/o theology. I highlight how U.S. Latina/o theologians creatively appropriated the experience of *mestizaje* as a space within which to name themselves and provide the diverse Latina/o communities a sense of cohesiveness as people. Their adoption of *mestizaje* discourse prompted U.S. Latina/o theologians to reclaim and revise their history of violence, conquest, oppression, and resistance. In doing so, U.S. Latina/o theologians initiated an innovative and creative theological process, a process that resulted in significant contributions to biblical hermeneutics, popular religious discussions, and theological methodology. U.S. Latina/o theologians' unique approach to the areas above will serve as background to highlight the creative and relatively new expression of U.S. Latina/o theology, as they challenged traditional approaches to theology as well as engaged in the struggle for justice and against marginalization.

In Chapter 2, I engage the theological proposals of four specific U.S. Latina/o theologians as they relate to *mestizaje*, highlighting the innovative character of their proposals, identifying the assumptions they make about *mestizaje*, and then also showing the limitations of their assertions. What tensions, gaps, and contradictions are there in U.S. Latina/o scholars' idealized notions of *mestizaje* that do not match the historical reality and context of Latina/o communities? This discussion continues into Chapter 3, with an analysis of self-identified Chicano/a scholarship. How did the work of José Vasconcelos influence the work of these scholars so as to provide the framework for articulating and conceiving *mestizaje* as the utopian direction of humanity where racist tendencies disappear and the inclusion of peoples from different cultural and ethnic groups takes place?

Chapter 4 examines the ambiguous character of *mestizaje* in recent debates among U.S. Latina/o theologians. I show how subsequent generations of U.S. Latina/o scholars appropriated the use of *mestizaje* and engaged in a more critical examination of the use of the term as they came to grips with the changing cultural and sociopolitical context of the U.S. Latina/o population. The second portion of this chapter outlines the particular indictments that recent scholarship in Latin America levels against the use of *mestizaje;* indigenous peoples, African descendants, and women reject romantic notions of *mestizaje*. These criticisms are points of entry for U.S. Latina/o theologians to engage in the painstaking task of evaluating their own theological articulations of *mestizaje*.

Finally, in Chapter 5, I briefly describe some of the concrete contributions that this study of *mestizaje* offers, and some of their implications for future developments of U.S. Latina/o theology. I dispel notions of a single, finished—albeit double—*mestizaje*. When considering the diverse cultural and ethnic constituency of the U.S. Latina/o and Latin American populations, it is more appropriate to speak of a plurality of processes of intermixture-*mestizajes*. Any process of intermixture must be interrogated as a plurality of processes of conflict and interaction, and such relations are always colored by power structures that reflect the interest of those with power. Focusing on the symbol of Guadalupe, I illustrate the complexity, ambiguity, and contested character of the *mestizo/a* interpretation of this important symbol when read from the perspective of the indigenous peoples. Finally, anticipating the future of U.S. Latina/o theology, I suggest pluri-vocal approaches to the theological task in order to engage as theological partners the various ethnic, cultural, and religious traditions within the U.S. Latina/o and Latin American peoples. The focus here is on the need for U.S. Latina/o theology to engage in deeper and intercultural intra-Latina/o approaches to theology, and the creation of intra-Latina/o interreligious conversations in order to recognize the influence and impact of the non-Christian roots among the U.S. Latina/o communities.

Most of my reflections in this study correspond to the articulations of *mestizaje* by self-identified Latina/o Catholic scholars. But U.S. Latina/o theology does not include only Catholics. Latina/o Protestants have also engaged and adopted *mestizaje*; their concerns and questions differ from those of their Catholic counterparts. Such study deserves its own analysis, but I do not engage it here. Thus, while there are great overlaps in the assumptions both groups of scholars make about the condition and idea of *mestizaje*, and my remarks must be understood as pertaining to Latina/o Catholic expressions and articulations of *mestizaje*, at some key points I allude to important Latina/o Protestant theologians and scholars to illustrate the extent to which *mestizaje* has become an understanding widely used by Latina/o theologians.

The background of this study on *mestizaje* is my acute awareness that the world is at a crucial moment of reconfiguration of peoples, cultures, identities, and ideas. The present reality of relocation of masses of people and the shrinking of the world or shortening of distances by way of technological developments in transportation, telecommunications, and the media contribute to an unprecedented (wanted and unwanted) clash and interaction of peoples from different places in the world.

More than ever before, we witness people from different ethnocultural and religious backgrounds thrown together and establishing relationships at the everyday level. As a result, it is becoming increasingly difficult to delimit the parameters of personal and ethnocultural identity. With the explosion of free-market economies and migration we are creating new ways for considering political borders, citizenship, and nationalism. These phenomena force us to reconfigure the way we understand, conceive, and articulate ethnocultural and political identities, construct society, and conceive religious expressions. They present us with concrete challenges for (re)thinking the implications and dynamics surrounding the encounters of peoples.

In other words, while this book is certainly significant for the U.S. Latina/o communities and theologians, it has implications far beyond that, to different world communities that have experienced and continue to experience the phenomena of intermixtures of peoples, ethnicities, and cultures. This work marks the celebration of nascent discussions of intermixture and interaction of cultures, ethnicities, and identities, particularly the central role of religion and faith experiences in their development. And the U.S. Latina/o theological discussions of *mestizaje* are a welcome contribution to these larger debates, including its analogues such as hybridity, creolization, negritude, and *mulataje*. This is particularly important in light of the present dangers of the commodification of differences by the forces of globalized capital systems. As Breny Mendoza warns us:

In the present, the process of globalization led by the United States and the quasi imperial economic, political, cultural and juridical reordering that characterizes it, requires racial theories that translate yesterday's biological fundamentalism into a multiculturalism or hybridity that allows the global commodification of the distinct races and cultures of the world—even when it does not bring to an end racial segregation under the regime of capitalist accumulation.

In following the development of *mestizaje* discourses and debates I share the concerns raised by liberation theologies, broadly understood, in unmasking the sociopolitical and economic structures that have led to marginalization, discrimination, and exploitation of entire communities in Latin America. Thus, I seek to show how the use of *mestizaje* can become a mechanism of liberation and/or oppression. I likewise use the framework of postcolonial studies, particularly its critical trajectory, teasing out the "Western" cultural elements that have influenced and continue to have a profound impact upon the construction of the U.S. Latina/o communities and identities and on the articulation of *mestizaje* discourse. Thus, I also seek to identify some of the ways in which *mestizaje* can become a tool of resistance against or continuation of the empire. I do not engage in a thoroughgoing liberationist or cultural study here, but I use these methods to guide my analysis of *mestizaje* discourse and its developments over time, and to understand and evaluate the manner in which *mestizaje* has been used theologically by U.S. Latina/o scholars.

Many of the ideas and reality addressed by the use of *mestizaje* in its biological, cultural, social, and political dimensions share strong discursive connections with *mulataje*. Originally used to speak about the intermixture between the African slaves and the Spanish conquistadors, *mulataje* shares key historical, biological, cultural, ideological, and sociopolitical reference points with *mestizaje*. But, while I will make occasional references to *mulataje*, I do not believe the two terms are interchangeable or synonymous. The discourse of *mulataje* has its own history and historical subjects, so it cannot be subsumed under a discussion of *mestizaje*. In discussing *mestizaje* I do not pretend to include the specific racialized cultural and sociopolitical issues pertaining to the historical African presence in Latin America and among Latinas/os. Nevertheless, while I do not intend this work to deal with the specific issues and concerns surrounding *mulataje*, in many ways much of what can be said about *mestizaje* is also relevant to the debates surrounding *mulataje*.

In this study I engage primarily U.S. Latina/o scholars in the Catholic tradition because they have incorporated *mestizaje* substantially in their theological work. They are part of the generation out which U.S. Latina/o theology first emerged. Protestant Latina/o scholars (for example, Justo González, Luis Pedraja, and Loida Martell-Otero) have raised similar concerns, questions, and discussions of *mestizaje* in theology. Their treatment of *mestizaje* deserves serious examination. But that is beyond the scope of this work. For this reason, while I make allusions to some of their writings, my remarks should be construed as primarily to reflect questions and debates among Catholic U.S. Latina/o scholars.

As is true of most authors, this work is about me. It is about the sources available in my journey toward (re)discovering and reclaiming my life story, and how they help me understand some of the gaps I found in traditional and contemporary ways of understanding personal and ethnocultural identity, including the discourse of *mestizaje* in theology and church. The considerations raised in this project were born out of a personal search for more adequate ways of describing who I am in relation to the different identity spaces I inhabit. In doing so, I have been forced to rethink and (re)claim my sense of identity, consciously aware of the gaps and tensions I have experienced in attempting to define myself as Guatemalan, Canadian, with American indigenous, Moroccan African, Spanish, and Italian roots, and Pentecostal with a Catholic and Presbyterian background.

Since I began this study I have become acutely aware of the particular intermixtures I have experienced. As a Guatemalan immigrant who lived in the United States and who has made Canada his home, I am not unfamiliar with the questions, concerns, and significance of the debates on *mestizaje*. Also, since the beginning of my doctoral studies, U.S. Latina/o theologians and colleagues have welcomed my presence among them and have invited me to participate in some of their conferences. This has fostered great relationships with some of them and has informed my own sense of identity. So I approach this project with the sensitivities of an insider, but mindful that I am also an outside critic, a representative of a new breed of Latino/a theologians that is just beginning to emerge in the context of Canada.

Finally, for the sake of clarity and consistency the first mention of an author will include both first name and surname; the last name only will be indicated in subsequent instances. In accordance with Latina/o and Latin American common practice, I mention the author's first name along with both last names, when available. Subsequent instances have only the two last names, following the alphabetical order of the first last name in the bibliography at the end. Also, unless otherwise indicated, all the English translations made from sources written in Spanish, Portuguese, and French are mine.

Works Cited

Alvar, Manuel. *Léxico del mestizaje hispanoamericano*. Madrid: Ediciones Cultura Hispánica, Instituto de Cooperación Iberoamericana, 1987.

Aquino, María Pilar. "The Collective 'Dis-Covery' of Our Own Power: Latina American Feminist Theology." In *Hispanic / Latino Theology:*

Challenge and Promise, ed. Ada María Isasi-Díaz and Fernando Segovia, 240–60. Minneapolis: Fortress Press, 1996.

————. "Theological Method in US Latino/a Theology: Toward an Intercultural Theology for the Third Millennium." In *From the Heart of Our People: Latino/a Explorations in Catholic Systematic Theology*, ed. Orlando O. Espín and Miguel H. Díaz, 6–48. Maryknoll, NY: Orbis Books, 1999.

Bloemraad, Irene. "Who Claims Dual Citizenship? The Limits of Postnationalism, the Possibilities of Transnationalism, and the Persistence of Traditional Citizenship." *The International Migration Review* 38, no. 2 (Summer 2004): 389–426.

De La Torre, Miguel A., and Edwin David Aponte. *Introducing Latino/a Theologies*. Maryknoll, NY: Orbis Books, 2001.

Elizondo, Virgilio. "Our Lady of Guadalupe as a Cultural Symbol." In *Beyond Borders: The Writings of Virgilio Elizondo and Friends*, ed. Timothy Matovina, 118–25. Maryknoll, NY: Orbis Books, 2000.

Goizueta, Roberto S. "Hispanic." In *Dictionary of Third World Theologies*, ed. Virginia Fabella and R. S. Sugirtharajah, 212–14. Maryknoll, NY: Orbis Books, 2000.

González, Justo L. "Latino/a Theology." In *Handbook of U.S. Theologies of Liberation*, ed. Miguel A. De La Torre, 204–17. St. Louis: Chalice Press, 2004.

Gracia, Jorge J. E. *Hispanic/Latino Identity: A Philosophical Perspective*. Malden, MA: Blackwell Publishers, 2000.

Itzigsohn, José. "Immigration and the Boundaries of Citizenship: The Institutions of Immigrants' Political Transnationalism." *The International Migration Review* 34, no. 4 (Winter 2000): 1126–54.

Klor de Alva, J. Jorge. "Colonialism and Postcolonialism as (Latin) American Mirages." *Colonial Latin American Review* 1, no. 2 (1992): 3–23.

Mendoza, Breny. "La desmitologización del mestizaje en Honduras: Evaluando nuevos aportes," 2001. http://www.denison.edu/collaborations/istmo/n08/articulos/desmitologizacion.html (accessed January 15, 2006).

Phelan, John L. "El orígen de la idea de Latinoamérica." Translated by Josefina Z. Vásquez. In *De Colón a Martí: Discurso y Cultura en América Latina*, ed. Olmedo España Calderón, 183–99. Colección Fundamentos. Guatemala City: Editorial Óscar de León Palacios, 1993.

Segovia, Fernando F. "Introduction: Aliens in the Promised Land: The Manifest Destiny of U.S. Hispanic American Theology." In *Hispanic/Latino Theology: Challenge and Promise*, ed. Ada María Isasi-Díaz and Fernando F. Segovia, 15–44. Minneapolis: Fortress Press, 1996.

Téllez, Dora María. *¡Muera la gobierna!: Colonización en Matagalpa y Jinotega (1820–1890)*. Managua, Nicaragua: Universidad de las Regiones Autónomas de la Costa Caribe Nicaragüense, 1999.

I

MESTIZAJE AS A *LOCUS THEOLOGICUS*

The Contributions of U.S. Latina/o Theologians to the Task of Doing Theology

> "Mestizaje" in the Americas seems to refer
> to both a strategic social construct and a
> generic but ambiguous type of collective
> identity. Acting strategically, mestizaje can
> function as a register (e.g., a myth) through
> which a new people can be brought into
> existence, or as an elucidating metaphor
> that helps to make sense of the masking that
> goes on when fusion fails to take place as
> different peoples meet under asymmetrical
> conditions.
>
> —J. JORGE KLOR DE ALVA

During the 1970s Mexican American theologians came up
with the notion of *mestizaje* in order to articulate the experience
of faith of the Mexican American people. They realized this was
inseparable from unmasking the conditions of impoverishment
and oppression these people experienced. Participating in the
struggle for social justice became a prerequisite to theological
articulations. At the same time, Puerto Rican and Cuban American theologians were beginning to show some interest in developing a U.S. theology for themselves. But it was only in the 1980s

that some Cuban Americans and in the 1990s that some Puerto Ricans expanded the notion of *mestizaje* beyond its mainly racial connotations to emphasize the centrality of culture. The Mexican American Virgilio Elizondo had already written about *mestizaje*, so his work figured prominently among other Mexican American theologians. As coalitions were built between Mexican American and the Cuban American theologians, Elizondo's proposal of *mestizaje* was turned into a useful theological category.[1] These theologians began to conceive of themselves as *mestizos/as*, affirming the centrality of culture and ethnic identity for the theological task. In so doing they carved a new sociopolitical and cultural space for themselves. They named themselves as a people and took a prophetic stance of resistance against the assimilationist dominant culture of the United States.

By adopting the category of *mestizaje*, U.S. Latina/o theologians were able to engage in a fruitful process of theological creativity. They gave their own theological task new impetus and direction by affirming the unique experiences and expressions of faith among the U.S. Latina/o communities. Their innovative proposals engendered a critique of dominant versions of theology by taking as their point of departure the way a particular people live the Christian faith, conceive of God, and interpret these experiences in light of their cultural traditions and ethnic identities. These theologians also challenged notions of pastoral practices that fail to incorporate people's cultural milieus and elements. In doing so these theologians carved a new religious space for themselves amid social injustice and marginalization in U.S. society and academy.

In this chapter I examine the way in which U.S. Latina/o theologians, searching for new and fresh ways for reflecting upon the Christian faith amid the struggle for social justice, deployed *mestizaje* as a fruitful category for constructing a collective identity and critiquing the dominant sociopolitical, ethnocultural, ideological, and religious context of the United States. In articulating the faith experiences and expressions of the U.S. Latina/o communities in terms of *mestizaje*, these theologians created a theological space from which they made and continue to make rich contributions to the task of doing theology. At the same time they challenged dominant approaches to doing theology that fail to take into consideration the central role of ethnic and cultural identity in people's faith experiences.

SETTING THE CONTEXT

U.S. Latina/o theology movements emerged at a time of many challenges for the task of doing theology. Many movements irrupted during the 1960s such as the civil rights movement, the Chicano Student Movement of Aztlán (MEChA), and the United Farm Workers movement. It was also during this time that the World Council of Churches began raising important questions on missions, evangelism, and our understanding of inculturation. The Second Vatican Council had finished in 1965, and it had redefined the understanding of the Catholic Church, missions, and the important role of the laity for evangelism.[2] It also made great inroads in incorporating peoples' cultures in their religious practices and liturgy.[3]

The so-called Third World had awakened to its reality of under-development and concluded that such conditions were intimately connected to its experience of being exploited and dominated. This awakening resulted in a wide range of theological perspectives that rejected the "universal" claims of the theology the Third World had inherited as not responding to the issues its peoples were facing in their local contexts.[4] And so these theologians broke away from traditional Eurocentric norms and epistemological frames for doing theology. They articulated a rich and creative variety of theological projects such as the creation of the Academy of Catholic Hispanic Theologians (ACHTUS) and the *Journal of Hispanic/Latino Theology*. They sought to reflect upon the expressions of faith of the Latina/o communities. The diverse starting points represented a shift toward reclaiming their unique cultural contexts as loci for theological reflection. Part of this shift included the emergence of U.S. Latina/o theology.

In the United States social change was taking place rapidly, sometimes violently. After the end of World War II the United States entered into an accelerated process of industrialization and urbanization nationwide. There was a heightened optimism for "progress." As heirs to the suffrage movement, women were fighting for greater equality at many levels—especially greater access to the labor force and equal treatment with men. During the same years there was a growing disenchantment with the U.S. involvement in Vietnam, and many peace movements exerted tremendous pressure to bring the war to an end. At the same time, the civil rights and Black Power movements were working against segregation in schools and public places and for greater social equality for the African American people. An important offshoot was the birth of black theology, as initially articulated by James Cone.[5] Inspired by the sociopolitical situations of injustice in the United States, black theology resonated with the theological movements from the Third World, looking for the relevance of the gospel message for the African American communities.

In relation to the Latinas/os in the United States, things changed dramatically after the United States asserted its status as a world power. After defeating Spain in 1898, the United States took control of the Spanish colonies of the Philippines, Cuba, and Puerto Rico the same year. By 1917 the population of Puerto Rico became U.S. citizens through the Jones Act, and many migrated to the continental United States.[6] Puerto Ricans and "Newyoricans" were added to the large sector of underpaid and exploited classes of Mexican Americans and African Americans. After the Cuban Revolution in 1959, many Cubans, primarily those centered in Florida, also made the United States their home, making the ethnic composition of the Latina/o people even more diverse.

For Mexican Americans the situation was changing rapidly as well. The terms of the Guadalupe-Hidalgo Treaty (1848) stipulated that the Mexican inhabitants of the regions of New Mexico, Texas, Arizona, and California receive automatic U.S. citizenship and the right to reclaim their lands.[7] In actuality their social status as U.S. citizens was little different than that of their African American counterparts. In a nation where the melting pot was the image for constructing national identity by the beginning of the twentieth century, Mexican Americans in the United States were expected to assimilate to the dominant Anglo-Saxon culture. They did not fit in the national image of the United States, constructed around the racialized white/black social binary.[8] They were unwanted! So much so that during the times of the Great Depression, the U.S. government initiated an "anti-immigrant" policy that forcibly deported back to Mexico as many as 500,000 Mexicans, including many who were U.S. citizens.[9] Discriminated against for being "half-breeds" and "foreigners," Mexican Americans began their own unique process of social-identity construction in the United States.[10]

While the U.S. government in 1970 officially subsumed Mexican Americans, Puerto Ricans, Cubans, and all the other immigrants from Latin America under the classification Hispanics, they were certainly not culturally or ethnically homogeneous. There were clear differences in the way these groups perceived themselves and each other. Nevertheless, these diverse communities sought ways of cooperating as they struggled against common social injustices and the racism of the elite and dominant Anglo-Saxon class. For example, during the 1950s and 1960s farm workers organized in the Southwest demanding better working conditions and wages, and during the 1970s Puerto Ricans organized to demand their rights in New York. Nationwide coalitions of minorities started to form, demanding to be treated as equals and seeking self-determination.[11]

In order to resist the U.S. dominant culture's intolerant agenda of assimilation and use of racialized codes of social structuring, the diverse U.S. Latina/o communities had to make alliances in order to have more political strength and to show a united front. So it was that during the later portion of the 1970s, in addition to terms such as *Hispanic* and *Latinos/as,* U.S. Latina/o activists and scholars adopted *mestizaje* as the common ethnocultural and religious banner of unity. For many of them, in theological and popular religious terms *mestizaje* was crystallized in the U.S. Latina/o interpretation of Our Lady of Guadalupe as the concrete expression of the faith of the people and the direct product of this "providentially driven" version of *mestizaje*. Interpreted as the perfect combination of Christian and indigenous religious elements, and as the symbol marking the reception of Christianity among the indigenous, Our Lady of Guadalupe became a key religious symbol for understanding the faith of the Catholic Latina/o people. Whether it was because at the time there where

very few Latina/o theological categories available, or because of
the building of coalitions among these groups, the relatively new
Puerto Rican population and the even more recent arrivals from
Cuba adopted the theological category of *mestizaje* emanating
from the overwhelming majority of Mexican Americans.

This was the ambiguous context in which U.S. Latina/o theologians found in the theological use of *mestizaje* a fruitful category for articulating their ethnocultural identity, struggle for
social justice, and faith. In the context of exclusion from the
social imaginary of the United States, and in the search for creative ways to name their reality, the category of *mestizaje* provided these scholars with a way to name themselves as social
subjects in resistance to the assimilatory policies of the U.S. government. As a collective of diverse ethnic and cultural groups,
mestizaje served as the symbolic term for cohering as a people
and for engaging the struggle for sociopolitical and economic
justice. They found in *mestizaje* a useful category for articulating people's experiences of faith in God. In line with the theological insights from Latin American liberation theology, their
discussions of *mestizaje* marked the intersecting spaces of "race,"
ethnic and cultural identities, and people's experience of
marginalization and oppression.[12]

THEOLOGICAL SKETCH:
THE ADOPTION OF *MESTIZAJE* IN THEOLOGY

I divide the development of *mestizaje* as a heuristic device in
theology among the four decades that separate us from the birth
of Latina/o theology. In 1972 and 1975 Elizondo had written
about the need for bicultural education for Mexican Americans.[13]
Already, he had hinted at *mestizaje* as a useful means for articulating the needs of Mexican Americans, but it was not until 1978
that he first proposed *mestizaje* as a theological category.[14] Focusing primarily on the biological condition of intermixture, his
articulation of *mestizaje* as a theological category emerged from
the historical consciousness of conquest and invasion shared by
the Latin American and the Mexican American people. Different
from Latin Americans, proposed Elizondo, Mexican Americans
underwent a second *mestizaje* with the U.S. Anglo–dominant

culture as a result of the events following the 1848 Guadalupe-Hidalgo Treaty, in which U.S. expansionism was crowned with the annexation of half the territory of Mexico.[15] Thus, for him, the reality of a double *mestizaje* not only set Mexican Americans apart from the rest of the Latin American *mestizos/as*, but also inspired in them resistance to the assimilationist tendencies of the U.S. Anglo–dominant culture. It also affirmed the in-betweenness that Latinas/os experience, feeling never fully part of either Latin American or U.S. Anglo–dominant culture.

In 1983 Elizondo relaunched his proposal in *Galilean Journey*, this time with a stronger cultural content, identifying the historical Jesus as a cultural *mestizo*.[16] In 1987, with no allusion to the work of Elizondo, Andrés Guerrero published his dissertation, *A Chicano Theology*.[17] Unlike Elizondo, Guerrero explicitly engaged the writings of Mexican José Vasconcelos, specifically his controversial essay of 1925, *La raza cósmica*.[18] Probably because its resonances were so close, and in fact seemed to replicate much of Elizondo's proposal, Guerrero's *Chicano Theology* was soon set aside.[19] Elizondo's proposal quickly became the standard source to explain the history of the *mestizo/a* people. His ground-breaking proposal set the agenda for Latinas/os theological reflections and contributions, many of which continue to offer great challenges to traditional approaches to theology.

In the same period, 1986–89, the Cuban American Ada María Isasi-Díaz first conceived her *mujerista* theology, already with direct allusions to the important role of *mestizaje* in the culture of the people and communities to which she claimed to give voice.[20] And John P. Rossing explicitly adopted *mestizaje* as a characteristic aspect of Hispanic American theology.[21] Unique to this decade is the configuration of *mestizaje* with strong cultural content, in large part because of the contributions of Cuban scholars to the discourse, a process that continued well into the following decade. At the close of the 1980s Elizondo made his categorical affirmation of *mestizaje* as a *locus* of theological reflection.[22] The 1980s can be identified both as the period of the entrance of Latinas/os into the U.S. theological academy and as the decade of the initial endorsement of *mestizaje* as a useful theological category. With their newly found sociocultural and political awareness as *mestizos/as*, U.S.

Latina/o scholars considered the dimension of culture in people's faith expressions as having rich theological import.

By the 1990s *mestizaje* was thoroughly and creatively adopted and expanded by U.S. Latina/o theologians. They turned it into a multivalent theological category useful for affirming the identity of Latinas/os in the United States, for reading and interpreting the biblical text, and for speaking theologically with a Latina/o "flavor." This was the most dynamic period for U.S. Latina/o theology in general and for the development of *mestizaje*. The year 1992 stands out; Allan Figueroa Deck labeled it the Year of the "Boom."[23] In 1993 and 1994, Cuban American Roberto Goizueta articulated *mestizaje* as a distinctly Latina/o theological method.[24] He contrasted Elizondo's version of *mestizaje* with that of José Vasconcelos, affirming the great potential of the former while critiquing the latter for its racist underpinnings.[25]

In 1993 Mexican-born María Pilar Aquino also adopted *mestizaje*, asserting that it opened the door for conceiving the role of women as producers of theological knowledge.[26] This was also the year that Ada María Isasi-Díaz wrote her *mujerista* theology manifesto, connecting *mestizaje* to questions of ethnocultural identity, gender, moral choice, and praxis.[27] Also, in 1993 Puerto Rican Eldín Villafañe hinted at the central role of *mestizaje* as an identity marker in the development of his social ethics.[28] By the middle of the 1990s a general consensus seems to have developed about *mestizaje* among U.S. Latina/o theologians. The endorsement of *mestizaje* in theology provoked the publication of the edited volume *Mestizo Christianity* in 1995, with an impressive lineup of accomplished Mexican American, Cuban American, and Puerto Rican scholars.[29] Also in 1995 Alejandro García-Rivera published his cultural semiotics focusing on the work *San Martín de Porres*, drawing significantly on Elizondo's work.[30]

The decade of the 1990s established U.S. Latina/o theology in the academy; Latina/o theology had come of age and Latinas/os were, in the words of Isasi-Díaz, "strangers no longer."[31] At the turn of the century, the complexity, sophistication, and important contributions to the general field of theology were illustrated by Miguel Díaz' masterful comparison of the work of Karl Rahner and the Latina/o theological method.[32] The decade of the 1990s established U.S. Latina/o theology in the academy; Latina/o theology had come of age and Latinas/os were, in the words of Isasi-Díaz, "strangers no longer."[33]

Despite the voluminous production of theological material, one finds very little critique of the notion of *mestizaje* by U.S. Latina/o theologians. They endorsed, deployed, and expanded *mestizaje* uncritically. By the end of the twentieth century *mestizaje* had become a central category without which U.S. Latina/o theology could not be understood or articulated. In 2001 Miguel De La Torre and Edwin Aponte wrote *Introduction to Latina/o Theology*, in which *mestizaje* figured prominently.[34] Other uncritical appropriations took place during this period: by Teresa Chávez Sauceda,[35] Benjamín Valentín,[36] and Oscar García Johnson.[37] Most important, during this period the category of *mestizaje* was expanded even further to include all of humanity, as we see expressed in the works of Valentín,[38] Elizondo,[39] and Jacques Audinet (himself not a Latina/o theologian).[40]

If one can say that the 1990s was the decade of the configuration of *mestizaje* into theological methodology, the first decade of the twenty-first century is characterized by serious challenges to many of the assumptions U.S. Latino/a theologians made of *mestizaje*. These challenges have emerged from within and without the Latina/o communities. We examine them in detail in Chapter 4, but for now, suffice it to say that by the turn of the century, *mestizaje* had become an increasingly problematic category demanding serious examination and rethinking.

MESTIZAJE AS A THEOLOGICAL CATEGORY

As *mestizaje* was appropriated by other U.S. Latina/o theologians, the condition of cultural *mestizaje* became central to theological consideration. Without exception, the adoption of *mestizaje* launched these theologians into a complex, uneven, messy, and painful historical revisionism and cultural reappropriation.

The seminal work of Elizondo positioned the U.S. Latina/o communities within the history and culture of *mestizaje*. It was these communities' experiences of sociocultural and political injustice, marginalization, and discrimination in their own country that U.S. Latina/o theologians sought to reveal, along with giving voice to their extraordinarily diverse expressions of faith in God. In other words, and in order to understand U.S. Latina/o theological perspectives, theological affirmations must be seen in relation to the consciousness of being themselves *mestizos/as* and from the position that as *mestizos/as* they have a privileged understanding of the unique theological import of culture and ethnicity. It is through these lenses that *mestizo/a* theologians understood history, read the biblical text, interpreted people's expressions of faith, and declared theological affirmations. What follows reflects the extent to which this category became fruitful in the articulation of U.S. Latina/o theology.

Mestizaje as a Theoretical Theological Framework

As the convergence of the U.S. Latina/o peoples' history, ethnocultural identity, and faith, *mestizaje* became the category from which to reflect theologically. This had several ramifications. As a theological category, *mestizaje* delineated the direction and limits for considering people's experiences and expressions of faith. U.S. Latina/o theologians insisted that abstract categories and theological conceptions were not appropriate for the theological endeavor if they were separate from concrete reality. For them, the theological task did not begin at the point of theoretical analysis but emerged out of the people's long history of faith traditions and expressions.[41]

By adopting *mestizaje*, U.S. Latina/o theologians uncovered the unique interconnectedness of the U.S. Latina/o people's history and faith, and proposed culture as constitutive of people's faith expressions. According to the U.S. Latina/o theologians, the cultural *mestizaje* of the people took place in the historical clash of different peoples: indigenous, African, and Spanish, and the subsequent amalgamation of their cultural elements. These theologians argued that the people's symbols and expressions were also constructed by incorporating aspects from each group's cultural and religious traditions. As they saw it, people's faith expressions and traditions are shaped, transmitted, and transformed as part of the sociocultural process engendered by all human collectives. Culture, then, functions as the medium through which religion is transmitted and expressed. U.S. Latinas/os' everyday life and *mestizo/a* ethnocultural context served as the space where the gospel was contextualized.[42]

The implication was that neither the gospel nor religious expressions of faith could be understood, engaged, or articulated apart from the realm of the cultural. Rejecting notions of culture as a finished product, by appropriating *mestizaje* U.S. Latina/o theologians sought to affirm culture as the *locus* of divine activity and theological considerations; hence Elizondo's pronouncement of *mestizaje* as *locus theologicus*.[43] U.S. Latina/o theologians now understood culture as being not only a central feature of people's identity but as the very place where people encountered God at work.

The interweaving of culture in the theological task and method offered new frames for conceiving the activity of God in humanity. Even more, it placed people's sociocultural reality in the theological arena, making the people the source and place for constructing theological assertions. This affirmation of culture and cultural context in theology contradicted modern notions of a theological meta-discourse above culture.[44] (In other words, given that *mestizaje* was seen by U.S. Latina/o theologians as inclusion of other marginal voices, any theological affirmation was bound by its cultural context.)

This was a revolutionary contribution; it reconfigured our understanding of revelation. It was not a postmodern relativizing of theological discourses, or a bold assertion that all cultures are the result of their own process of intermixture *(mestizaje)*, though they are.[45] It set new parameters for understanding the self-disclosure of God. In line with Latin American liberation theology, U.S. Latina/o theologians asserted that revelation took place as people engaged in the actual living of the faith, and in particular in their struggle against injustice. They added, however, that the encounter with the divine came within the limits of the cultural material of believers. In other words, what the gospel is and how people reflect the content of the good news cannot be understood or articulated separate from the cultural reality of the people.[46]

By using *mestizaje* as a theological category, U.S. Latina/o scholars made the bold assertion that no cultural group had a complete view of God, "no one culture can embrace the fullness of the mystery of God."[47] All theological notions are incomplete, and only by coming together, by entering into conversation with other cultural groups as equals, could U.S. Latino/a scholars' unique understanding of the reality of God be better appreciated. As they saw it, within the space of *mestizaje*, no cultural group could claim to have the last word of God's self-disclosure and no cultural group could claim to have a monopoly on understanding and discoursing about God.[48]

The initial adoption of *mestizaje* by U.S. Latina/o theologians was a move away from ethnocentric theological views. As they saw it, they could no longer emphasize one culture as a finished product but instead focused on the ancestral cultural strands that had contributed to the formation of the Latina/o cultural expressions. So they focused simultaneously on two things: first, that *mestizaje* is the dynamic and complex process of cultural intermixture; and second, since this cultural intermixture takes place at the level of the people, that the emphasis on *mestizaje* interprets the people themselves as the locus of divine disclosure, the carriers of the good news. U.S. Latino/a theologians valued people's faith experience and their theological import. In their analysis of religious expressions the use of *mestizaje* also affirmed the central role of the people in the production of theological knowledge. So for them, the critical reflection on the praxis of the faith, the task of theologizing, is not the province of intellectuals alone, although they are an important component in the process of knowing God. The people, at the level of the banal everyday specific concreteness of their faith in God, already offered refreshing ways of seeing the divine at work.[49] This is an extremely innovative and challenging notion when one considers the role of the biblical text and of the Spirit in people's expressions of faith.

To the best of my knowledge, only one of the U.S. Latina/o theologians explicitly states that the Bible plays a lesser role when it comes to engaging people's expressions of faith.[50] This may be related to the importance given to the people as interpretive community and the situating of the Bible within the larger Catholic tradition, so that the Bible is rarely central when considered alone. While Aquino does not list the Bible as one of the sources of U.S. Latina/o theology, a closer examination of U.S. Latina/o writings does demonstrate their intimacy with the scriptures.[51] I will discuss this later; for now, let me just say that by placing the people in intimate relation with the divine self-disclosure, U.S. Latina/o theologians have offered an unfinished reflection of revelation. At the same time, they argue for the continuing divine self-disclosure: the divine continues to encounter the people; God's divine creative process continues. It is part of the continuing creation of the future *mestizo/a* people, where there will be a place for everyone, and where the injustices that separate people because of their gender, "race," ethnoculture, class, sex, and religious traditions will be removed.

Mestizaje as a Biblical and Historical Hermeneutical Key

Mestizaje becoming a theological category placed the ethnocultural identity of the U.S. Latinas/os at the center of the task of doing theology. It resulted in a radical rereading and reinterpretation of history and of the biblical narrative. On one hand, adopting *mestizaje* launched U.S. Latina/o theologians into a slow and painful process of (re)claiming their historical past as the province of God's creative work. Their reading of history, while highlighting the bloody invasion and conquest by the Spaniards and Portuguese, has providential overtones, as Elizondo's work illustrates, pointing to the creation of the *mestizo/a* Latino/a people.[52] To him, although the encounter between the indigenous and Spaniards had violent and destructive effects, primarily for the indigenous people, it also produced unexpected results: the *mestizo/a* people. Accepting Elizondo's proposal, these theologians interpreted the birth of the *mestizo/a* people as a divine act of creation.

By affirming *mestizaje* Latina/o theologians claimed the legitimacy of the *mestizo/a* people in the sight of God and U.S. society. Within the context of racialized social and cultural exclusion in the United States, Latina/o theologians adopted *mestizaje* to create a space within which they could stand as people, with dignity, and resist the sociocultural and religious assimilation forces of the dominant culture. Drawing from the pre-independence context of Mexico (and Latin America), where *mestizos/as* were discriminated against and where to be *mestizo/a* was seen in derogatory ways, U.S. Latina/o theologians redeemed and reclaimed *mestizaje* to name their ethnic, cultural, and historical uniqueness as a people.

For U.S. Latina/o theologians *mestizaje* also announced the utopic future of a polyphonic society. They considered that *mestizaje* marked a coming together of dissimilar ethnocultural groups, that *mestizos/as* embodied the future era of ethnocultural plurality. Their birth, they affirmed, was a concrete divine act of continuing creation, a concrete expression of the divine desire to remove sociopolitical injustices resulting from intolerance. *Mestizaje* proclaimed a new way for constructing peoples and societies of love and inclusion rather than of exclusion and discrimination. For them, being *mestizo/a* meant to welcome other voices into the theological arena and not to silence them.[53] It meant the creation of a new humanity, the humanity of inclusion, where all peoples would find a place to celebrate the divine. The divine process continued in the ongoing act of creating a *mestizo/a* people, so as to establish a cosmic order characterized by *mestizaje*.[54]

The theological reinterpretation of the history of Latinas/os in light of *mestizaje*, their pains, suffering, struggles, and present conditions of oppression and marginalization within the context of their own home country, the United States, opened the door for engaging the biblical text in new and fruitful ways. U.S. Latina/o scholars began to read the biblical text to elucidate questions of power. This is what Justo González has called "reading the Bible in Spanish."[55] He comments that the goal of this perspective is to acknowledge the activity of the divine in the midst of the messiness of history and human actions; it is a "non-innocent reading of history." He proposes that when reading the Bible in "Spanish" there is little room left for ideological constructions that deny the history and reality of violence.

The revolutionary element of this approach is the very people that interpret the text. According to González, the "unglamorous" history of U.S. Latinas/os does not permit U.S. Latina/o scholars and people to romanticize the biblical narrative, for they know that history is messy and oftentimes painful and bloody. The people read the Bible not to find flawless heroes but actual people.[56] Moreover, he argues, the goal is not to read the biblical text to justify notions of power that preserve the status quo. The Bible is not politically neutral. González insists that all interpretations of the Bible are tainted with economic, social, and political interests, which often have obscured the message of the good news in the biblical text. The biblical text is profoundly political, which means that the text deals directly and unabashedly with matters of power and powerlessness, and these understandings shape the biblical text and our comprehension of it.[57]

In this way, then, González sets new interpretive parameters for reading the biblical text, in light of the history and experiences of the members of the community of faith, for it is this history and these experiences that shape the questions that people ask of the Bible. For him, there is no universal, ahistorical reading of the biblical text.

In *Santa Biblia* González uses *mestizaje* as the hermeneutical key for finding cultural intermixture in the biblical narrative. That is, cultural intermixture is an ever-present element in the biblical narrative. Thus, for example, identifying *mestizaje* in the Bible sheds light on the ministry and work of the apostle Paul, who would not have been able to move back and forth between Hellenic Jews and Gentiles were he not himself a cultural *mestizo*.[58] In the same way, he insists, *mestizaje* is part of the biblical reality that helps us read many Old Testament passages that had previously gone unnoticed. For example, he suggests Jewish and Persian Esther as a cultural *mestiza*. He asserts that it was her status as a *mestiza* that helped her prevent the destruction of the people of Israel. He also insists that there are some important parallels between the notions of frontier and border in the United States and the destruction and invasion of the land of Canaan by the people of Israel. In light of this, he writes, *mestizaje* provides us with valuable clues for interpreting Deuteronomistic history.[59]

A similar interpretive approach of *mestizaje* is found in the work of Robert Maldonado. With his "identity hermeneutics" he proposes a closer examination of culture and identity issues as they relate to questions of canon. He claims that people's identity and culture set the boundaries to the questions and concerns they ask of the biblical text and traditions. In examining the "dynamics of the canonical economy of interpretation," people's identities must be seen as interconnected with the interpretive process. "To the extent that the identity of the interpreter sets boundaries around the hermeneutical project, this identity is reflected in the process of interpretation."[60]

Since Maldonado notes there is a sociocultural component to one's identity, the history of the community of one's identification is a significant piece of the identity-hermeneutical project. For U.S. Latina/o people, it is the history of *mestizaje* that sets the boundaries upon and provides the questions to ask of the biblical narrative. For Maldonado, this is particularly evident in the way issues of conquest and exodus relate to the history of *mestizaje* and the *mestizo/a* people. The use of *mestizaje* refines how these central biblical themes are interpreted and contextualized. In the case of U.S. Latina/o communities, the use of *mestizaje* evokes a backward look at their own history of conquest/exodus toward the affirmation of their own identity as people.[61] In this way U.S. Latinas/os find themselves in the biblical narrative.

By interrogating the biblical narrative for what it reveals in light of *mestizaje*, that is, highlighting the presence of cultural intermixture in the biblical text, U.S. Latina/o theologians also laid out a new course for interpreting the significance of the Jesus event. The interpretive richness of this approach is epitomized in Elizondo's *Galilean Journey* (1983), where Jesus' Galilean *mestizo* cultural background is interpreted as analogous to the experience of the Mexican American people.[62] A full analysis of Elizondo's proposal goes beyond the scope of this book; suffice it to say his is a contextual reading of the relevance of the Jesus event for the experience of oppression and discrimination of the Mexican American people and that he does this by highlighting the sociocultural dimensions of the life and ministry of Jesus. For Elizondo, the use of *mestizaje* sets the agenda and interpretive framework for understanding both the history of his people and the New Testament narratives of Jesus, as outlined in the first two divisions of his book. The crux of his argument is that *mestizaje* is a central notion for understanding Jesus' life and ministry. As Maldonado put it (thirteen years after that book's publication), by seeing Galilee as a marginal center of cultural intersections and intermixtures, and by seeing Jesus as a cultural *mestizo*, Elizondo reclaims the divine legitimation of the *mestizo/a* people.[63]

Elizondo's analogy follows this logic: First, Mexican American people have experienced a double *mestizaje*. Jesus was born and raised in the context of Galilee, a marginal place, but also a geographical center of cultural intermixture, which made Jesus a *mestizo*. Second, for Mexican Americans *mestizaje* was accompanied by discrimination and rejection by both Mexico and the U.S. Anglo–dominant culture. For Jesus, rejection came from both Rome, which was the power that occupied the land of Israel, and from Jerusalem, which was the center of power for the Jewish people. Third, and here Elizondo inverts the order, God in Jesus challenges the structures of power by bringing salvation from the margins. What people rejected and killed, God chooses as God's very own by sending Jesus and by raising him from the dead. By analogy, the Mexican American people are the rejected "border" communities out of which God may bridge the great divide between Mexicans (really Latin Americans) and the United States.[64]

From Elizondo's analogical study of the Jesus event three principles emerge: the Galilean principle, the Jerusalem principle, and the resurrection principle (discussed in the last section of his book). Essentially, these principles celebrate the role of *mestizaje* in making concrete God's divine act of creation of a new humanity: the *mestizo/a* humanity (the Galilean principle); the church's prophetic role in unmasking the roots of the oppression of peoples on the basis of their ethnocultural background (the Jerusalem principle); and the reality of God's love and presence manifest in the peoples' expressions of faith (the resurrection principle). For Elizondo, then, *mestizaje* brings together the realities of identity and culture, of suffering, death, and new resurrected life. In the life, ministry, and mission of Jesus *mestizaje* represents a new creation and a new existence. Indeed, the cross unveiled the evil and sinfulness of the system founded upon human self-centeredness, discrimination, and violence. The resurrection, however, represented God's liberating alternative of life. In the *mestizo* Jesus the *mestizo/a* people are validated, and *mestizaje* represents the beginning of a "new Christian universalism."[65]

In these and many other ways the lens of *mestizaje* has offered U.S. Latina/o theologians rich perspectives on interpreting the Bible. Taking the specificity of their sociocultural and religious context, they developed creative new ways for engaging the biblical text and for understanding the intimate relationship among the faith of the people, their ethnocultural background and history, and the presence and activity of the divine. In no other place is this more evident than in the concrete religious symbols, expressions, rituals, and practices of the U.S. Latina/o people. To these I now turn.

Mestizaje as Paradigm for Interpreting People's Experience of Faith

U.S. Latina/o theologians adopted the preferential option for the poor and oppressed. It was this option that opened the door for the theological appreciation of popular religion and popular religious expressions. This, perhaps, is the most important element of U.S. Latina/o theology; it traces the intersections of culture, identity, and faith, as well as the theological import of these intersections. For these theologians, adopting *mestizaje* has played a key role in engaging theologically popular religious expressions. Although this refers primarily to the rich Catholic traditions and expressions of the Latina/o people, it would be a mistake to assume that the Protestant and Pentecostal communities do not have popular versions and expressions of their faith in God. It is in this way that adopting the category of *mestizaje* has contributed to a greater appreciation of the unique ways in which different peoples live and express their faith in God. Using *mestizaje* helps us understand popular expressions of faith as important vehicles of the Christian tradition and message.[66]

For U.S. Latina/o scholars the reality of *mestizaje* in popular religion goes back to the original biological-cultural encounter between the indigenous and the Spanish peoples. Elizondo, for example, claims that Mexican American people experienced a double *mestizaje*—and that means that they also experienced a double evangelization.[67] U.S. Latina/o theologians view the religious and cultural legacies of both periods of evangelization and *mestizaje* as easily detected in the amalgam of Spanish and indigenous (and African) religious elements displayed in the religious expressions, traditions, and symbols of the U.S. Latina/o population.[68]

Initially, theological reflection on popular religious traditions received a stimulus from Vatican Council II, evident in Elizondo's reflection on the role of culture in pastoral ministry.[69] At the beginning some U.S. Latina/o scholars also sought for ways to promote popular religion as legitimate expressions of the *sensus fidelium*.[70] For example, Espín went so far as to insist that U.S. Latina/o popular religion is not only a legitimate way of "being Catholic," but, in fact, that it has no "significant differences" with the official doctrinal position "if one keeps in mind the role that culture plays in always contextualizing the faith and every expression of it."[71] Whether Espín would hold to this position today is a matter of debate. But the affirmation shows a corresponding relation between popular religion and issues of identity. The focus on popular religion provides U.S. Latina/o theology with its own historical specificity. For U.S. Latina/o theology, popular religion and religious practices are the way in which Christianity is lived in a truly Latina/o way.

This is particularly true of the symbols of Jesus and Our Lady of Guadalupe, which play a key role in defining U.S. Latina/o popular religious practices and identity. It is in light of these two symbols that Goizueta writes that if "popular religion is the dimension of Latino culture most deeply 'ours,' [popular religious practices] are the aspects of particular symbols, narratives, and rituals that are more deeply ours than others."[72]

In the case of Jesus, Goizueta writes that people's everyday sociopolitical and economic struggles and devotions serve as the place for reflecting upon and understanding their celebrations during the Holy Week Triduum. Focused on the community of San Fernando in San Antonio, Texas, he contends that during this event the people's accompaniment of the image of the crucified Jesus becomes a sacramental space of divine self-disclosure. It is also the place where people unmask the violence and injustice in the world and in the U.S. society that excludes them. These people, claims Goizueta, are the privileged bearers of the "transcendent God," "because their historical suffering and struggles are the only obstacle to the . . . identification of U.S. society with the reign of God."[73] In this "empathic fusion," between the crucified Jesus they accompany and the Christ that accompanies them in their daily struggles, the people's popular religious symbols and traditions become the place for encountering God and defining their humanity.

The innovative character of U.S. Latino/a theologians and their adoption of *mestizaje* are expressed most richly in their interpretation of the symbol of Guadalupe. For example, Elizondo sees her as *mestizo/a* symbol par excellence. He sees the symbol of Guadalupe as "the perfect synthesis of the religious iconography of the Iberian peoples with that of native Mexicans into one coherent image."[74] As such, she represents the *mestizos/as,* their struggles and dreams, and embodies the divine endorsement of *mestizaje*. Guadalupe represents the spiritual birth of the *mestizo/a* people. For U.S. Latina/o theologians this is not simply another way of finding a unique nuance of "Christian" symbols as they intermixed with indigenous elements, although that is certainly true of Guadalupe. Since Guadalupe was the "evangelizer" of the indigenous peoples, and since the evangelization of the indigenous peoples took place as a result of her apparition, then Guadalupe is "nothing less than an American Gospel."[75]

Although U.S. Latina/o scholars mention the violence of the conquest, when it comes to dealing with the symbol of Guadalupe, she is described in almost providential terms. She is the peaceful synthesis of indigenous and Spanish cultural elements. It is in light of their appreciation of the popular devotion to and expressions of Guadalupe that U.S. Latina/o theologians affirm the evangelistic power of popular religion.

Elizondo expresses it quite well. First, Guadalupe's offer of love and hope for the people parallels that of Jesus. She welcomes people not by threats of eternal punishment but by offering comfort, protection, and good news to the poor and marginalized.[76] Second, he adds, as the *mestizo/a* symbol par excellence Guadalupe points to the evangelizing power of the *mestizo/a* people. The tradition of Guadalupe is the ongoing incarnation of the gospel, not according to conquest and domination, but by the evangelizing witness of the converted poor and marginalized *mestizos/as*. The *mestizos/as* in their traditions, practices, and symbols announce the good news. "It is through the Christianity of these groups that America is still being Christianized and Christianity is being genuinely Americanized."[77] At this point Elizondo is close to saying that the *mestizo/a* people are the truest or among the truest expressions of being American (here he refers to the American continent).

U.S. Latina/o theologians offer important contributions by engaging theologically the people's expressions of faith. These theologians do not seek to produce universal principles applicable differently to different communities everywhere. They contend that it is impossible to enter the theological arena and do theology outside of people's experiences of faith as reflected in their daily, concrete, historical, and culturally bound expressions. To do otherwise is to turn theological reflections into an intellectually abstract exercise that holds no specific relevance for the very people who are the object of such reflections. Thus, writes Goizueta, the adoption of *mestizaje* by these theologians exhibits a different rationality and a construction of truth that emerge from the understanding of the person-as-full-human-being in connection to his or her respective community, which, in many ways, is contrary to and critical of "Western" individualistic and reason-centered approaches.[78]

This means that for U.S. Latina/o theologians, *mestizaje* functioned as catalyst for appreciating the amalgam of indigenous, Spanish, and African elements in their diverse religious expressions. By appropriating *mestizaje* these scholars acquired the lenses through which to gain theological insight into the people's celebrations, feasts, religious activities, and veneration of particular religious symbols. In this way these symbols, traditions, and practices became sources of theological knowledge and loci for encountering the presence and work of God amid the *mestizos/as*.[79] By emphasizing the popular religious dimension of faith, U.S. Latina/o theologians demonstrated the impossibility of universal theological formulas. They insisted that their theological reflections had to emerge from their own cultural, particular, and historically situated faith communities.[80]

By adopting the category of *mestizaje*, U.S. Latina/o theologians signal a new course for articulating and understanding the faith, religious symbols, and practices of the people. They insist that people's expressions of faith are a source and object of theological reflection, and that the people, those who practice the faith, are the subjects of the theological task. U.S. Latina/o theologians introduced new interpretive patterns for reading the biblical text. Their perspectives shed light on the particular cultural dynamics taking place in the biblical narratives. Even more, by focusing on questions of ethnocultural dynamics and faith as expressed in *mestizaje*, U.S. Latina/o theologians help us appreciate the rich cultural context within which Jesus announced the good news. They also invite us to engage the biblical text as a cultural document that contains a relevant message for our present cultural challenges and questions of biological and cultural intermixture today.

2

U.S. LATINO/A THEOLOGY
AND THE DISCOURSE(S)
OF *MESTIZAJE*

Despite the ideological valorization of mestizaje, the racism inherent in both U.S. and Mexican societies certainly circulated in the "Mexican-American" [and Latina/o] communities. In a North American context, this meant that the members of these communities were under pressure to assimilate particular standards—of beauty, of identity, of aspiration. In a Mexican context, the pressure was to urbanize and Europeanize. Which is to say that in order to belong to larger imagined communities of the nation—particularly in the United States— "Mexican-Americans" and [Latinas/os] were expected to accept anti-indigenous discourses as their own.

—ELISEO PÉREZ-TORREZ

Although most Latina/o theologians are not Latin Americans in the United States, the latter group borrowed the concept of *mestizaje* from Latin America, emphasizing the historical connections they shared with the Latin American population to warrant their adoption of the term. Yet they also emphasized

23

their distinctiveness as people, and they worked hard at distancing themselves from Latin America and Latin American liberation theology.[1] Elizondo's notion of "double *mestizaje*" eloquently articulates this distinctiveness: theirs was a "new" type of *mestizaje*.

However, as U.S. Latina/o theologians developed, adopted, and recreated the notion of *mestizaje*, they failed to engage questions of *mestizaje* inside and outside of the borders of the continental United States. Resolved to distance themselves from Latin America, U.S. Latina/o theologians paid no attention to the way in which the idea of *mestizaje* had become a tool of oppression in many places in Latin America, a mechanism for "whitening" the population and bringing about cultural homogeneity, even to becoming the official policy of some local governments. With the exception of the messianic idealized notion of a universal *mestizaje* described by Vasconcelos and scant allusions to Octavio Paz, the older and larger debates of *mestizaje* in Latin America were entirely absent from their theological writings.

U.S. Latina/o theologians borrowed the category of *mestizaje* from Latin America without engaging the actual sociocultural and political history of the term; they uncritically adopted an ideal and reified version of *mestizaje* that they conceived as being capable of bringing about cultural inclusivity and removing racist tendencies. And they failed to interrogate their own context in light of the different racialized tensions among Latinas/os. Specifically, they did not challenge the U.S. Latina/o homogenizing imaginary that excluded indigenous peoples and African "Latina/o" communities.

Were U.S. Latina/o theologians aware of the rich diversity of the Latina/o population from the beginning in the late 1970s? The fact is that they presented a unified front, as a result of which many of the internal tensions of the U.S. Latina/o communities were diminished. In the words of De La Torre and Aponte, a "conscious decision seems to have been made by Hispanic theologians to minimize [the] differences [among national groups] and, instead, concentrate on areas of commonality. Pan-Ethnic unity was sought at all costs, masking those areas that threatened to tear Latinos/as apart."[2] By diminishing the rich ethnic and cultural diversity in these communities, and by assuming *mestizaje* to be a category that reflects all of the U.S. Latina/o population, these scholars presented a false sense of unity and homogeneity of these communities. They occluded the complex political, social, and cultural issues at play in the different U.S. Latina/o communities—in relation to one another, in relation to the United States government and the larger population in the churches and the academy, and in relation to Latin America.

But it was not only their own that they represented falsely; they unwittingly reinscribed earlier silences of the indigenous and African descendant voices alive in the U.S. Latina/o communities and in Latin America. They also masked the diverse ethnic-cultural roots of the many peoples that constitute the Latin American and U.S. Latina/o populations. Oftentimes their articulations of *mestizaje* displayed some of the same tendencies toward homogenization and whitening of the population as some of their counterparts in Latin America, tendencies that are only recently being critiqued by younger Latina/o theologians such as Rubén Rosario Rodríguez and Benjamín Valentín.

For these reasons I examine in this chapter how four U.S. Latina/o Catholic theologians used *mestizaje* in theology.[3] First, I explore their theological affirmations that highlight their uncritical and romantic assumptions about *mestizaje*. And second, I follow the implications of their theological assertions as unwittingly denying the richly diverse cultural composition of the U.S. Latinas/os, and by extension of the Latin American population, at times perpetuating tendencies toward the homogenization of the U.S. Latina/o communities. Through their uncritical totalizing and idealized assumptions, U.S. Latina/o theologians reify *mestizaje* as having the capacity to remove homogenizing and racist tendencies. The same idealized assumptions about *mestizaje* play a significant role in blinding U.S. Latina/o theologians to self-reflective analysis of the particular racialized tensions that exist among the U.S. Latina/o communities.

Whether Mexican American Virgilio Elizondo gave the U.S. Latina/o theological movement its original impetus is the subject of debate, but there is consensus that he provided U.S. Latina/o theology with the first and most extensive theological articulation of *mestizaje*.[4] His theological intuition of *mestizaje* gave U.S. Latina/o theologians the conceptual framework for articulating the faith experience of Latinas/os in the United States. For other U.S. Latina/o scholars of the same generation, his work represented the auspicious moment for Latinas/os to make their presence felt in the theological academic arena. It is thanks to his initial intuition of *mestizaje* that other U.S. Latina/o theologians engaged the term, adapted it, and transformed it into a category for theological reflection and critical analysis. To this we now turn.

Although Elizondo's seminal work influenced U.S. Latina/o theologians in the most fundamental way, the theologians I discuss here have incorporated *mestizaje* more substantially in their theological work and are part of the generation out of which U.S. Latina/o theology first emerged.

MESTIZAJE AS A *LOCUS* OF THEOLOGICAL REFLECTION: VIRGILIO ELIZONDO

Characterized by Mary Doak as a public theologian,[5] Elizondo originally proposed a *new* understanding of *mestizaje* as a fruitful descriptor of the lived-faith reality of the Mexican American people. He begins by examining the earliest negative understanding of *mestizaje*, emphasizing that *mestizo/a* children were discriminated against during colonial times—and continue to be—as a result of a sociopolitical emphasis on purity of blood and culture. While acknowledging that the term has carried negative overtones for those who are mixed, he redeems the term as the appropriate self-imposed category for reclaiming and reappropriating the dignity and the unique culture and faith experience of the Mexican American people. In this way *mestizaje* parallels the earlier African American claim that "black is beautiful."

In 1978, in his doctoral dissertation, Elizondo begins his recounting of this mixing with the original violent and genocidal encounter between the indigenous people of today's Mexico and the Spanish forces led by the conquistador Hernán Cortéz. For him, the encounter brought about the reality of miscegenation between indigenous people and Spanish people. Although he recounts the violence of the conquest in Mexico, he interprets the events of the Spanish invasion in reconciliatory terms. As he puts it, Mexican Americans "have come to appreciate the final battle of Tlatelolco, not in terms of defeat or victory, but in terms of the painful birth of a new race."[6] The violent encounter between the Spanish and indigenous and the suffering of the latter Elizondo interprets as the first foundational *biological and cultural mestizaje* that gave birth to the *new "raza mestiza."*[7] He adds that as the Mexico–U.S. war came to a close with the signing of the Guadalupe-Hidalgo Treaty, the Mexican people in the United States entered into a second period of *cultural* intermixture, by which they became second-class marginalized citizens. This he identifies as a second *mestizaje.*[8]

It is these two clearly distinguishable and historically measurable periods of admixture that gave birth to the Mexican American people who live in a kind of cultural in-betweenness, says Elizondo.[9] Mexican Americans have the arduous task of assimilating Mexican and U.S. dominant cultures, not by denying their past, but by transcending it. As people of faith they "have no choice but to see it as the providential coming together of two peoples who had never come together before."[10]

In Elizondo's theological scheme each of these periods is also marked by a complex process of evangelization. The first was characterized by the radical destruction of indigenous religions and the imposition of European forms of Christianity. But with the appearance of Our Lady of Guadalupe to Juan Diego, the indigenous people interpreted and appropriated Christianity for themselves by producing their own *mestizo* (mixed) symbol par excellence that represents the cultural and religious birth of *la raza.*[11] The indigenous people disappear in Elizondo's proposal, and their memory survives only in the *mestizo/a* cultural symbols and religious expressions.

The second period of evangelization imposed European (Catholic and Protestant) forms of religious expressions and practices on Mexican Americans in order to force them to abandon their cultural traditions, language, and religious expressions and symbols.[12] Elizondo argues that this second evangelization had a more detrimental effect on Mexican Americans, because it sought to erase their very identity and replace it with a foreign one. But as the *mestizos/as norte americanos/as* continue to resist marginalization and push for social equality in the United States, and as they develop their own religious symbols, they mature, marching "toward the future that has already begun [with *mestizaje*]."[13] Who these new *mestizos/as* will become, in Vasconcelos's view, lies in the future.[14]

It is out of this dialectical tension between the present reality and the quasi-providential messianic future reserved for the (doubly *mestizo*, doubly rejected) Mexican American people that Elizondo was inspired to conceive the faith experience of his people in a new light. Convinced that they had to create their own knowledge and understanding of their religious beliefs, he founded the Mexican American Cultural Center in 1971 to promote the unique culture, religious beliefs, and theological articulation of the Mexican American people.[15]

Referring to the tradition of Mexico's colonial caste society, Elizondo claims that for *mestizos/as* the condition of *mestizaje* initially had a stigma attached to it, that of being second-class citizens, backward people. The "*new mestizaje,*" he says, marks the birth of something new, the result of both *mestizajes*. Elizondo equates *mestizaje* with biological and cultural intermixture, a meaning other U.S. Latina/o theologians later expanded. For Elizondo, *mestizaje* is about the *mixture* of disparate elements.[16]

The creativity and richness of Elizondo's *mestizaje*-as-mixture proposal is evident in his 1983 *Galilean Journey*, in which he argued that the present double marginalization and rejection experienced by Mexican Americans result from their condition of being *mestizos/as*. The condition of *mestizaje*-as-intermixture can be useful in two ways: for articulating the struggle against discrimination and inequality, and for finding the legitimation of the culturally conditioned religious symbols of the Mexican American people. Similarly, *mestizaje* functions as a lens through which to interpret the biblical text. These three approaches to *mestizaje* are held in tension in Elizondo's work.

The double *mestizo* (mixed) character of Mexican Americans is illustrated in their faith experience. Their Christian communities—mostly Catholic but some Protestant—have their own *mixed* religious symbols and practices that are uniquely vital and creative. This reality would be impossible to explain without the previous *mestizajes*. Therefore, any theological reflection must emerge from the wealth of the collective faith experiences, identity, and wisdom of the *mestizo/a* people. Their historical and cultural location as *mestizos/as* colors their reading and interpretation of the gospel message.[17]

Two theological assumptions operate in Elizondo's reading of the biblical text. First, his understanding of *mestizaje* as a providential creation of a "new race" allows him to argue for God's activity in cultural and historical processes—as we can see in Our Lady of Guadalupe. *Mestizaje*-as-intermixture is the vehicle through which God brings into existence (creates) the Mexican American people and culture. Second, it follows that *mestizaje* is the place where we find the divine at work on the side of the oppressed and marginalized. Hence Elizondo's dictum: *mestizaje* is a *locus* of theological reflection.[18] In this way Elizondo's reading of the gospel message and the person of Jesus turns *mestizaje*-as-mixture into a hermeneutical key through which he raised questions of culture and context in the life of Jesus, elements that were not commonly part of dominant approaches to biblical hermeneutics.

This has concrete implications for Elizondo's reading of the biblical narrative. According to him, when reading the gospel narratives from the perspective of *mestizaje*, Jesus' Galilean *Sitz im Leben* can be seen to parallel the Mexican American *mestizo/a* communities. In finding a cultural correspondence of intermixture between the reality of Jesus and that of the Mexican Americans, he idealizes the historical-cultural situatedness of Jesus' Galilee as "a crossroads to cultures and peoples with an openness to each other."[19] And he goes even further! In ways that resemble Vasconcelos's criticism of the U.S. white-Anglo refusal to intermix with other ethnocultural groups, he states that for "pure-minded" Jerusalem Jews the "natural *mestizaje* of Galilee was a sign of impurity and a cause of rejection."[20]

This is really the turning point in Elizondo's work in regard to the person of Jesus and his relevance for the Mexican American people. Galilee represents marginalization and rejection, but it also represents the birthplace of salvation in the person of Jesus. The Galilean *(mestizo)* Jesus, understood as the historical in-breaking of God in human affairs, represents at once the rejected and the divine siding with the rejected ones. Jesus is rejected and marginalized because he is a Galilean *(mestizo)*, born poor, and not a member of the elite Jerusalem Jewish religious caste.[21] Being God incarnate, Jesus ushers in the reign of God symbolized in the restoration of the human dignity of the marginalized and poor and the establishment of a unique relationship with those whom society rejects. Using messianic overtones, Elizondo affirms that it is from these rejected people, the Galileans *(mestizos/as)* who follow Jesus, that God will found a *new* social system based on equality, radical love, and forgiveness. The Galileans are the new chosen people who go out and proclaim the way of Jesus. For Elizondo, here *mestizaje*-as-mixture means inclusivity; *mestizaje* announces a "new universalism" by excluding no one because of "race," culture, nationality, class, or color.[22]

Elizondo's argument continues by suggesting that (the *mestizo*) Jesus represents the divine alternative to systems of oppression and marginalization, which the *mestizo* Mexican American people also confront. Jesus' life, death, and resurrection illustrate the divine scheme of things. We have seen that Elizondo elaborates this in three principles: the Galilean principle, the Jerusalem principle, and the resurrection principle.

The *Galilean principle* emphasizes the specific divine legitimation of peoples' ethnocultural identity: "what human beings reject, God chooses as his very own."[23] This reverses traditional ways of excluding *mestizo* peoples and systematic attempts at erasing their histories, cultures, and religious traditions. This principle fits the *mestizo*-mixed identity of Mexican Americans as the contemporary Galileans chosen to bring unity to both sides of the American continent. Their cultural identity finds its ultimate meaning in the Galilean *(mestizo)* Jesus. The *mestizo* condition and the accompanying suffering of the Mexican Americans illustrate their part in bringing these two sides of the Americas into a relationship of appreciation and love of each other. *Mestizaje* ultimately is the condition for reconciliation.

The *Jerusalem principle* is ecclesiological in focus. It teaches that God *chooses* the oppressed and marginalized people to establish a new community and to confront, transcend, and transform the structures that oppressive societies establish and that violate human dignity. For Elizondo, the church, the "people of God," is the "birth place" of the *mestizo/a* people, because they embody inclusion, equality, and new creation. The church is the *mestizo* par excellence because "it strives to bring about a new synthesis of the earthly and the heavenly. . . . It is the 'third' or new people, which assumes the good that was before and gives it new meaning."[24] As such, the church functions as the social conscience that rejects and condemns racism, capitalism, and other social maladies that dehumanize people. So, for Elizondo, *mestizaje* means intermixture and the synthesis that occurs as a result of different elements coming together and being synthesized. *Mestizaje* further points to the divine providential creation of a new reality in which all peoples are welcome and there is no racism.

Finally, the *resurrection principle* is the redemption of the suffering of the *mestizo* Mexican American people. Just as Jesus' humiliation and death were turned into a source of life and joy in the resurrection, God will bring life and health out of the *mestizo*-mixed people's suffering and death. This is what happens when the poor and marginalized people encounter the risen Lord. This principle shows the voiceless finding their voice and unmasking the forces that suppress them and marginalize them. The principle of resurrection is the struggle for life that opposes exclusion and death, and opts for celebration, life, and inclusion, which is indicative "of the eschatological *mestizo* identity: they are the ones in whom the fullness of the kingdom has already begun, the new universalism that bypasses human segregating barriers."[25]

In Elizondo's work the original historical intermixture of the indigenous peoples and the Spaniards identified as *mestizaje* undergoes a radical metamorphosis. It quickly becomes an ambiguously complex and fluid concept, as we can see by outlining the three different elements that he includes in the descriptor *new mestizaje:* first, those pertinent to the Mexican American people; second, those that relate to the task of doing theology; and third, those that Elizondo finds have important "universal" implications.

First, the descriptor *mestizos/as* for the Mexican American people recognizes their double history of conquest and invasion, as first and second *mestizaje*. In this initial articulation of *mestizaje*, starting in 1975, Elizondo claims that this double history of conquest and invasion differentiates Mexican Americans from all the other Latin American communities, who are also *mestizos/as* but only of the first kind.[26] The *new mestizos/as* are bicultural and have what DuBois labels a "double consciousness."[27] Not only culturally but also geographically these are people who live in a state of existential in-betweenness. They are neither Mexicans (indigenous and Spanish) nor U.S. white-Anglo-European North Americans—and yet they are both. They represent the *new humanity* legitimated by God in the person of Jesus. Through their religious symbols and practices they preserve and give life to their cultural identity.[28] They are bicultural, and this means different approaches to religious education and unique pastoral opportunities as they live their Christian faith.[29] This first division refers to the historical specificity of the Mexican American people and their unique identity as culturally *mestizos/as*-mixed.

Second, as to the task of theology, *mestizaje*-as-mixture proves to be disruptively useful for Elizondo beginning in the mid-1980s in that it reclaims the history of the Mexican American people, their struggles, their conditions of discrimination and oppression, and their religious experience. In other words, there is no such thing as one type of theology applicable for all cultures. By including the human experiential dimension of culture, Elizondo makes it difficult for any future articulation of theology to make general claims without paying attention to the cultural context of the people.[30]

Third, relating primarily to his later works, in the 1990s and up to the present (although there are hints of this direction in his earlier writings), Elizondo reflects upon the worldwide implications of the notion of *mestizaje*. He connects *mestizaje*-as-mixture to the phenomena of migration. He argues that the present flow of people is creating the conditions for a *mestizaje* on a global scale.[31] Other scholars have reached the same conclusion; Jacques Audinet, for example, sees *mestizaje* as the logical, if not the inevitable, next step of multiculturalism.[32] But according to Elizondo, *mestizaje*-as-intermixture is as "old as the planet itself."[33] And because of its inherent *inclusive* nature, racism is neutralized and interreligious considerations are guaranteed. The *new* creation that is on the verge of formation in the *new mestizo* family of the Americas will be a place where there "will be rich racial and ethnic diversity, but not discrimination . . . ethnic identity but not ethnocentrism."[34] He sees in the Americas the birthplace of a utopian universal *new* humanity. This is a place that promises to be ecumenical, where "all the religions which live in this land . . . will come together . . . to take counsel and listen to the divine spirit at work in us."[35] This third aspect, therefore, reveals Elizondo's assumptions about the inclusive and utopian character of *mestizaje*.

Andrés Guerrero arrives at a conclusion similar to Elizondo's in this third phase of *mestizaje*, but he takes a stronger ethnocultural stance: Guerrero claims that *La raza* is a symbol of "cosmicity," of specific universality; *mestizaje* promises to exclude no one. The *mestizos/as* Chicanos/as symbolize the unity of all of the Latin Americans and provide the conceptual framework under which all Latin Americans can unite. More specifically, the "beauty of *La raza cósmica* lies in its literal colourblindness." Chicanos/as will "naturally" include other people; they are the mixture of many peoples, and therefore their *mestizaje*-intermixture is the antidote to racism and the solution to racial prejudices.[36]

> We have one foot in the rich world and one in the poor world. We experience both because we live in both. Racially we are all the different colors of people. Economically we are poor in a rich country. Politically we are millions of people but invisible. Culturally we are a combination of four major cultures. Socially we interact with many people who have also been mixed and look like us. Spiritually, because of our *mestizaje*, we have characteristics that encounter and include others.[37]

Not everything is as coherent in Elizondo's work as it appears. Certainly in his reconstruction *mestizaje* becomes a useful and plastic category for cultural, political, and religious analysis and theological discursive articulations. *Mestizaje* is variously a hermeneutical key; an affirmation of the Mexican American culture and religious symbols; the space from which to struggle for equality and against marginalization; a symbol of the church;

and the promise of the universal inclusion of all peoples. The identifiable icon of divine "chosen-ness" along with the *mestizo* Galilean Jesus is Guadalupe, the *mestizo/a* symbol par excellence. But the historical realization of such *mestizaje* lies in the future, as does that of the liberation and full potential of Chicanos/as.[38]

This creates great tensions and contradictions for Elizondo. He insists that the first and second *mestizajes* are clearly historically definable. At the same time, he insists that Mexican Americans are in a state of cultural maturing.[39] Elizondo rejects notions of culture as static and monolithic, endorsing instead an understanding of culture in constant flux. Yet, in speaking of a well-defined, almost-finished double *mestizaje*, he suggests that cultural change and development can be measured. At the same time, he disapproves of the present inroads that "fundamentalist" churches are making among the Mexican American people, identifying them as a negative third evangelism because of their destructive attitude toward the religious symbols and practices of the people.[40] However, using his framework of the fluctuating character of culture, it would make better sense to speak of subsequent *mestizajes*-as-intermixture, and not limit them to a specific number. The dialectic tension between the finished-unfinished character of Mexican American culture does not allow him to see in the reality of intermixture new processes that bring about radical *new* changes to cultural collectives.

More to the point, by speaking about the second *mestizaje* of Mexican Americans as yet unrealized, and in affirming that the *future is mestizo* (mixed), Elizondo unwittingly echoes José Vasconcelos's universalizing and assimilating *cosmic* dream. On the one hand, he lessens the effect of the violence of the Spanish conquest by invoking the inscription at the Plaza of the Three Cultures, stating that what happened there was "neither a victory nor a defeat, but the painful moment of birth of the Mexico of today, of a race of Mestizos." This reminds us that, for Vasconcelos, the benefits of the conquest were greater than the violence it represented. But as González declares: "The famous inscription, no matter how beautiful it may be, does not tell the truth. There were victors and vanquished. And the vanquished and their descendants have suffered for centuries the consequence of their defeat."[41]

On the other hand, he insists that "cultures will not die or disappear but simply continue through the new flesh and spirit, in the new body and soul of the *mestizo* children."[42] In this way *mestizo/a*-mixed people will be the heirs of the cultural elements of their parents. But this creates important implications for the way he conceives *mestizaje* through the "providential" lenses. By seeing the divine as the impetus of the reality of intermixture, the violence, genocide, and atrocities of any intercultural encounter can be explained away: at worst as necessary evil, and at best as collateral damage. Stated this way, *mestizaje*-as-intermixture, including the violence with which it happened, is divinely sanctioned.

By ascribing universal characteristics to *mestizaje*, Elizondo comes dangerously close to making absolutizing claims that run contrary to his theological proposal. He turns *mestizaje* into a catch-all category for speaking about intermixture, thus all but divorcing the term from the original distinctively historical-social-political specificity of Latinas/os in the United States. This uncritical use of the term reduces the notion of *mestizaje* to a mere abstract synonym of *intermixture*, interchangeable with notions like hybridity, heterogeneity, inclusivity, and creolization, but with no historical foundation.[43] It says very little about the power dynamics at play when different peoples clash.

MESTIZAJE AS THE CONCRETE RELIGIOUS EXPERIENCE OF THE PEOPLE: ROBERTO GOIZUETA

Like Elizondo's, Goizueta's philosophical-theological proposal represents a paradigm shift in the manner in which theological knowledge is conceived and articulated. Starting in early 1992, this Cuban American sought to distance himself from intellectual individualistic approaches rooted in a "dualistic epistemology" that reduces reality to opposing elements.[44] He argued that these dichotomies—the individual against society, community against institution, affect against intellect, morality against intelligence, body against mind—must be rejected because they are fundamentally at odds with the U.S. Latina/o experience and have served as ideological instruments to oppress U.S. Latina/o communities.[45]

Methodologically speaking, he proposed that the historical experience of U.S. Latinas/os is the grounding for U.S. Latina/o theological knowledge and articulation. What does this mean for theology? First, the experiences of the people place limitations on theological knowledge. His affirmation is a bold assertion in favor of theological plurality. He rejects univocal ahistorical theological articulations that function under the pretence of universality and become their own standard.[46] In other words, all theologies are colored by their historical context and location.[47] And U.S. Latina/o theology is a conscious attempt at recovering this critical aspect of theology.

Second, the experience of the people as the point of departure of theology recovers the long-lost interconnection between praxis and theory, and praxis and poiesis. Goizueta's innovative proposal draws on Enrique Dussel's anadialectical method in his understanding of praxis as liberative subjective action of "openness toward an Other," placing praxis (human activity in relation to other humans) and poiesis (human productive activity in relation to nature) at the service of the oppressed other.[48] At the same time, he seeks to (re)define the limits of theological discourse (theory) by recovering the connection between religious expressions and practices (form), and theological reflection (content).[49] The alternative to dominant intellectual notions of theology that reduce reality to the sphere of reason alone is a theology that intentionally emerges from the preconceptual dimension of life (or theopoetics).[50] The historical everyday experiences of Latinas/os, in which the divine is revealed prior to its conceptual articulation (theology), are the ground of Latina/o theology. By itself, this assertion also moves away from restricted notions of revelation that fail to envision the divine at work in the sphere of the everyday reality.

Third, popular religion is the place where people express their experience concretely. For Goizueta, this is consistent with the liberationist "epistemological privilege of the poor." For him, it follows that if the poor have a privileged access to *knowledge* of the divine, they also have a privileged access to the *form* of such revelation. Such revelation is embodied in the people's religious practices, symbols, and images—which is to say that theological reflection, ethics, and aesthetics are in dialogue with popular religion. For Goizueta, this is the intersubjective human praxis of the U.S. Latinas/os.[51]

Here *mestizaje* plays a central role in Goizueta's reflections. As he puts it, *mestizaje*-as-miscegenation provides the context for the experience of the people. He adopts Elizondo's proposal of a double *mestizaje* emphasizing the biological and cultural dimensions of intermixture. From the vantage point of miscegenation, *mestizaje* is fraught with negative connotations, as it is the consequence of "centuries of rape, violence, forced exile, and conquest."[52] In the same way *mestizaje*-as-mixture provides the material content reflected in popular religious expressions and symbols as the amalgam of indigenous and Spanish elements.[53]

These religious expressions represent the birth of a new, rich culture; they are the fruit of the "people's unquenchable hope."[54] So in Goizueta's work *mestizaje* as miscegenation and *mestizaje* as intermixture exist in fine tension. The resolution takes place at the level of everyday life and in the religious practices and symbols of the people. In this way, he claims, the condition of *mestizaje*-as-mixture has uniquely equipped the people to envision reality in a new *inclusive* way. So he sees *mestizaje*—as expressed in popular religion, specifically in Our Lady of Guadalupe—as the people's redemptive space from the violent experience of miscegenation. His underlying assumption is that the negative effects of the Spanish conquest, invasion, and violence have been subverted by the intermixture-*mestizaje* of Spanish and indigenous elements concretely manifest in the religious expressions of the people. Consistent with Elizondo, the forces of assimilation that cause marginalization and discrimination in the United States are countered by merging these human-cultural traditions—Iberian, indigenous, and white-Anglo—into a new cultural expression: Latina/o culture and people. *Mestizaje*, as he understands it, represents the hope of inclusivity.

Goizueta is not unfamiliar with the tensions and ambiguities inherent in the use of *mestizaje*, whether of biological intermixture or of cultural and religious exchanges. In order to speak of these two dimensions, early in his career (1994) he proposed *mestizaje* as a category of analysis. This permitted him to connect the biological with the cultural, and to engage the intellectual at the same time. That is why, despite the serious weaknesses of racism and idealism that Goizueta finds in Vasconcelos's version of *mestizaje*, he insists that *mestizaje* as a category of analysis is fruitful for speaking of the experience of the people.[55] Appropriately, he cautions U.S. Latina/o theologians that the term cannot be appropriated *uncritically* without grounding it in the *historical experience* of the U.S. Latina/o communities. Not to do this, he claims, runs the danger of becoming accomplices in the oppression of the people.[56] So, contrary to Vasconcelos's aesthetic and ahistorical notion of *mestizaje* as the result of empathic fusion, U.S. Latina/o theology must also reflect upon the experience of *mestizaje* from the perspective of the sociopolitical and economic reality of the U.S. Latina/o communities. As Goizueta asserts, it is only by taking the historical experience of *mestizaje* in its relation to all dimensions of life, that Vasconcelos's abstract idealism can be corrected and overcome, and the category of *mestizaje* can then become concrete and liberative.[57]

But at this point Goizueta's critical edge begins to break down. He urges U.S. Latina/o theologians to develop new categories that mediate the cultural and philosophical with the socioeconomic dimension of praxis. He does not realize that the very assumptions of inclusivity he holds true about *mestizaje* are part of the problem. He appropriately points out the contradictions between the reality and the assumptions about the intellectual category; he is right in connecting degrees of cultural intermixture with class allegiance by saying that among U.S. Latinas/os those "least mesticized"—by which he really means those with lighter skin—have greater opportunities to acquire wealth. The opposite is also true; those "more mesticized"—by which he really means those who look more indigenous or African—make up the bulk of the lower classes.[58] But here Goizueta echoes earlier notions that connected lighter pigmentation with a lower degree of intermixture, as illustrated in the caste paintings.[59] In my view, this is a myth, for it conceals the various degrees of intermixture that European and Anglo U.S. ethnic and cultural groups have undergone among themselves, which in many ways are not as easily detectable as are intermixtures with indigenous and African groups.

Similarly, Goizueta concedes that to say that the indigenous people are equal to the Spaniards without critiquing the violence the latter perpetrated on the former can also mean that U.S. Latina/o theology promotes rape.[60] He does not follow the logical implications of this assertion. He fails to realize that the problem and contradictions are inherent in the construction of *mestizaje* itself. He conflates the sociocultural reality of the people with the utopian dream of inclusivity and equality in his idea that intermixture-*mestizaje* results in promoting equality and inclusion. *Mestizaje* is a rhetorical mirage that claims to represent equality among ethnic groups, but when compared to the reality and experience of Latinos/as, and specifically when measured against the reality of the Cuban community to which he belongs, intermixture-*mestizaje* has not brought about the equalizing of people at the economic level, nor has it removed racial discrimination or promoted inclusivity.

The difficulty in untangling the manner in which Goizueta has braided these three meanings together has to do with the collapsing of the *biological reality of miscegenation* and the *cultural dimension of intermixture* within *mestizaje* as *intellectual category*. Part of the problem is that his emphasis on the historical experience of *mestizaje* of the people as mediated by popular religion is far too simplistic. He is right in asserting that

> the future of *mestizaje* depends not only on an increased openness to other cultures and races, not only on sympathy, not only on the development of an aesthetic sense, and not only on intermarriage, but also on a critique of and struggle against those structures that have for centuries impeded the development of *mestizaje* by forcing us to choose between equally unthinkable alternatives of assimilation or exclusion.[61]

But in paying attention to the situation of marginalization of the U.S. Latinas/os based on the historical emphasis of purity of blood in the United States, Goizueta fails to critique the notion of *mestizaje* itself. The assumption is that the condition of being mixed-*mestizo/a* brings about equality. He pays too much attention to the structures and institutions that have prevented intermixture-*mestizaje* from developing in the United States, but he misses the reality of racialized sociopolitical and economic differences among U.S. Latinas/os. The issues that emerge here go beyond the scope of this discussion, and it is important to review the fruits of this research. Thus, I will engage them at greater length in a later chapter.

For now, let me just say that the term *mestizaje* is particularly attractive for Goizueta and U.S. Latina/o theologians because it provides the material discourse with which to resist the dominant culture of the United States. The notion of *mestizaje* helped them counter the dominant culture's definition of humanity and "American" society as "white" and monocultural. Indeed, Goizueta contributes to the construction of a new theological space in which the historical experience of marginalization and discrimination of the U.S. Latinas/os can be articulated. He sees the vitality of the experience and expressions of faith and cultural activities of these peoples as resistance. *Mestizaje*-as-resistance expresses the stubborn determination of these communities not to be assimilated by the dominant culture.[62] In line with Elizondo, *mestizaje* means the retrieval and reclaiming of their unique history of violence and conquest, but also of resistance and hope.[63]

Mestizaje as a category of analysis is useful for countering intellectual dualistic notions. Goizueta tells us that *mestizaje* provides the material for conceiving reality outside of the Cartesian either/or model and more like a both/and approach. As far as he is concerned, *mestizaje*-as-intermixture challenges monocular views of reality and replaces them with a binocular perspective. More to the point, Goizueta conceives *mestizaje* as removing the oppositionalism inherent in the U.S. dominant culture and society.[64]

Note that Goizueta finds in *mestizaje* such disruptive force precisely because of the assumptions informing his intellectual exercise. His logic is this: First, while miscegenation (biological *mestizaje*) is the violent coming together of two peoples, it is a coming together nonetheless, and not a preservation of purity of blood. At this point he agrees with both Vasconcelos's and Elizondo's critiques of the U.S. white-Anglo dominant culture that prohibited "biological intermixture." Second, he reasons that along with miscegenation came the intermixture of cultures (cultural *mestizaje*). This notion of intermixture, he claims, challenges essentialist monolithic notions of identity formation and recognition. But here he fails to address the fact that the "encounter" did not take place between equals; he does not engage the power relations at play. He claims that it is as a result of such intermixture that the identity and reality of the U.S. Latinas/os must be conceived; it encompasses the historical-cultural elements of their ancestry, both biological (Spaniards and indigenous) and cultural (Spaniards, indigenous, white Anglos of the United States). Third, the concrete expressions and amalgams of the legacy of their common ancestry are found in popular religion and cultural practices. These include bold expressions of resistance to assimilation into the dominant U.S. culture. Popular religious expressions display great flexibility, in which Spanish and indigenous cultural-religious elements are incorporated by the people in the production of a new *inclusive* way of life. Fourth, this new way of life as resistance by inclusivity reveals the divine activity. The experience of *mestizaje* of the people, along with their everyday intersubjective praxis reflected in their popular religion, is the *locus* and ground of theological reflection.[65] Fifth, the concept of *mestizaje* refers to a voluntary or willful "coming together," which carries the implication that the category of *mestizaje* is inherently inclusive and breaks away from dualistic exclusionary notions. Here, he makes no attempt to see the exclusive dimensions of the historical discourses of *mestizaje*. Sixth, and last, theological articulations must be based on the historical experience of the people. Historical experience means at least four things for Goizueta: the initial experience of invasion and conquest, the U.S. invasion of Mexico, the present experience of marginalization and discrimination, and the present state of the people's religious expressions and future possibilities.

Part of the limitations of Goizueta's proposal is that in attempting to name the distinctiveness of the experience of the U.S. Latinas/os as *mestizaje*, he leaves unchallenged the particular racialized tensions among Latinas/os. Indeed, the discourse of *mestizaje* leads to the exclusion of significant sectors of the Latina/o population. And for Goizueta, emphasizing the *dual* identity of Latinas/os in the United States excludes the possibility of *including* the African ancestry as a legitimate third prong in the process of identity formation of the U.S. Latinas/os. From this perspective the experience of *mestizaje*-as-miscegenation is true only for a portion of the U.S. Latina/o population. There are other groups that do not fit under the rubric of *mestizaje*.

In seeing *mestizaje* as a dual both/and reading of reality, Goizueta also repeats traditional binary oppositional views between the indigenous and Spaniards; he simply reconciles them. He tries to ameliorate the situation by synthesis, yet he fails to notice the rejection of *mestizaje*-as-synthesis among particular indigenous communities that do not want to lose their own unique identity in the United States.[66] In this case, in promoting *mestizaje* he runs the risk of reproducing the type of racism that excludes these indigenous communities. In failing to evaluate the larger lineage of violence in *mestizaje*, his innovative notion of maintaining praxis and theory together breaks down.

Goizueta rightly suggests that *mestizaje* cannot be taken uncritically. He distinguishes between authentic and unauthentic *mestizaje*, the former referring to critiquing the sociopolitical and economic dynamics connected with *mestizaje*. From the perspective of the indigenous and African descendant, who is excluded from the discourses of *mestizaje*, Goizueta's proposal reinscribes the idealization he was trying to avoid in the first place.

This last point seems critical for Goizueta, as he highlights that the experience of *mestizaje* relates also to his vocation as a U.S. Latino theologian. As a U.S. Latino theologian his version of *mestizaje* is not just an intellectual category but also sheds light on his own (and that of U.S. Latina/o scholars in general) experience as an academic. As a theologian he experiences a sense of in-betweenness in relation to the U.S. Latina/o community to which he belongs, and in relation to the theological community. In terms of the former, his vocation is one of solidarity with the people and their experience of marginalization. In terms of the latter, his responsibility is that of bringing that solidarity face to face with the dominant culture that excludes. Thus, he adds, "the experience of *mestizaje*, which has taught us to refuse easy dichotomies, becomes a source of strength in the struggle for liberation."[67] Such existential ambiguity prevents U.S. Latina/o scholars from becoming only intellectuals with no activism, but it is an occasion for maintaining both their activism and intellectual life in close relation. As he states: "If . . . our reflection is not firmly rooted in the historical experience of Hispanic communities in the United States, in our experience of *mestizaje*, and in popular religiosity through which communities live out their faith, we likewise betray our people and become accomplices in their oppression."[68]

I agree with Goizueta's initial claim that theological reflection must emerge from the experience of the people. He also claims that just as "the *mestizo/a* has a history, so does the very concept of *mestizaje*."[69] But for some reason, he does not follow the retrieval of the messy and oppressive history of *mestizaje* discourse that disallows the unqualified use of the term in the fashion in which he and other U.S. Latina/o scholars suggest. A careful examination of the history of the people makes it problematic to use *mestizaje* to describe appropriately the diverse U.S. Latina/o communities. Such use reproduces the absences of great sectors of the U.S. Latina/o population. To use *mestizaje* in such fashion is tantamount to Goizueta's own charge of producing a dehistorized ethics and theology.[70]

MESTIZAJE AS SOURCE AND FOUNDATION OF LATINA FEMINIST THEOLOGY: MARÍA PILAR AQUINO

Aquino identifies herself simultaneously as a U.S. Latina feminist theologian, a Latin American feminist theologian, and a Latina/Chicana scholar. That is, when writing from the perspective of women in Latin America, she tends to write as a Latin American feminist liberation theologian.[71] For Latina women in the United States, she speaks as a Latina feminist scholar.[72] And when she places herself in the tradition of Latin American women and women of Mexican descent in the United States, she uses the Latina/Chicana designator.[73] This seriously limits her work. On the one hand, she is uniquely versatile in responding to the diverse challenges that oppressed women face in the different contexts she navigates as a Latina feminist theologian; she sees her theological observations reaching both sides of the Mexico-U.S. border. On the other hand, it is unclear with whom she identifies in some of her writings; is it with U.S. Latina/o theology (as Latina, Chicana, or Mexican American), or as a Latin American theologian in the United States? This ambivalence undercuts the effectiveness of some of her work and brings into question the nature of her commitment to either theological tradition. This ambivalence in identity is particularly true when she is discussing the issue of *mestizaje*.

Aquino's version of *mestizaje* is central to her personal commitments and entire theological work, which began to surface around 1988. She has invested much of her energy countering social and intellectual patriarchal and kyriarchal structures that promote women's exclusion from equal participation in society.[74] While she upholds a plurality of commitments, in every context her primary concern is the oppressed women of Latin America and U.S. Latinas. Contrary to abstract theological expressions that fail to relate to the complexity and messiness of reality, she proposes a "sentient" theology whereby reason and the senses are but two steps in theological articulation.[75] She pursues an organic and embodied theology that incorporates women's bodies and sexuality, along with everyday struggles and experiences of oppression as sources for theological reflection. And she is also particularly invested in reclaiming women's subjectivity as producers of theological knowledge.

A central feature of Aquino's theology is the everyday *(lo cotidiano)* experiences of the people.[76] For her, *lo cotidiano* is the level at which women encounter violence and injustice, but also the context within which women struggle and find grace and hope.[77] She would say that the present globalizing kyriarchal system of market capitalism has exacerbated the oppression of women by promoting their threefold discrimination along the axes of sex, class, and race,[78] and by reducing them to conditions of mere survival in which they have become simply collateral damage.[79] Violence against women is indeed the most unspoken, the most hidden, and even justified as natural!.[80]

Aquino's theology is an intra-ecclesial conversation within Catholicism. She argues that the present structures of the institution exclude women from participating in ordained ministry and authority structures of the church. In order to change these structures, she insists, there is need for reformulating the understanding of church as a "community of equals" where "laity" becomes a dimension of the entire church.[81] Chiding her male Latin American liberation counterparts, she brings into the open their lack of support for women's theological efforts. This is contradictory to their liberation claims, she points out, for "there cannot be a liberation theology that configures itself at the expense of silencing women."[82] For her, then, the church as an institution is divided by class, race, and sex, which results in the everyday exclusion and discrimination of women inside and outside the church. Her theological critique includes the globalizing capitalist system for perpetuating the subaltern and oppressive situation of women.

At this juncture, in 1992, Aquino turned to *mestizaje* as a critical category and hermeneutical key in her theological reflections. Her theology condemns the many kinds of oppressions against U.S. Latina/o and Latin American women, who, for the most part, are indigenous, black, and *mestizas*.[83] She problematizes the oppression of women, including the racialized ethnocultural dimensions. In other words, her experience of oppression as *mestiza* (and that of many other *mestizas*) plays a central role in her theological reflections.[84]

By connecting the concerns of Latin American women and U.S. Latinas in her work, Aquino becomes vulnerable to a double criticism. Her proposal of *mestizaje* does not address the particular dynamics of identity recognition and *mestizaje* among the diverse populations of Latin America and U.S Latinas/os. She does not acknowledge the complex and oppressive role that *mestizaje* discourse plays within the Latin American population, at times promoting the "whitening" and de-indigenization of the African descendants and indigenous populations correspondingly.[85] In Latin America not to be part of the dominant *mestizo/a* culture is to be part of the diverse marginalized and exploited indigenous groups or African descendants.[86]

More important for our purpose, Aquino points out that in the United States most non-white Latinas (indigenous, blacks, and *mestizas*) are exploited and underemployed. Her criticism is directed mainly at the white dominant society and Latinos/as as the oppressed peoples. But she does not deal with the inherent group identity obstacles introduced by the notion of *mestizaje* among the Latina/o communities. Subsuming U.S. Latinas under the category of *mestizaje* effectively covers up the concrete ways in which social, cultural, and racialized differences among Latinas result in expressions of racism among them.[87]

Aquino appropriately points out that when Africans were brought to the Americas, they came in chains as slaves, so that the enslaving of the African people and the genocide and oppression of the indigenous peoples were seen positively only by the Europeans and their descendants.[88] The complexity of the issues in Latin America is such that the *mestizo/a* population, the descendants of the Spaniards-Europeans and indigenous, continued with the work of conquest and cultural genocide of the indigenous peoples, as exemplified by Dora María Téllez, and as testified to by the increasing literature emerging from Latin America.[89]

Resonating with most Latina/o theologians, for Aquino the question of *mestizaje* clearly relates to the amalgam of the African, indigenous, and Spanish-European peoples and cultures. She tells us that *mestiza* theology inevitably leads us to recover the ancestral indigenous and African cultural legacies.[90] She adds, "The growing strength of our theology can be appreciated, among other factors, in the appropriation it has made of indigenous, African, and European traits as constitutive dimensions of its being."[91]

At this point, Aquino's understanding of *mestizaje* turns dangerously into an idealized, dehistoricized, abstract notion. The "cultural legacies" of the indigenous and African peoples are not vestiges of a distant past preserved among the *mestizos/as;* they are present among those communities that do not identify themselves with the label of *mestizas/os*. The tensions inherent in her affirmations are between the ancestral indigenous and African heritage, and today's marginalized indigenous and African peoples. The indigenous and African peoples among the U.S. Latina/o communities show that the label of *mestizaje* cannot be applied to the whole population.

Aquino's appropriation of indigenous and African traits and cultural heritage resonates with Mexico's cultural renaissance immediately after the revolution of 1910, which promoted a cultural indigenism without giving any attention to the continuing impoverishment and social exclusion of the indigenous people. Taking pride in indigenous ancestry and cultural heritage was key in asserting *mestizo/a* identity. In order to affirm their *mestizo* identity, Mexican intellectuals thought that the displacement, dislocation, or assimilation of the indigenous people was necessary, celebrating their replacement by the *mestizo/a* population.[92] In the same way, during the revolution the national identity of Mexico was built by excising the African heritage from the national *mestizo/a* imaginary.[93] Hidden beneath the Latina/o theologians and Aquino's use of *mestizaje* is a similar construction of U.S. Latina/o identity that displaces indigenous and African peoples. To use *mestizaje* as the defining category of Latinas/os effectively masks the internal power asymmetry by which the indigenous and African communities are excluded from the Latina/o *mestizo* imaginary.

Further, Aquino supports reconfiguring the limits and understanding of *mestizaje*, as Zipporah Glass articulates.[94] My concern is the direction of such reconfiguration. Glass proposes the adoption of *mestizaje* to speak about the reality of intermixture among the African Americans. She also challenges the reigning images of U.S. Latinas/os by highlighting the African roots and presence in many of them. Glass notes that U.S. Latina/o African descendants have a different understanding of themselves than other African Americans. As she sees it, this is partly because these groups have had different experiences and history. She counters the rhetoric of blackness from the 1950s and 1960s, which assumed a "homogeneous black people who shared a common identity and history" in the United States.[95] Her proposal, then, is the adaptation of *mestizaje* as a key rhetorical category for identifying the plurality among African Americans in the United States.[96] Here she resonates with Alice Walker's comment that U.S. African American people are the *mestizos* of North America.[97] Glass and Walker show that there are other experiences of intermixture and violence that resonate with what U.S. Latina/o theologians are trying to say with *mestizaje*.

Two important points emerge here. First, Glass's initial recognition of African roots and presence in Latin America and among U.S. Latinas/os subsumes these peoples and their experiences under the discourse of *mestizaje*. Suzanne Bost illustrates this tendency as she reconfigures and acknowledges the rich diversity of Puerto Rico with *mestizaje*.[98] Bost's categorical move risks subsuming under the discourse of *mestizaje* the unique and separate history of the African people and their descendants, their slavery, and their struggles of resistance. Although closely connected to issues of *mestizaje* and intermixture, I suggest that the discursive spaces of the African descendants among Latinas/os refer specifically to the discourse of *mulataje*.

Second, to assume *mestizaje* as a useful category for speaking about diversity among African Americans, as both Walker and Glass argue, problematizes and relativizes the use of *mestizaje*, because the experience of intermixture is not unique to the U.S. Latina/o communities. This demands that U.S. Latina/o scholars engage in conversation with other groups who are using the term in order to create new spaces of conversation beyond dominant binary oppositional and essentialist constructions of ethnic and cultural identity. But this also shows that U.S. Latina/o theologians' use of the category of *mestizaje* for any type of intermixture runs the danger of reifying *mestizaje* as an abstraction separated from its historical rootedness, universally applicable for any context of intermixture. The historically specific underpinnings of the experiences of different peoples must accompany any uses of *mestizaje*.

Admittedly, symbols often escape their origins and take on new and different meanings. But all symbols must be evaluated against their sociohistorical and political expressions. In this case, the unqualified use of *mestizaje* to speak of the different experiences of intermixture among African peoples in the Americas is highly problematic. Such use of *mestizaje* does not take seriously the unique historical baggage of violence and exclusion under which *mestizaje* was initially conceived and later came to be used as a mechanism of assimilation, de-Africanization, and de-indigenization.

To use *mestizaje* to speak of the African presences of the Americas denies the unique history of slavery, exploitation, and intermixture experienced by the African American communities. These need to be reflected upon and articulated in their own right. Not to do this represents a practical erasure of the violent historical baggage of *mestizaje* as a homogenizing ideology and ensures the continuing invisibility and silencing of the African peoples. U.S. Latina/o theologians must reconfigure *mestizaje* so that it clearly does not purport to speak for all U.S. Latina/o populations and other ethnocultural intermixtures.

This leads me to another use of *mestizaje* by Aquino. Most common among U.S. Latina/o scholars is the idea that *mestizaje* means inclusion. In this second period in the development of Aquino's theological thought, the inclusion she speaks about emerges from a gender critique of the male-centered traditional theological structures and methods and determination to create coalitions of marginalized women. To her, *mestiza* theology is a critical appropriation of Latinas deriving from their *mestiza* (read: culturally mixed) condition, which is itself a cry of struggle on the side of the poor and oppressed. It is also the recognition that as women participate in the articulation of their own experience they contribute to the production of new theological knowledge. By using *mestizaje* here, Aquino not only shows discomfort with traditional approaches to theology, but also with the theological subjects that traditionally have excluded women in the Latin American and U.S. Latina/o contexts. *Mestiza* theology is, then, a space where women from different cultural backgrounds can stand together and unmask the injustices of the systems of oppression and gender exclusion.[99]

This view of *mestizaje* as inclusion falls in line with Aquino's view of *mestizaje* in the direction of interculturality. In this latest use of *mestizaje*, in 2002, she points to the adoption of a theological method which "consciously opts for inculturality as central methodological axis."[100] Aware of the debates on inculturality, pluralism, diversity, and multiculturalism, she proposes that *mestizaje* is "better equipped" to respond to the questions emerging from "our own historical reality," which, following Fornet-Betancourt, she calls *intercultural*. Here she tells us that she is referring not so much to the biological *mestizaje*, but to the cultural and intellectual *mestizaje* that has created the new *intercultural* reality. Yet, she makes clear that using *mestizaje* as a category of analysis cannot be separated from the biological condition of *mestizaje*.

Aquino makes two problematic assumptions about *mestizaje* here. First, she adopts Elizondo's discursive understanding of *mestizaje* as inclusion. She writes that while the dominant cultures have given *mestizaje* a social value worthy only of exclusion, "a *mestizo/a* theology will highlight the vital synthesis which 'new peoples' have interculturally created in order to explain their own vision and their own identities."[101] Note the play between the singular "synthesis" and the plural identities. The implication of Aquino's proposal is that in identifying new identities as *mestizas*, *mestizaje* becomes an overarching category making it impossible for these *new* identities and particularities to be defined as anything but *mestizas*. This construction turns *mestizaje* into the rigid absolutizing and homogenizing mechanism that makes it impossible for different cultural universes and identities to exist outside of *mestizaje*. Under such understanding, inclusion is a myth. It amounts to saying that "*mestizos/as* only have one culture" (that is, that all cultures are mixed in many different combinations and permutations)—that of *mestizaje*, as Espín puts it.[102] Although one can say that no one "mixed" culture is like any other, to conclude that U.S. Latina/o communities have one, albeit mixed, culture obscures the internal cultural diversity of the Latina/o peoples. Seen this way, *mestizaje* does not lead to a sociocultural heterogeneity, as Aquino would like to think, but its exact opposite.[103]

Aquino's second assumption relates to the terms and conditions upon which people enter into such "intercultural" relations. Aquino recognizes the asymmetrical character of social relations at every level. She is certainly not naive concerning the past violence that gave birth to the original *mestizaje*. This is why she asserts that "*mestizaje* is a historical fact that still opens-up old wounds." In the same sentence she argues that *mestizaje* is also "the opportunity to build an intercommunicative platform with other voices who speak from their own irreducible cultures."[104]

The issue is that the reality of power asymmetries and assimilation of a Spanish-European (first *mestizaje*) and/or an Anglo-European (second *mestizaje*) version of culture and society are not only a matter of the past. The idea of *mestizaje* not only opens up "old wounds" of "bad old violent days," but reminds us of national ethnic and cultural imaginaries against which the indigenous and African descendants and communities struggle in order not to be absorbed into and erased from the U.S. Latina/o sociocultural fabric.

Aquino operates with an idealized understanding of *mestizaje*. She does not detect the power differential that mediates the "coming together" of peoples. She writes: "Where different cultures and experiences converge, each carrying its history of suffering and struggle against the powers of death, *mestizaje* becomes the privileged space for a theology that navigates on the currents of solidarity among peoples who seek to confront their suffering."[105] She assumes that such "convergencies" are always voluntary. In the history of the conquest of Latin America, the invasion of Mexico by the United States, and in contemporary U.S. society, violence and injustice have been the underlying forces under which people have intermixed and continue to intermix. Thus, such "coming together" is myth and has meant incalculable suffering for the indigenous peoples and African descendants. Therefore we must call into question Aquino's understanding of *mestizaje*.

MESTIZAJE AS AN ETHICAL-MORAL CHOICE: ADA MARÍA ISASI-DÍAZ AND *MUJERISTA* THEOLOGY

Starting roughly in the second half of the 1980s, the work of Isasi-Díaz reveals a rich tapestry of sensibilities and commitments that resonate with diverse theological traditions. Her work intersects with feminist discourses against sexism, liberation theological emphasis against classism, and, in line with U.S. Latina/o theological work, against ethnic prejudice/racism.[106] More specifically, her *mujerista* theology (a label she coined in 1989) is a bold departure from traditional approaches in that it proposes a theology grounded upon the people's life experiences and struggles.[107] The most important tenets of her theology are the everyday experiences of the people *(lo cotidiano)*, *mestizaje-mulatez*, popular religion, the understanding of theology as praxis, and the recognition that theology is a communal endeavor. These tenets play central roles in how she conceives, constructs, and articulates her theology.

As Aquino does, Isasi-Díaz also insists that the everyday experiences of Hispanic women are the ground, the source, and *locus* of *mujerista* theological reflection.[108] It is at the everyday level that women experience discrimination at home, the church, and society, simply because they are women, Hispanic, and poor.[109] For Isasi-Díaz, the experience of Hispanic women reveals the fundamental role of cultural identity/ethnicity in the way they confront reality and express their faith in God. In her view, ethnicity is a social construction and not simply the result of inherited natural characteristics. It is an organizational tool, "a way of gathering the social forces that go into forming Hispanic women in the U.S.A."[110] Spanish language, popular religion, "social-cultural-psychological survival," economic oppression, and our vision of the future are the elements that, although in constant flux, give the Hispanic community its cohesiveness in the United States.[111] These are the building blocks of her *mujerista* theology's most important feature, namely, *mestizaje-mulatez*. *Mujerista* theology is built upon and finds its center of gravity in *mestizaje-mulatez*.

The early Isasi-Díaz preferred using the label *mestizaje* because she was convinced it was sufficient as a descriptive and prescriptive category of analysis. For example, this is the label she used in her popular *En La Lucha* in 1993. Soon after, in 1996, she proposed that *mulataje* or *mulatez* should be subsumed under *mestizaje*.[112] In 2004, in *La Lucha Continues,* and with the help of Fernando Segovia, she adopted the dual label *mestizaje-mulatez* as a way of acknowledging and naming the African cultural heritage in Hispanic culture.[113]

In *mujerista* theology there is a parallel between the everyday as a source and *locus* of theology, and *mestizaje-mulatez* as *locus* of theology. This is not accidental. The everyday is the reality where worlds collide. The everyday is the place where people experience ethnocultural discrimination, and the space where people struggle against such discrimination. The everyday is the existential location where people come to understand the world and come to know God from their unique ethnocultural context. Like the category *mestizaje-mulatez*, the everyday becomes a place for doing theology. Thus, together with Elizondo, she advocates *mestizaje-mulatez* as central for U.S. Latina/o theology.[114]

Isasi-Díaz's creative version of *mestizaje-mulatez* needs to be untangled because of the numerous meanings she ascribes to the term(s). I divide them into two groups: *mestizaje* as related to the historical roots of intermixture (from the late 1980s to mid 1990s), and *mestizaje* as an intellectual category (from the mid 1990s to today).

In the first group, *mestizaje-mulatez* relates to the historical intermixture among indigenous, African peoples, and the Spaniards-Europeans, and to the children resulting from these intermixtures.[115] This allows Isasi-Díaz to make a number of important assertions. First, influenced by Elizondo, she interprets the conquest in reconciliatory terms stating that *mestizaje-mulatez* marks a "coming together" of peoples and cultures, the creation of a new people, *La raza*.[116] *Mestizaje-mulatez* "was and is a natural result of the coming together of different races. It is not the attempt of one race to make the other disappear."[117] Second, the biological intermixture implicates the cultural aspect as well. Affirming *mestizaje-mulatez* places the theological task in contact with three histories: indigenous, African, and Spanish.[118] And it also means that *mestiza/o-mulata/o* culture is the amalgam of these three different traditions. That is, there is a range of cultures, each mixed in different combinations and proportions. To understand Hispanic people, she claims, it is not enough to go back to their ancestors; one must go to the *mestizo/a* people themselves.[119] Third, since both the indigenous and African peoples had their own religions, they mixed these with European-Spanish Christianity. The adoption of *mestizaje-mulataje* means the embracing of these groups' religious heritages in the form of popular religions as the concrete expressions of this intermixture, which, instead of calling them syncretistic, she identifies as *mestiza/o* religions.[120]

These three different meanings of *mestizaje-mulatez*—biological, cultural, and religious *intermixture*—serve as the platform for the rest of Isasi-Díaz's theological reflections on *mestizaje-mulatez*. From her perspective *mestizaje-mulatez* functions as a hermeneutical tool in understanding the complexity of the Hispanic communities, and as a paradigmatic scheme for the self-representation of these communities.[121] *Mestizaje*, she claims, functions as an instrument of differentiation from the rest of the

U.S. population, and it also sets the parameters for understanding Hispanic faith experience and religious expressions. In this
way *mestizaje-mulatez* is a *locus theologicus*, bringing questions
of ethnicity and culture to the forefront of the theological task.
For her, this is not only a question of the centrality of ethnicity
and culture in human experience. Rather, she perceives everything in the Hispanic communities as being *mixed/mestizo-
mulato*. In other words, to be Hispanic is to be *mestizo/a*. "The
Hispanic understanding of the divine, the human, the meaning
of life, emerge from this *mestizaje*."[122]

In the second category of meanings Isasi-Díaz seeks to broaden
the theological understanding and use of *mestizaje-mulatez*.
Consistent with her proposal, she abandons the original historical specificity of the initial *mestizaje-mulatez*. For her, in the
United States *mestizaje-mulatez* no longer refers to the original
indigenous-Spanish (and African) mixtures. Hispanic culture also
contains cultural elements of the dominant Anglo and Native
American, black, and Asian American.[123] Here, while she echoes
Elizondo's *second mestizaje* of the Anglo-dominant cultural group
with the Mexican Americans, her version is more far-reaching in
scope, although still operating with a rigid view of *mestizaje* and
mulatez as finished products.

For Isasí-Díaz, culture has to do with a living reality, "and as
such it must grow, change, adapt"; the same thing is true of the
Hispanic communities as they undergo a "new" *mestizaje* and
mulatez in the United States, which is an expression of their "actual ongoing growing."[124] So, for her, cultural intermixture is a
continuing process for U.S. Latinas/os. And *mestizaje-mulatez*
has a broader applicability, pointing to any sort of cultural *mixture* among the U.S. Latina/o communities. This is a different
mestizaje-mulatez, however; it includes the indigenous, African,
and Spanish original elements but also extends much further than
that. "*Mestizaje* and *mulatez* also have become a paradigm not
only for our racial diversity but for all the diversity we have in
our Latino/Hispanic communities."[125] Consequently, to embrace
mestizaje-mulatez is to welcome difference.

Working against any notion of purity of culture, and in order
to highlight the fact that Hispanics in the United States are discriminated against because of their ethnicity, Isasi-Díaz proposes

welcoming diversity as an act of subversion of the dominant culture. For her, to embrace *mestizaje-mulataje* is itself a political stance of resistance against a U.S. Anglo–dominant culture of exclusion. Embracing difference, she claims, means rejecting assimilationist and dominant essentialist versions of difference articulated in oppositional terms of mutual exclusion. Difference is more a question of relationality and not a matter of substantive categories that can be listed.[126] For this reason, embracing difference means also the rejection of categories and terms laden with racialized prejudices that result in marginalizing entire segments of society.

Isasi-Díaz asserts that *mestizaje-mulatez* is the Hispanic communities' act of embracing and valuing diversity and difference. *Mestizaje-mulatez* means much more than the biological intermixture of indigenous and African people with the Spanish; in socio-practical terms *mestizaje-mulatez* means the fair and inclusive distribution of opportunities, resources, and benefits. This is the contribution of these communities toward the construction of a culturally plural society.[127] In the same way, for *mujerista* theology, promoting *mestizaje-mulatez* is also the concrete way in which the people hope for their own liberation, and this allows them to be in solidarity with other marginalized groups. *Mestizaje-mulatez* is a critique of the dominant culture's inflexibility towards other cultural groups.[128]

Since for Isasi-Díaz theology is intimately connected with praxis, embracing *mestizaje-mulatez* (difference, multiplicity, and plurality) is a matter of moral choice. For Hispanic women, adopting *mestizaje-mulatez* is the concrete expression of their preferential option for the poor and is intrinsic to their Hispanic identity. When these women opt for *mestizaje-mulatez*, they also opt for themselves and for "Hispanic-ness." "We have the opportunity of defining ourselves, of opting to be *mestizos*, opting to be *for* Hispanics, opting to be Hispanics. . . . I look at the need for the poor to choose the poor, for Hispanic women to choose Hispanic-ness and *mestizaje* as an expression of their option for the poor and the oppressed, an option to which I believe the poor and the oppressed are also called."[129] In this way Isasi-Díaz turns adopting *mestizaje-mulatez* into a matter of personal moral choice. She runs the risk of conflating the option for the poor and for Hispanic identity with the adoption of *mestizaje-mulatez*, which here really means being committed to the struggle for justice, inclusion, and recognition of more complex "mixing" among U.S. Latinas/os. So, for her, it is possible to adopt *mestizaje-mulatez* and not be biologically *mestizo/a*. But she leaves herself vulnerable to serious criticism. Since for her the test of the "moral truth-praxis" of her *mujerista* theology and theological reflections is the adoption of *mestizaje-mulatez*, and since adopting *mestizaje-mulatez* is also to opt for being Hispanic, it follows that Hispanics will, almost instinctively, opt for *mestizaje-mulatez*.[130] This suggests that there is no other way to be Hispanic but to be *mestiza/o-mulata/o*.

It is difficult not to notice the inner tensions in Isasi-Díaz's multilayered understanding of *mestizaje-mulatez*. Her distancing from the historical specificity of *mestizaje* and *mulatez* and from late twentieth-century U.S. reality leaves her paying the cost of contradiction. She has indeed managed to broaden the meaning of the term. Yet in part, this has been possible only by neglecting the reality of exclusion and unique history of *mestizaje* and *mulatez*. By subsuming all other sorts of mixtures under *mestizaje-mulatez*, she uncritically reduces the term to its lowest level of signification. She treats *mestizaje* and *mulatez* as synonymous. But each term is the result of distinct sociohistorical developments, which cannot be reduced to a superficial acknowledgment of the indigenous and African cultural heritage within the Hispanic culture.

Dealing with *mestizaje* and *mulatez* is not simply a question of naming the African presence in the Hispanic culture, as she does, following Fernando Segovia.[131] It is not only a question of highlighting the rich tapestry of Spanish, indigenous, and African cultural elements in U.S. Hispanic culture, as Segovia and other U.S. Latina/o scholars do.[132] Engaging *mestizaje* and *mulatez* calls for a serious critical analysis of the history of each term, both of which go back to Latin American colonial times. True, Isasi-Díaz argued that *mestizaje-mulatez* put *mujerista* theology in contact with three different histories. But that necessitates retracing the violent and at times genocidal attitudes and social, political, and economic structures that gave birth to these terms. Instead, she romanticizes the histories and results of *mestizaje* and *mulatez* by stating that they were and are "a natu-ral result of the coming together of different races."[133] This downplays the violence that gave birth to *mestizaje* and *mulatez* and fails to expose the asymmetrical power differential even to-day, as people are thrown together because of immigration and discrimination.

Isasi-Díaz also fails to follow the internal logic and tenden-cies toward homogenization in her own proposal. No doubt she is convinced that *mestizaje* and *mulatez* promote inclusion and multiplicity. With positivist overtones, she reiterates a type of evolutionary Messianism (similar to Vasconcelos) stating that *mestizaje-mulataje* (once it is global) will represent "the going forward of humankind."[134] Using the work of Goizueta as her interpretive lens on Vasconcelos, she asserts that *mestizaje-mulataje* is the result of an "empathic fusion" of different races, which to her speaks of unity in diversity. She argues that even for Vasconcelos the "*mestizo* community goes beyond a homo-geneous community."[135] As she sees it, this explains why, for Goizueta, "the *mestizo*" does not impose unity but achieves it though this empathic love. She can affirm this position only by holding contradictory elements in the same hand. For both Vasconcelos and Elizondo, fusion or synthesis carried the impli-cation of bringing together diverse groups toward the formation of *some-one-thing* that contains the *mixture* of the whole, which to me sounds too much like homogeneity. So, to affirm *mestizaje-mulatez* as "fusion" runs dangerously close to reinscribing Vasconcelos's own proposal of "voluntary extinction" in the case of the African and indigenous communities.[136]

Isasi-Díaz qualifies her adoption of *mestizaje* by hinting at how the rhetoric of *mestizaje*-as-inclusion has contributed to the development of numerous local agendas that seek to erase indig-enous people from the geo-sociopolitical landscape of Latin America. She is aware that *mestizaje-mulatez* is not always seen as a positive element in Latin America. She points to the am-bivalent embracing of *mestizaje* in Peru and Mexico, by their appropriation of their indigenous "great past" at the same time that they continue to create laws to oppress indigenous peoples.[137] Hers, however, is a "new" *mestizaje-mulatez* that emerges from the need of Latinas/os to struggle against discrimination in the

United States. But she connects *mestizaje* in Latin America with the Latina/o version, claiming that *mestizaje*—as articulated by Latina/o theologians— is also the result of the seeds planted "in our countries of origin regarding the races that have come together in those lands."[138]

So there is an idealized and romanticized interpretation of *mestizaje* at work in her proposal. A careful look at the everyday reality of the people, the "everyday" that Isasi-Díaz affirms as a source of *mujerista* theology, demands a more critical stance toward the historical development of *mestizaje* and *mulataje*. The idea of *mestizaje* continues to be used in exclusionary ways to promote a homogeneous view of national and cultural identity in Latin America and in that fashion continues to penetrate the United States through immigration. Most important, in the context of the U.S. Latina/o communities, the use of *mestizaje-mulataje* continues to exclude a good number of peoples who do not identify themselves with such categories.

Isasi-Díaz embraces *mestizaje-mulatez* without critically engaging the present historical expressions of the term in the specific communities included in her *mujerista* theology: Cuban Americans, Puerto Ricans, and Mexican Americans. A brief look at the social situation in each of these communities quickly reveals that in many places the use of *mestizaje* and *mulatez*, instead of removing racialized discrimination and ethnic prejudice, in fact reinscribes earlier racialized hierarchies among groups, placing the white European at the top of the racialized pyramid. By failing to engage the distinct sociocultural and historical contexts of these communities, Isasi-Díaz leaves herself vulnerable to the critique that she continues the inherent exclusionary and homogenizing force of *mestizaje*. She unwittingly removes all difference by reducing the terms to the level of *mixture*—perhaps only a slightly more sophisticated version of the much derided "melting pot."[139] In the final analysis, she reifies *mestizaje*. She ascribes too much confidence to people's capacity to *inter-mix* as the antidote to the "illness" of racism and discrimination.

These brief surveys of Elizondo, Goizueta, Aquino, and Isasi-Díaz show a plurality of different meanings ascribed to *mestizaje*. These scholars transformed *mestizaje* into a multivalent, powerful critical category of analysis and theological reflection. In responding to the material conditions of their time, U.S. Latina/o theologians used *mestizaje* to open the space for giving discursive theological context to the Latina/o communities' experiences and expressions of faith. But as these theologians used *mestizaje*, they failed to identify the tensions and contradictions engendered by the use of the term. Through their theological contributions they added new meanings to the term, which led to a confusing web of contradictory and competing meanings that make the use of *mestizaje* increasingly problematic. Though sometimes they spoke of *mestizaje* in terms of inclusion and preservation of diversity, in their writings the indigenous peoples and African Latina/o peoples are absent.

These, then, are some of the ways in which U.S. Latina/o theologians used *mestizaje* uncritically, and some of the implications of their claims based on an idealized understanding of *mestizaje*. These theologians failed to examine critically the historical baggage of violence, its inherent logic of exclusion, and its seductive yet destructive façade of inclusion, effectively hiding the presence of racism among U.S. Latinas/os.

By differentiating themselves from Latin America, and by following the dominant Mexican American thrust of the debates at the time, U.S. Latina/o theologians constructed a romantic version of *mestizaje* that naively promised the inclusion of all peoples but effectively silenced the rich diversity of the U.S. Latina/o population. By uncritically taking Vasconcelos as their only connection to the larger debates on *mestizaje* in Latin America, U.S. Latina/o theologians failed to foresee potential problems for using *mestizaje* as a liberative theological and analytical category.

3

MESTIZAJE AMONG MEXICAN AMERICAN CHICANO/A SCHOLARS

The mestizaje valued within Mexican nationalist ideology returns with a vengeance
in a contemporary Chicana/o context. Not
only do different cultures (indigenous,
Mexican, American, colonial Spanish,
gypsy, African, pre-Cortesian), not only do
different languages ("standard" forms of
English and Spanish, mexicanismos, slang
and working class English, caló, regional
Mexican Spanish, chicanismos, regional
Chicano Spanish, indianismos), but also different social, economic, political conditions
(impoverishment contrasted against luxury,
disempowerment against the powerful, the
voiced against the voiceless) come together
to form the Chicana/o.

—RAFAEL PÉREZ-TORREZ

U.S. Latina/o theologians adopted *mestizaje* in order to give
voice to the experiences and struggles of the U.S. Latina/o communities but failed to critique their sociocultural and political
context. So they articulated a naive notion of *mestizaje* that promised to include other cultural groups and end racism, without

interrogating their own assumptions about the term. How did self-identified Chicano/a authors use the term, and was their dependence on the work of José Vasconcelos any different?[1] I focus here particularly on Gloria Anzaldúa's proposal in her *Borderlands/La Frontera*, because very few Chicano/a scholars have had as profound an impact in Chicano/a scholarship as she has.

SETTING THE CONTEXT:
HISTORICAL BACKGROUND

The 1848 Guadalupe-Hidalgo Treaty between Mexico and the United States serves as the historical marker of the birth of the Mexican American people. This event, along with its sociopolitical ramifications, became a rallying point against the U.S. Anglo-European expansionist agenda and oppression of the Mexican American populations. On both sides of the Mexico-U.S. border it marked the violent, even traumatic, experience of separation from family, the fragmentation of territories, and loss of lands, traditions, cultural practices, and identities.

Mexican Americans and Mexicans share much in common by way of experience, culture, history, and identity as a people. For many years these border communities related as if there were no political separation between them. But as the U.S. government established stronger measures to keep Mexican immigrants out of the United States, the relations between them became tense. The political barrier between the two communities strained and oftentimes ruptured the connection of Mexican Americans with their ancestral land. This break forced Mexican Americans to find new and creative ways of asserting their identity as people.

In the Southwest, U.S. peoples were highly segregated, and Mexicans and Mexican Americans shared the bottom rung of society. Mexicans were unwanted in the United States; during Operation Wetback in 1954 the U.S. government deported large numbers of Mexican immigrants. Things changed as the onset of the Second World War resulted in a shortage of farm workers. This forced the U.S. government to enter into an agreement with Mexico—commonly known as the *bracero* program—to allow Mexican seasonal farm workers into the United States. Many of these *braceros* found ways to stay in the country.[2] According to Adolfo Carlos Vento, they were not always welcome. There were differences and tensions between Mexicans and Mexican Americans: to the former, the latter had sold out to the U.S. culture and were not true Mexicans; the latter were oblivious to the social and political plight of the former. Also, the presence of the *braceros* and other types of immigrants angered some of the most assimilated Mexican Americans, who at times used the pejorative term *mojados* (wetbacks) to speak of them.[3]

As Mexican Americans became more aware of the extent to which they were being exploited and marginalized, they began to voice their concerns. César Chávez, Reies López Tijerina, Rodolfo Corky González, the Raza Unida political party, the PADRES and the Las Hermanas organizations, and the Farm Workers movement became symbols of the new struggle for justice and equality. And when it came to articulating their identity and historical origin, they looked for clues, in particular in the long and rich intellectual legacy of Mexico.[4] It was then that the Chicano/a movement was born, a movement that sought to articulate the struggles of the Mexican American population. According to J. Jorge Klor de Alva, the black struggle for civil rights, the ascent of feminist radicalism, the various movements against the Vietnam War, the widespread appeal of anticapitalism, and the growing counterculture of urban insurrection of the baby-boomers "all made the moment ripe for Chicano political protest."[5]

The *Plan Espiritual de Aztlán*, adopted in March 1969 by the First National Chicano Liberation Youth Conference, expressed this concretely. It was a defiant manifesto claiming the Chicano/a community's right to self-determination. It was a political and cultural program that connected issues of class, land, sovereignty, and political organization. For Klor de Alva, the creation of the myth of Aztlán was "the most brilliant maneuver of the Chicano cultural nationalists," as they sought symbols that would distinguish them from other movements and unite them under one banner.[6] Under the banner of Aztlán, Chicano/a people found ways of reclaiming their indigenous Nahua ancestry, while at the same time distinguishing themselves from U.S. Anglo and Mexican cultures.[7]

According to the Aztec legend, Aztlán was the homeland of the Nahua people, whence they migrated south to Tenochtitlán

(Mexico City). The region of Aztlán, claimed Chicanos/as, was the U.S. Southwest. They asserted that the Chicano/a people were the direct descendants of the Nahua people prior to their contact with the Spaniards.[8] In this fashion they bypassed their connection to the Mexican people after the conquest and paid little attention to Mexico's contemporary sociopolitical situations.

The *Plan Espiritual de Aztlán* inspired many movements and numerous forms of activism, but the goals of separating from the United States and becoming self-determining did not come to fruition. However, it managed to rally masses of people under the banner of *la raza* and *mestizaje*. While the *Plan Espiritual de Aztlán* differentiated the Chicano/a people from Mexicans, the ideas behind and labels of *La raza* and *mestizaje* were preserved, and these have played key roles in constructing Chicano/a identity and ethnocultural discourses.

In preserving these two concepts as descriptors of Chicano/a identity, the Chicano/a movement aligned itself with the intellectual influence of Mexico, which dated back to the times of the Porfirista dictatorship and the positivist Los Científicos of the fourth quarter of the nineteenth century. The work of Andrés Molina Enríquez (1868–1940) equating Mexican national identity with being *mestizo/a* epitomizes this.[9] It is during this period of intellectual-nationalistic and anti-U.S.-expansionist revival that the (albeit European assimilationist, positivist) constructions of *mestizaje* eventually became the grand alternative to Mexico's (and the rest of Latin America's) "indigenous problem."[10] Without great changes to its racist implications, these racially homogenizing nationalistic views of *mestizaje* were turned into a well-structured globalizing-messianic and providential project in Vasconcelos's work *La raza cósmica* during Mexico's Revolution.

MESSIANIC SYNTHESIS: VASCONCELOS'S PARADIGM OF *MESTIZAJE* AS *LA RAZA CÓSMICA*

José Vasconcelos's work responded to issues more directly related to the historical context of Mexico. He protested against the imperialist expansionism of the United States, which years earlier, in 1848, had appropriated large Mexican territories. He reacted against the liberal reform of the mid 1800s, which had removed the privileges of the Catholic Church in Mexico.[11] Most important, Vasconcelos set out to counter the elite intellectuals who had concocted their own version of positivism mixed with notions of Spencer's social Darwinism as ways to justify and preserve the Porfirista dictatorship.[12] These intellectuals, known as Los Científicos, insisted that progress (as defined by Europe and the United States) and the use of the hard sciences were the measures of advancement. Headed by Justo Sierra, this group asserted that the progress and the social evolution of Mexico depended greatly on educating the "backward" masses of indigenous peoples.[13]

After completing his studies in law, Vasconcelos became a founding member of the Ateneo de la Juventud (October 28, 1909).[14] As a member of the Ateneo he came to affirm the African, indigenous, and Spanish ancestry of Mexico, and developed his anti-European and anti-U.S. sentiments.[15] In (re)constructing their own identity, something thoroughly and uniquely theirs, the intellectuals of the Ateneo began to postulate *mestizaje* as a key for constructing Mexican culture, identity, and nationalism.[16] Vasconcelos eventually built an entire system of thought in which *mestizaje* was the central feature of his "aesthetic monism."[17]

As a deeply religious person, and as part of his determined war against positivism's rejection of religion and metaphysics, Vasconcelos could not conceive of reality outside of a cosmic divine force that gave coherence to everything that exists. He "yearned for . . . an experience capable of justifying the validity of the spiritual within the field of empiricism itself."[18] Rejecting the scientific strictures and epistemological limitations of positivism, he insisted that spirituality (religion and faith) and experience (emotions, feelings, and beauty) were appropriate epistemological and hermeneutical sources. He opposed reason alone as the highest measure and criterion of knowledge, and he rejected abstract notions of metaphysics. Reality, he argued, was not reducible to the ability of the *Cogito*.[19] Vasconcelos was looking for something new and different that offered an alternative to the racist ideas he had been taught. And he sought a framework that could explain the mechanisms at play in the universe.[20] In articulating this framework he postulated God and God's activity behind phenomena as his points of departure for understanding the world and human history.

In Vasconcelos's proposal this meant that God is still actively infusing the world with the creative spiritual energy that seeks to bring all things together. God pushes existence toward its divine goal, namely, synthesis. For Vasconcelos, this meant at least three things: First, in this self-proclaimed Platonist frame, he insisted that the creation was infused with the spiritual creative energy that engendered and moved it in the direction of the divine intent. God is more like an artist still in the process of perfecting a work of art.[21] Second, rejecting notions that promoted the unity of what is homogeneous and the rejection of what is different, he argued that the divine intent of synthesis meant the unity of heterogeneous elements.[22] He insisted that when heterogeneous elements unite, they do not keep their essential elements intact. Something else is produced that is not just the sum of its parts but is something entirely new. For him, this synthesis is a kind of spiritual existence, which is best illustrated by the reality of the divine itself.[23] Similarly, this synthesis is also illustrated by music and other artistic disciplines as they bring together heterogeneous elements that produce wonderful works of art.[24]

Third, the improvement of the world is the impetus behind synthesis. The world is on its way along its divine predetermined trajectory. In this internal dynamic order and "faculty of synthesis," as things find their mission, they are affected by and affect synthesis.[25] Consciousness of the divine intent and its accompanying result of improvement inspires things to engage in synthesis, which for Vasconcelos meant that things enter into the aesthetic spiritual dimension of existence. For him, the consciousness of and search for synthesis was the way to fulfill the divine intent.

Vasconcelos proposed this to be the way human history should be understood. He argued that there have been four stages in human history.[26] Using racialized genetic categories, he insisted that these four stages are represented by the four racial families we have today: black, Indian, Mongol, and then white, the last one to arrive and the most advanced. According to him, each racial group has a mission in history, and when it fulfills its mission it declines and disappears. At the present, we are in the era of the white family group, and it, like other groups, will also pass away, but not just yet.

As Vasconcelos puts it, the function of each group is to pass down civilization to the next group, so that humans can reach their superior divine goal. In this case it is no accident that the white family group with its scientific advances and technologies has become the invader of the world; this group has not realized it is to serve a higher purpose. It has a transcendental mission: to serve as the bridge creating the appropriate *material* and *moral* conditions so that "all the [human] types and all cultures may fuse in a fifth universal race."[27]

Oblivious to the Spanish imperialistic overtones of his own proposal, Vasconcelos forged his perspective over against U.S. imperialist sentiments. He explained that out of the white family group the mission has fallen upon the two strongest branches: the English and the Spanish. Of these two, the Spaniards were the most apt. Despite the great nation the U.S. Anglos had become, with their concerns about purity of blood they committed the *sin* of killing the indigenous people of North America.[28] Indeed, it may seem as if God guides the English, but their material mission has come to its zenith. It is only a matter of time before the English begin their decline and are absorbed by the fifth race.

On the other hand, since the Spanish mixed with and assimilated the indigenous peoples, they are closer to the divine transcendental purpose. The Spaniards, obedient to their divine mandate, still have a mission to fulfill. When they came to the Americas they had no racial prejudice, and out of an "abundance of love" they desired to intermix with the natives in order to elevate them.[29] In this kind of utopian Messianism, the Spaniards represented the salvation of the indigenous peoples. They came to save them from their own tyrants (in the case of Mexico this meant salvation from Montezuma).[30] Vasconcelos contended that the Spaniards desired to intermix with the indigenous peoples and, in so doing, provided a solution to the problem of the indigenous peoples being an inferior group.[31] In mixing with the natives the Spanish created a "new race" in which the white race was preserved and Western culture disseminated. Yet, their mission was not finished. They were still responsible for constructing the birthing place of the fifth race. For being more faithful to the divine mission in America, the Latin people were the ones called to consummate it.[32] For Vasconcelos the direction of human history had a clear purpose, namely, synthesis-*mestizaje*. And contrary to Spencer's idea that miscegenation produced inferior children, he contended that all the racial groups of the world will intermix and produce the superior fifth race.

Some contradictions begin to appear at this point. First, the master plan of the fifth race, product of a global scale *mestizaje*, lies in the future; it is in the process of becoming.[33] The already mixed people of Latin America are only an imperfect shadow of what is to come. Moreover, Vasconcelos does not mean intermixture in the most general, unqualified sense. For the final fifth race to replace the four existing ones, the best qualities of each individual racial group will be preserved. But for him, this racial fusion means that the "inferior" and "uglier" groups—African descendants and the indigenous groups—will have to be elevated by mixing with the superior ones.[34] Since inferior groups cannot escape their condition of inferiority by themselves, once *conscious* of the divine intent, they will see in intermixture their redemption. These groups have little to contribute to the fifth race, so their passage from inferiority to superiority will have to be a "voluntary extinction." In other words, Vasconcelos's *mestizaje* functions as a type of eugenic cleansing process whereby the inferior characteristics of the inferior group will be removed.[35]

As is already apparent, in his attempt to articulate something uniquely Mexican (and Latin American), Vasconcelos offers a complex hermeneutical system for interpreting world phenomena and human history, and looking to the future from the location of Latin America. As Haddox tells us, his is a philosophical-theological system.[36] Indeed, he thought that in *mestizaje* he had found the antidote to any kind of racism and an affirmation of the inclusion of all human groups.[37] For him, because the fifth race is the amalgam of the best qualities of all groups, it is also the one better equipped for true "fraternity, and [capable] of a really universal vision."[38]

In the final analysis Vasconcelos proposed the systematic erasure of the indigenous and African peoples. He was unapolo-
getic about his proposal for the "inferior" African progeny and
indigenous peoples of Latin America. His solution for the indigenous peoples is their *latinización y españolización*.[39] Yet he did
not intend—and in fact considered it impossible—to erase the
historical indigenous heritage of Mexico. Mexican as well as Latin
American identity is rooted in the Spanish *present* and the indigenous *past*, but there is no point in bringing it back. The hope of
the indigenous people is *mestizaje*.[40] But they should be happy,
for they are being elevated. In his philo-theological scheme, because the Spaniards wanted to mix with the natives, out of their
love, because they were conscious of their divine mission, and
because what the Spaniards brought was better than what they
destroyed, it follows that the violent, heinous, and dehumanizing treatment of the indigenous and African peoples was a necessary evil. The atrocities the Spaniards committed must be left
in the past. Therefore, his proposal for *mestizaje* was an open
invitation to historical amnesia.

THE CHICANO/A IDENTITY CONSTRUCTION
AND VASCONCELOS

Vasconcelos was not the only writer who engaged questions
of *mestizaje*, nor was he the only one who saw in *mestizaje* an
alternative for articulating Latin American identity and self-perception, and for constructing society. Others, in fact, engaged
and criticized his myopic views, among them José Carlos
Mariátegui in Peru.[41] However, because of the connection with
Mexico, Vasconcelos's notion of *mestizaje* as *La raza cósmica*
became for many the fruitful formula for communicating, affirming, constructing, and articulating Mexican American and
Chicano/a national identity and experience in the United States.
Similarly, no other book had interconnected the terms of *La raza*
and *mestizaje* as Vasconcelos's work did. Because of its anti-U.S.
sentiments this book served well as the material source for constructing Chicano/a ethnic identity in contrast to that of the U.S.
white Anglo-European-dominant society and culture.[42]

As Chicanos/as articulated their struggles, three issues gained prominence during the 1960s and 1970s: they reclaimed the indigenous ancestral heritage represented by the legendary Aztec civilization; they adopted notions of *mestizaje* and *La raza* to articulate their experience of miscegenation and cultural intermixture; and they reappropriated Our Lady of Guadalupe as the divine *mestizo* symbol par excellence that announces emancipation.[43] These three issues crystallized the claims of the Chicano/a people and are also the sources from which Chicano/a identity and experience of faith were expressed and articulated.

Indeed, for a few Chicano/a scholars and U.S. Latina/o theologians the work of Vasconcelos has been a useful source when discussing *mestizaje*. Most have been critical of the explicitly racist overtones and implications promoting an ethno-racial and cultural whitening. Few have engaged and critiqued the very structure and logic of inclusion in Vasconcelos's entire philosophical-theological approach to *mestizaje* that finds its way into the writings of most scholars.

For example, in the second chapter of his *Mestizo Democracy*, John Francis Burke juxtaposes the racialized aesthetic work of Vasconcelos, Virgilio Elizondo's "extremely hopeful" vision, and Gloria Anzaldúa's "agonal" content.[44] Just like Roberto Goizueta years before, Burke finds Vasconcelos's proposal flawed for the construction of a truly inclusive society.[45] Yet, he takes for granted the entire logic of inclusion in *mestizaje* as a useful category "providing the experiential and intellectual basis for engaging in multicultural relations in a *democratic fashion*."[46] In my view this is highly problematic, because the reality of intermixture among Latinas/os has not removed racialized prejudices or promoted a non-hierarchic organization of society. This means Burke's proposal is historically unsubstantiated.

Andrés Guerrero took the connection of Vasconcelos and *mestizaje* a step further. In *A Chicano Theology* he insisted that Vasconcelos was responding to the context of social Darwinism that had dominated the Mexican intellectual arena since the mid-nineteenth century. Vasconcelos intended to provide a cure for racism by asserting that the mixture *(mestizaje)* of different ethnocultural groups did not produce inferior beings. Unaware of his own racial prejudices, he ended up repeating the same racist sentiments against which he tried to fight. Therefore, Guerrero intended to articulate a "non-racist" version of *mestizaje*.[47]

The weakness in Guerrero's analysis, just as in the case of Burke, lies in his uncritical use of the logic of inclusivity and inoculation of racism by way of *mestizaje*. He correctly criticizes Vasconcelos on the basis of his racist idealization of *mestizaje*, but he fails to examine the impact that Spencer's social Darwinism had upon the categories of inclusion and intermixture. Vasconcelos rejected Spencer's conclusions that intermixture produced inferior groups as part of the intrinsic evolutions of societies. He takes the opposite direction: intermixture produces superior groups. Thus, for him, *mestizaje* (intermixture and inclusion) was the next step in the social evolutionary ladder of humanity.[48] Vasconcelos never abandoned the Euro-Hispanocentric evolutionary underpinnings of *mestizaje*; that is why *La raza cósmica* was still in the future. For him, the Latin American nations constituted the *cosmic race* only in potentiality, not in actuality. The operating assumption was that the closer the Latin American people got to the *cosmic race*, the more they abandoned their "backward" indigenous and African roots. The members of the Ateneo de la Juventud and the intellectuals supporting the earlier dictatorship of Porfirio Díaz echo this.[49]

Moreover, most critiques of Vasconcelos deal with the superficial racialized overtones of his work but leave unchallenged his notion that the Spaniards were more open to intermixture.[50] Chicano/a (and Latina/o) scholars generally critique the tendency to compare intermixture in the United States to Latin America, as if the former's intermixture was an expression of a lack of racist prejudices, as Esteva Fabregat suggests about the Spanish conquistadors.[51] They critique the white race supremacy inherent to Vasconcelos, but say very little about how intrinsic to *mestizaje* the superiority of whiteness remains in practice.

In order to understand this better, it helps to examine the rationale behind the rejection of intermixture in the United States, where it was not rejected wholesale. Even staunch "purists" such as Madison Grant and Arthur de Gobineau did not reject intermixture altogether.[52] Gobineau, for example, thought that intermixture was acceptable if it took place between more "compatible" superior groups.[53] What he rejected, and what racist notions in the United States have resisted, is the intermixture between a "superior" white race, characterized by the Anglo culture, and "inferior" races and cultures, whether European, African, indigenous, or other. *Mestizos/as* are rejected not strictly because of their mixed condition, but because they carry traces of an "inferior" blood.[54]

Resistance to this type of intermixture is part of the complex web of racialized processes and codification that privilege white versus non-white. It is in fact an ideological, ethnic, and cultural "war" against the "inferior" races, the indigenous, and African descendants. Among Chicanos/as (and Latinas/os) this war is still going on: with very few exceptions, the indigenous and African Chicano/a and Latina/o voices are generally absent from Chicano/a (and Latina/o) scholarship. More important, to my knowledge these scholars seldom acknowledge or condemn the presence of racism and discrimination among their communities, privileging those with lighter skin who (consciously or unconsciously) are considered racially better and more aesthetically attractive. This reality demonstrates unequivocally that even among the members of *La raza*, intermixture-*mestizaje* has not removed racial prejudice, which is a central concern to any notion of inclusion. In no other Chicano/a author are these issues as conspicuously present and as specifically connected to the Eurocentric intellectual framing of reality as in the work of Gloria Anzaldúa.

GLORIA ANZALDÚA: *LA CONCIENCIA DE LA MESTIZA*

In 1987, the same year that Guerrero's *A Chicano Theology* was published, Anzaldúa's *Borderlands/La Frontera* was also published.[55] This is one of the most sophisticated articulations of *mestizaje* since Vasconcelos. In it, Anzaldúa sketched a new horizon for articulating and formulating questions of identity. Her work is an *autohistoriateoría*.[56] In weaving together poetry, cultural theory, autobiography, and other literary genres, as well as Spanish, English, and some Nahuatl terms, her work is at once complex and ambiguous.[57] She uses all of these components as literary devices to communicate the unsettling complexity of the issues she is addressing. Anzaldúa's primary preoccupation relates to what she calls the *borderlands/las fronteras*. In the first instance, *borderlands* refers to the geographical "open wound" *(una herida abierta)* that is the Mexico–United States border established after the Guadalupe Hidalgo Treaty in 1848.[58] The border is the contemporary symbol of the historic exploitation of and discrimination against Chicano/a communities.[59] Most important, she tells us that the treaty is the culmination of a series of displacements that have contributed to the oppression of Chicana women: first by the Aztecs, then by the Spanish Conquistadors, and then by the U.S. invasion of Mexico.[60] During each of these periods, it is the indigenous women who have been most victimized, but they have also resisted.

In a second instance, and more in line with questions concerning *mestizaje* as discourse, the borderlands also refer to sociocultural and conceptual spaces. Here Anzaldúa shifts from understanding the borderlands as a set of geographic and physical spaces, to a "series of psychological, sexual, and spiritual sites, present wherever two or more cultures edge each other, where people of different races occupy the same territory, where under, lower, middle, and upper classes touch, where the space between two individuals shrinks with intimacy."[61] More specifically, the borderlands represent the created spaces erected by the dominant groups to exclude the other. In Anzaldúa's experience, the Chicano culture opposes the Aztecs' more matrilineal cultural legacy.[62] Chicano culture, she avers, makes women subservient to men, prescribing specific norms of conduct for women to follow—but leaving them only the options of being in the church as virgin-nuns, at home as mothers, or in the streets as whores.[63] She reclaims her indigenous roots, stating that Chicana identity "is grounded in the Indian woman's history of resistance."[64] Her resistance is threefold. As a Chicana, she rejects notions that make the indigenous women the traitors of the people and therefore suppress the indigenous cultural legacy that amounts to self-hatred.[65] As Catholic she opposes the Catholic heterosexual script imposed upon her and the portrayal of women not only as sexual objects but as those who are closer to evil and who for this reason must be protected.[66] And as part of the U.S.

dominant Anglo-European culture she resists narrow, racist notions of identity that disallow her Chicana experience and identity. For Chicanas, this is a stance of resistance against "cultural tyranny," against inflexible hegemonic frames of interpreting reality and the world that end up excluding those whose identity does not fit such air-tight socially constructed conceptual frames.

Anzaldúa is raising issues particular not only to women or Chicanos/as. Her proposal has broader implications.[67] She advocates a paradigm shift in order to resist the dominant culture's attempt to reduce reality to dualistic frames, which do not permit the conception of multiple identities in people. This explains why she adopts the metaphor of the borderlands when it comes to issues of identity recognition and construction. The implication is twofold: first, the borderlands mean "conceptual structures of oppositionalism" used by the powerful and dominant groups.[68] The notion of borderlands unmasks the intellectual web of categories designed to peg people's relationships in oppositional terms. And second, the alternative solution is a counterstance characterized by a new *mestiza* consciousness that demands standing in the borderlands in order to unmask and resist those structures. It means standing in the interstices, the multiple "spaces between the different worlds" people inhabit.[69]

Anzaldúa reclaims the metaphor of the legendary Aztec symbol of Coatlicue, the ancient serpent creator goddess who holds opposite elements in fine tension without excluding anything. She is the goddess of birth and death, the one who both gives and takes away life; she is the "incarnation of cosmic processes."[70] The problem, as she sees it, is that Coatlicue was fragmented and replaced, first by the Aztecs' patriarchal system, and later by Our Lady of Guadalupe.[71]

Anzaldúa is not concerned with the deity, as such, reestablishing the ancient cultic practices. She is concerned with the conceptual paradigmatic shift that this symbol entails. Proposing Coatlicue means that ambiguity is made present and that opens the possibilities for resistance by holding in tension the dualisms men/women, body/spirit, virgin/whore, death/life created by hegemonic dominant cultures. This goes beyond the adoption of an ancient religious symbol from Aztec mythology. The metaphor of Coatlicue means entering a mental space where ambiguity and contradiction reign, and where reality and identity are irreducible to fixed categories, conceptual frames, or rigid terms. Any attempt at defining her reality and true identity means going outside prescribed norms and frames; it is to "kick a hole" out of the old boundaries.[72] With the use of the metaphor of Coatlicue, Anzaldúa offers a (re)interpretation and reconfiguration of what she calls serpent that wound metaphors by turning them into sites and vehicles of resistance.[73] By entering ambiguity she can identify the "serpents that wound," the dualist, inflexible, reductionist frames upheld and protected by the dominant culture that discriminates against Chicanos/as. She can also identify the internalization of a corrupted identity that they (the Chicano/a communities) have come to see as their own, and which has provoked self-hatred. This internalized distorted identity, or Shadow Beast, is a lie, she claims. Chicanos/as are neither ugly nor inferior; indigenous women have not betrayed their people; Chicana queer women are not devious or abnormal; and women carry no "evil" inside.[74]

For Anzaldúa, to enter the Coatlicue state means allowing the "serpent" of ambiguity to devour her. Unlike the dominant culture, the solution is not to control Coatlicue-ambiguity, but to surrender to its disruptive power; this means not to attempt to define it, but rather to be defined by it. This leads to developing *la facultad*, which is the capacity to search for the deep structure of surface phenomena usually hidden behind rigid conceptual frames. *La facultad* is "a kind of survival tactic that people, caught between the worlds, unknowingly cultivate," a deeper awareness developed by those who do not feel physically or psychologically safe in this world. "Those who are pounced on the most have it the strongest—the females, the homosexuals of all races, the dark skinned, the outcast, the persecuted, the marginalized, the foreign."[75]

According to Anzaldúa, the power in unmasking the Shadow Beast and the awareness, survival, and resistance of *la facultad* give birth to *la conciencia de la mestiza*. This is both a *mestiza* consciousness as well as a consciousness of the *mestiza*. As the former, it is a description of the everyday practice of *mestizo/a* people as they attempt to find coherence despite their sense of being torn between cultures and identities, what she calls "mental nepantilism." The consciousness of the *mestiza* stands against notions of cultural or ethnic purity, and it means engaging in the construction of a conceptual *tapestry* by which aspects from different cultures are brought together, reflecting the complexity of human identities and reality. This is an inclusive consciousness that, despite being in "uncharted seas," has discovered that it cannot "hold concepts or ideas in rigid boundaries."[76] For this reason, argues Erika Aigner-Varoz, while one reclaims one's voice even within one's own psyche, the *mestiza* consciousness also "serves as a mode of self-critique."[77] Instead of making reality fit one single mold, *la conciencia de la mestiza* displays a movement away from "set patterns and goals and toward a more whole perspective, one that includes rather than excludes." The *new mestiza* copes by developing a sense of tolerance for contradictions and for ambiguity. "She learns to juggle cultures. She has a plural personality, she operates in a pluralistic mode—nothing is thrust out, the good the bad and the ugly, nothing is rejected, nothing abandoned."[78]

I agree with Claudia Milian's insistence that there are important points of connection between the work of Anzaldúa and DuBois, particularly around matters of borderlands and "double consciousness." But I also want to point out that Anzaldúa's proposal goes far beyond dualistic understandings of consciousness.[79] As Aigner-Varoz puts it, Anzaldúa constructs "inter-referencing metaphors from more than two cultures," which avoids "defining ethnicity in a binary system."[80] She goes far beyond notions of mental dualism or cultural schizophrenia. Her position is far more fluid, resembling Bernice Zamora's dictum: "You insult me, when you say I'm Schizophrenic. My divisions are Infinite."[81]

It may appear that by insisting on the possibilities of multiple identities Anzaldúa is suggesting the utter disconnection among them. That is not the case at all! A synthesis occurs that brings about resolution. The resolution, however, takes place in the most hidden areas of the mind, in the subconscious. The *mestiza* is abruptly yanked out "of ambivalence by an intense, and often painful, emotional event which inverts or resolves the ambivalence." As a result, the radical shift turns the space where the *mestiza* stands, "where phenomena tend to collide," into a space where "the possibility of uniting all that is separate occurs."[82] This is not an assembly where separate pieces merely come together. In an attempt to work out a synthesis, argues Anzaldúa, the self has added a third element that is greater than the sum of its parts.[83] "That third element is a new consciousness—a *mestiza* consciousness—and, though it is a source of intense pain, its energy comes from continual creative motion that keeps breaking down the unitary aspect of each new paradigm."[84]

In promoting *la conciencia de la mestiza*, Anzaldúa is proposing new ways for conceiving identities. She is not promoting a complete blueprint of what constitutes "Chicana-ness/Chicano-ness."[85] She displays great flexibility in the process of identity construction. She has no problem appropriating elements from her own cultural background, as in the case of borrowing from Vasconcelos. And she also has no difficulties in breaking open traditional conceptual frameworks in order to create something different that is more consistent with the reality of the numerous groups in the periphery of U.S. dominant culture. In other words, *la conciencia de la mestiza* is a deconstruction and a reconstruction, an appropriation but also a transformation through resistance to the established "traditional" norms.[86] As the result of a painful "kneading" *(un amasamiento)*, argues Anzaldúa, *la mestiza* is designed for preservation and activity under a variety of conditions, contexts, worlds, and identities. This symbolizes the birth of new multiple identities, which amounts to an indefinable and unpredictable "morphogenesis."[87]

Anzaldúa's *mestizaje* promotes openness and the ability to conceive identity not as a monolith but as plural in sources. Yet her controversial proposal quickly turns into an intellectual abstraction without historical grounding. Arturo Aldama argues that it would be a mistake to assume that Anzaldúa speaks from no context, that her point of reference is the U.S.-Mexico border.[88] And Anzaldúa graphically claims that in these borderlands women are "raped, maimed, strangled, gassed, shot," showing her own historical context.[89] There is a sense in which she becomes hostage to the ambiguous nature of identity construction. For her, the synthesis of the different pieces occurs at the level of consciousness, but such synthesis says nothing of their historical expressions. In my view, it is at the level of their historically specific expression in the form of everyday activities, practices, customs, rites, celebrations, and so forth, that different cultural elements become part of a larger cultural whole. The resolution that Anzaldúa is trying to achieve takes place in history and not only or primarily in the intellectual sphere. Her use of *mestizaje* allows her to conceive the abstract-ambiguous and fluid character of identity constructions, so that she can inhabit many identity spaces. Yet, she does not ground her claims on her own particular historical specificity. She writes:

> As a *mestiza* I have no country, my homeland cast me out; yet all countries are mine because I am every woman's sister or potential lover. (As a lesbian I have no race, my own people disclaim me; but I am all races because there is the queer in me in all races.) I am cultureless because, as a feminist, I challenge the collective cultural/religious male-derived beliefs of Indo-Hispanics and Anglos; yet I am cultured because I am participating in the creation of yet another culture, a new story to explain the world and our participation in it, a new value system with images and symbols that connect us to each other and to the planet.[90]

In a very individualistic vein she gives the impression that she picks and chooses elements of identity just as she has "chosen" her queerness. But that minimizes the profound impact that specific communities have upon a person and communities during the lifelong and complex process of socialization. By using *mestizaje*, Anzaldúa claims to do away with binary categories and instead to champion hybridity and the creation of new multiple identities. She envisions a different kind of future than Vanconcelos does, "a world where all worlds fit" (resolution of the Zapatistas). The potential danger of her claims is the promotion of infinite new identities that remain in the abstract and fail to ground themselves concretely in history. Without specific historical grounding, her work risks the same limitations of abstraction and idealization as Vasconcelos's fifth race.

There is no question that Anzaldúa transcends and transforms Vasconcelian notions of synthesis and inclusion in *mestizaje*. She appropriately constructs a platform for articulating identity discourse differently. There is a sense, however, in which her postmodern approach betrays her proposal in some significant ways. She still operates within a "metaphysics of presence" by which Coatlicue (the embodiment of ambiguity-*mestizaje*) is the force pushing reality forward, the "incarnation of cosmic processes."[91] So there is a sense of inevitability in her notion of new *mestizaje*. This parallels Vasconcelos's "divine energy," by which everything moves toward a coherent synthesis and pushes all racialized groups toward intermixture-*mestizaje*. This, in turn, implies that *mestizaje* is unavoidable and even "natural," and, as Vasconcelos held, can be accelerated by imposition.

Another problem with Anzaldúa's proposal is how she conceives cultural phenomena and how she disconnects these phenomena from history. For example, she is right in asserting the fluctuating nature of identities and cultures. This is befitting, as she is writing at a time of cultural, political, and spiritual transitions, where "new" cultures, identities, spiritualities, and politics have not yet crystallized. So her work testifies to the separation of reality from theory and the limitations of traditional approaches to define people's identities. But she remains in the intellectual-abstract sphere, making it difficult to connect the *mestiza* consciousness, as the promotion of multiple identities, to the specific historical grounding of *mestizaje* resulting from the conquest and eventual national identity discourse as expressed by the Latin American countries and the Chicano/a communities.[92] If, indeed, the work of Anzaldúa intersects with a number of different histories, as Ian Barnard asserts, then her work must be evaluated in terms of those histories with which she intersects in using the category of *mestizaje*.[93] There is a historical baggage that accompanies *mestizo/a consciousness*, that, while alluded to, is never made explicit in a way that would lead to self-criticism among the *mestizos/as*.[94]

Anzaldúa claims that *mestizos/as* were born of the mixture between the indigenous peoples and the Spaniards. (She refers exclusively to the *mestizos/as* born as a result of the arrival of Hernán Cortés to the shores of today's Mexico in 1519.) This new *mestiza/o* race, she tells us, inherited Central and South America. What remains unsaid are the conditions under which the *mestizos/as* "inherited" such regions of the continent, namely, the displacement, rape, and exploitation of the indigenous populations. In constructing their own consciousness, identity, and sociopolitical and economic space, many *mestizos/as* were complicit with their Spanish fathers in asserting their power over the indigenous masses and, not long after, over the African slaves and their descendants.

One finds in Anzaldúa's writing the same characteristics of *indigenismo* that once played a central feature in the Mexican version of *mestizaje* as national unity and identity.[95] She appropriates indigenous images and symbols, and she even insists that her Chicana identity is grounded upon the indigenous women's acts of resistance. Yet, the connection is made only in relation to an ancient and long-gone mythical civilization that she (re)claims for herself. This is tantamount to saying that *mestizo/a* Chicanos/as are the proper guardians of the indigenous cultures and traditions today. Such notions silence the contemporary impoverished and marginalized indigenous groups that resist being identified as *mestizos/as* because of the historical assimilatory expressions of the term.

Indeed, with her "new *mestiza* consciousness" Anzaldúa announces the fluid, incomplete, and dynamic process of identity construction. She breaks open binary understandings of *mestizaje*. But she gives us no practical ways to historicize this "new" *mestizaje*. In my opinion, her proposal of a "new" *mestiza* consciousness of inclusivity is only possible by denying the messy and bloody history behind *mestizaje* discourse in Mexico and the rest of Latin America. If, indeed, this new *mestiza* consciousness leads to self-critique (as I believe Anzaldúa would claim), then a historical examination of the manner in which the rhetoric of inclusion has meant exclusion in Latin America must provoke interrogating such conceptual framing of *mestizaje* as it is deployed among the Chicanos/as and U.S. Latinas/os.

Part of the reason *mestizaje* discourse is so pervasive among Chicanos/as relates to their connection to Mexico's history and intellectual tradition, as demonstrated by Guerrero and Anzaldúa, among others. The self-perception of Chicanos/as as *La raza* and the use of *mestizaje* have been discursive staples since the Guadalupe-Hidalgo Treaty. This historic event marks the birth of a new people and of the Mexican American and Chicano/a

identities. In a way, for those who became U.S. citizens over-
night, the abrupt separation from Mexico brought about an identity crisis; they could no longer consider themselves only Mexicans.

In their new sociopolitical context, Chicanos/as came to perceive themselves in connection with Mexico (and Latin America)
and the Anglo-U.S. world and culture. The same is true of U.S.
Latina/o theologians as they sought to define themselves differently from Latin America and the dominant Anglo-U.S. culture
and world. But these communities constructed idealized notions
of identity built upon the terms of the dominant Anglo epistemological and cultural universe, which operate undisputed in their
writings. In an oblique way, even by creating disruption, the notion of *mestizaje* functions as a form of intellectual control prescribing the parameters of the debate between the dominant culture and the peripheral marginal Chicanos/as and Latinas/os.

Anzaldúa attempted to overcome these pitfalls by accounting
for the different identity spaces people inhabit in ways that go
beyond binary oppositional understandings. She announced new
ways of conceiving the process of identity construction as irreducible to rigid airtight conceptual categories. But she leaves us
without a mechanism by which we can take seriously the historical situatedness of people's identities. In light of this, I suggest there is need to exercise a healthy dose of self-reflective criticism on the very framing of our reflections on *mestizaje* in ways
that take seriously the historical reality of Latinas/os. This can
help us avoid reproducing the silencing of the indigenous and
African peoples among the U.S. Latina/o population.

4

THE SHIFTING SHAPES
OF *MESTIZAJE*

Navigating the Contested Spaces
of *Mestizaje* Discourse(s)

I believe that the idea of mestizaje or transculturation was and is guided by the dictates of power. If we agree that "culture" acts as a form of institutional power, then the alleged exchange and mutual assimilation . . . between colonizer and colonized, exploiter and exploited, rich and poor, European and non-European, East and West, or North and South can never be true transculturation [or *mestizaje*], for such relations will always be mediated by privilege and assigned value. To advocate transculturation [and *mestizaje*] without attempting to change the systems and institutions that breed the power differential would simply help to perpetuate the utopian vision that constructs Latin America . . . as the "continent of hope" [always in the future, never in the present].

—Lourdes Martínez-Echazabal

Until now I have focused on the tensions and contradictions in the theological use of *mestizaje* by U.S. Latina/o theologians. In *mestizaje* they found alternative and new paths for discussing the experience of faith of the Latina/o communities in the midst of sociopolitical marginalization and ethnocultural discrimination in their own country, the United States. But in articulating their theological proposal these scholars failed to question their assumptions about *mestizaje*. Drawing from idealized constructions of *mestizaje* in Latin America, and without engaging the sociopolitical context of the region, U.S. Latina/o scholars reified *mestizaje*, claiming that intermixture-*mestizaje* led to the inclusion of other cultural groups. Their assumption was that the condition of *mestizaje* excluded racist tendencies. Seeking to present a united front among U.S. Latina/o theologians and scholars, *mestizaje*-intermixture quickly became characteristic of the U.S. Latina/o communities and obscured the "unmixed" and "differently mixed" indigenous and African voices among the U.S. Latina/o populations.

This was possible in the earlier U.S. social landscape where the Latina/o population experienced great economic and political disadvantages and cultural marginalization. But the sociopolitical and cultural conditions that initially provoked the use of *mestizaje* in theology have changed. Some Latinas/os today occupy key places in the highest echelons of U.S. society, and some have become quite wealthy. Although the majority of the U.S. Latina/o population is still socially marginal, Latina/o communities have also gained significant social presence, and now have become a powerful cultural and political force with which the dominant culture must reckon. For these reasons, the conditions for articulating *mestizaje* have changed, and the ways in which *mestizaje* was originally deployed by U.S. Latina/o theologians must be interrogated to reflect more adequately the ethnic and cultural composition of U.S. Latinas/os.

At the same time, and in various ways, indigenous, African, and women's voices are beginning to challenge the dominant versions of *mestizaje* in the different countries of Latin America. They bring serious indictments of hegemony, homogenization, racism, and sexism to the way *mestizaje* has been conceived and articulated differently by Latin American elite. They are also recasting the limits of *mestizaje* in order to make room for the diverse ethnic and cultural traditions that constitute Latin America. These recent reconfigurations and criticisms of *mestizaje* are ones U.S. Latina/o theologians must engage and take seriously.

How then are U.S. Latina/o theologians beginning to interrogate the uncritical and romantic use of *mestizaje* in theology? How are they responding to the hegemonic, racist, and discriminatory indictments against *mestizaje* emerging from the indigenous, African, and women's voices in Latin America? While a self-critical attitude has developed in recent U.S. Latina/o scholarship concerning the ways *mestizaje* discourse promotes false notions of a homogeneous U.S. Latina/o population, a thorough critique of how the use of *mestizaje* occludes racialized classism, sexism, and ethnocultural discrimination tendencies among the U.S. Latina/o population has, in my opinion, yet to take place.

I turn first to the particular self-critical responses by U.S. Latina/o theologians to the uncritical uses of *mestizaje* in order to delineate the complexity of the debates about *mestizaje* presently taking place among U.S. Latina/o scholars. Then, I show how particular criticisms and reconfigurations of *mestizaje* emerging from Latin America by indigenous and African peoples and women highlight particular gaps of *mestizaje*.

THE CONTINUING DEBATES ON *MESTIZAJE* AMONG U.S. LATINA/O THEOLOGIANS

As subsequent generations of U.S. Latino/a theologians emerge, they also appropriate *mestizaje*, most times uncritically, for its adaptable multivalence for theology. This second generation of U.S. Latina/o theologians formalized systematically theological reflections encompassing discussions on spirituality,[1] Christology, anthropology, pneumatology, social ethics, and biblical hermeneutics, all of which pointed to the richness of *mestizaje* as a theological category.

Despite the particular contributions to theology by subsequent generations of U.S. Latina/o theologians, clearer understanding of *mestizaje* has remained elusive. These theologians spoke of *mestizaje* as self-evident. As they ascribed new meanings to *mestizaje*-intermixture, they turned *mestizaje* into an abstraction open to all kinds of uses and contexts and paid little attention to its violent historical specificity.[2]

Awareness of the contested nature of *mestizaje* has never been absent from U.S. Latina/o theological writings. From the beginning these theologians acknowledged some of the limitations in giving a term very broad connotations that could become a "pan-Latino" or "pan-Hispanic" ethnocultural identity concept, and in turn subsume the rich diversity of the U.S. Latina/o population.[3] This is in line with Andrew Irvine's criticisms, and Benjamín Valentín and Rubén Rosario Rodríguez's concern about the potentially racist overtones of *mestizaje*.[4] For Irvine, the insistence on the U.S. Latina/o ethnocultural identity can be counterproductive, becoming a type of ethnocultural ghettoism. By the same token, he argues, by using *mestizaje* to counter the characterization of U.S. Latinas/os by the dominant culture, U.S. Latina/o theologians have uncritically adopted essentializing characteristics of the dominant culture, portraying it as homogeneous. That is to say, these theologians operate with an imaginary that has yet to be interrogated for its assumptions about the U.S. dominant culture.[5]

Valentín's criticism is directed to the public role of U.S. Latina/o theology. He detects overemphasis on the ethnocultural identity of the U.S. Latina/o communities. For him, such notions of ethnocultural identity operate around culturally essentializing categories that tend to obscure the diversity of these communities. Further, the excessive emphasis on the "Hispanic" and/or "Latina/o" ethnocultural identity creates a social barrier that can potentially further marginalize these communities from U.S. society.[6] Though I agree with Valentín that an overemphasis on Latina/o identity can work negatively, I am cautious about the degree to which Latina/o theologians would like to enter the public sphere of the United States, as anything other than Latina/o. Is it not in this very way that they can offer a public voice and remain rooted in Latinas/os history in the United States without succumbing to the assimilationist requirements of the dominant culture?

Others have been more specific in their criticisms of *mestizaje*. Goizueta, for example, explores the connections and differences between the work of Vasconcelos and the theological proposal of *mestizaje* by U.S. Latina/o theologians. Goizueta argues that adopting *mestizaje* means a retrieval of the history of *mestizaje* to avoid a "naïve cultural romanticism, or 'mestizolatry,' inattentive to the history of this category."[7] While he refers only to the use of *mestizaje* in Latin American philosophy, his comments apply to the entire history of *mestizaje* in Latin America—from the conquest to the colonial period, to the wars of independence, to the later development as nations and national identity, all of which were influenced in one way or another by discourses of *mestizaje*. So Goizueta is right in inviting us to engage both the history of the *mestizo/a* people and of the concept of *mestizaje*.[8] Yet, somewhere along the way, he and the rest of the U.S. Latina/o theologians laid aside this important principle as Vasconcelos's ideas became the starting point in the discussions of *mestizaje*.[9]

Without engaging the voluminous writings on *mestizaje*, these theologians thought it sufficient to use as their sources one or two Mexican authors, without engaging the longstanding history, debates, and concrete developments of the term either in Mexico or in the rest of Latin America. They thus assumed a homogeneous ethnocultural composition of the U.S. Latina/o population and also unwittingly suppressed the violent process of sociocultural-sexual power interaction between the Europeans and the indigenous peoples, portraying it as a "romantic" intermixture of equals.

Another more focused criticism came from Orlando Espín in his overview and evaluation of particular developments within U.S. Latino/a theology during its first two decades.[10] He examines the current state of U.S. Latino/a theology, highlighting its birth, sensibilities, theoretical and theological contributions, accomplishments, and future trajectories. He stresses idealized uses of *mestizaje* that, in his view, have led to "an essentializing definition of *latinidad*," while at the same time hiding all "sorts of denigrating, violent and dehumanizing behavior in which Latinos/as themselves engage."[11] Espín's preoccupation advocates the de-romanticisation of *latinidad* so as to encompass the rich

diversity of the different U.S. Latino/a communities synonymous
with *mestizaje*. His critique goes even further. He insists that
using such encompassing-essentializing terms has prevented U.S.
Latino/a communities from seeing the discriminatory and racist
practices among themselves.[12] But Espín did not pursue this further. Nor has his warning received the attention it deserves, as
many U.S. Latina/o theologians have continued articulating
mestizaje using the same uncritical tendencies he so strongly cau-
tioned against.

In 1994 Loida Martell-Otero expressed her discomfort with
the use of the terms *mujerista* and *feminista* to describe U.S.
Latinas. She argued that both terms "do a great injustice to the
rich diversity of beliefs and backgrounds among us."[13] To her,
because of the theological approach each represents having
emerged from secular movements, and because both terms describe a Catholic constituency, they do not represent the Protestant voices or their theological perspectives. She suggested a third
term to describe those women, like herself, that identify with the
Protestant tradition: Hispanic *mujeres evangélicas*.[14]

In another paper, locating herself under the rubric of
mestizaje/mulatez, she suggests an addition that could have
brought important delimitations to the use of *mestizaje*. She argued that, for the context of Puerto Rico, questions related to
mestizaje are not historically relevant. With a large population
of African descent, the Caribbean Islands have to deal more with
questions of *mulataje*.[15] And in the context of her native Puerto
Rico, the term *sato/a* is commonly used to describe, in a derogatory manner, someone who is not "pure," someone of mixed
descent.

But what does Martell-Otero mean by people of mixed descent? She seems to assume that in Puerto Rico there are people
who have never been mixed. This is also true among other
Latino/a theologians who assume that people of light skin are
less mixed. Yet her critique of the use of *mestizaje* to encompass
all of the U.S. Latina/o peoples remains valid, given that *satos/as*
in the context of Puerto Rico are people who are rejected, de-
spised, and relegated to the margins of society. In such a context
this label *(sato/a)* indeed "catches well the spirit with which terms
such as *mestizaje* and *mulatez* were first proposed."[16]

The problem with her proposal is that *satos/as* as a category loses its critical edge as she simply runs along the discursive lines of *mestizaje*. This ends up reducing *satos/as* to just another, parallel term without going deeper into questions of historical and ethnocultural and religious specificity evoked by the use of the term itself. In her paper she tells us that she was looking for a term that could communicate similar ideas as *mestizaje* but be more appropriate for the Puerto Rican context, yet she does not pursue this to its conclusion and seems to content herself with making similar claims as those made about *mestizaje*.

For different reasons, Manuel Mejido has also criticized the use of *mestizaje* in theology. Evaluating the status of U.S. Latino/a theology in academia, he expresses concern about U.S. Latina/o theologians entering into a self-reflexive and self-critical process in relation to the mainstream theological arena.[17] Part of this self-reflection relates to the different usages of *mestizaje*, which, to Mejido, sometimes refers to anti-racist attitudes and at other times has assimilationist implications. To bring his point across, he points to "slippage" in Elizondo's *Galilean Journey*, where Elizondo sometimes "signs this nomenclature in such a way that gives it an integrationist-liberal meaning and other times in such a way that gives it an emancipatory-liberationist one."[18] Mejido illustrates the need for further clarification of the different uses of *mestizaje*.

Another recent and substantial criticism comes in Rubén Rosario Rodríguez's dissertation. He agrees with Irvine's and Valentín's criticisms, above, that *mestizaje* essentializes U.S. Latina/o conceptions of race and cultural identity. Drawing on Irvine's work, he insists that the myth of an experience shared by all Latinos/as in the United States does not acknowledge the rich ethnocultural diversity of the communities included under such a general term. He suggests that a better understanding of *mestizaje* could be gained if *mestizaje* were located within the context of the broader history of racism, race consciousness, and identity politics in the United States. For him, there was a time when the nationalistic overtones of *mestizaje* served a purpose in bringing together the diverse U.S. Latino/a communities. That is no longer the case. The sociopolitical conditions of the country have changed. Following Isasi-Díaz, he proposes that the defining characteristic of *mestizaje* should be that of a moral-political act. He wants to reconfigure *mestizaje* so that its "emancipatory" potential not be inseparably linked to a "literal understanding of *mestizaje*" but rather be "interpreted as a moral and political possibility regardless of a person's biological [and cultural] heritage."[19]

Taking the works of Isasi-Díaz and Pedraja, Rosario Rodríguez suggests "reconstructing *mestizaje* as a set of relationships rather than a static identity moving beyond the narrow ethnocentrism and striving for a genuine mutuality between cultures." For him, this means that group identity is not limited to "either biological identity or static view of culture, but is understood as something constantly negotiated by the *mestizo* in relation to both parent cultures."[20] As he acknowledges, this brings the dangerous implication of reducing the *mestizo/a* identity to actions of autonomous individuals. Seen this way, *mestizaje* or to be a *mestizo/a* means to make specific moral and political choices, which are not necessarily connected to a specific historical ethnic or cultural tradition, or to the history of a particular ethnocultural group.

Rosario Rodríguez admits that there are dangers involved in using *mestizaje* indiscriminately, particularly that it "occludes more than it reveals" about the reality one attempts to describe. Nonetheless, he insists that it exposes "something very important about racism in the North American context." He continues to use *mestizaje* because "(1) it is the dominant metaphor for cultural identity employed by U.S. Latina/o theologians, and (2) it reminds us that existing social stratifications are built upon an ideology of white supremacy."[21] In this way, and against his better judgment, he preserves the general structure of *mestizaje* discourse.

Rosario Rodríguez's assumptions about the leveling power and promise of inclusion of *mestizaje* betray the logic of his argument.[22] Admittedly, he writes that "while . . . hybridity or transculturation are suitable conceptual alternatives, the use of *mestizaje* is a subversive act that empowers those labeled as racially 'other' (and therefore less than human) to resist cultural and political domination by valuing their difference."[23] Yet he fails to see that germane to the history of *mestizaje* and of the *mestizos/as* is a social stratification and cultural identity construction built upon similar ideological rules of racial superiority that he so adamantly condemns.

This is precisely the reason why Goizueta's assertion that the concepts of *mestizaje* and the *mestizo/a* have a history must be taken seriously in order that we not lose the historical specificity of the term. Most important, U.S. Latina/o theologians have gone beyond simply stating that *mestizaje* "needs thoroughgoing critique and reconstruction," as Rosario Rodríguez wants.[24] They are at a stage where *mestizaje* can potentially become a tool of the empire. An uncritical deployment of *mestizaje* can counter the liberative efforts initiated by the U.S. Latino/a theological movement. U.S. Latina/o scholars have yet to engage those groups of people who are most negatively affected by *mestizaje* in Latin America. And they have yet to confront the presence of racism amid fellow Latinas/os toward those who are different and who do not easily fall under *mestizaje* or want to identify themselves as *mestizos/as*.

Some of these concerns have been recently put forth by Manuel Vásquez in *Rethinking Mestizaje*, which, to my knowledge, is the most recent critique coming from the context of the U.S. Latina/o communities. He begins his argument by citing the U.S. census data showing the richly diverse composition of the U.S. Latina/o population. Although he follows traditional national nomenclature, he also displays some sensitivity to making room for other groups that until now have not been among those national labels.[25] Taking Elizondo's and Isasi-Díaz' versions of *mestizaje* (and *mulataje*) as points of entry to the debate, he challenges U.S. Latina/o theology to consider seriously particular indictments against *mestizaje* coming from Latin America. To support his claim he mentions the works of Jeffrey Gould and Charles Hale, both of whom pointedly reject notions of *mestizaje* as the proper description of Latin America's ethnocultural and sociopolitical landscape.[26]

While Vásquez considers it unwise for U.S. Latina/o theologians to abandon *mestizaje*, he still cautions against the "silences, exclusions, and power asymmetries that criss-cross any *mestizo* discursive and institutional formation." In other words, while he critiques the teleological discursive trajectory in U.S. Latina/o theology, presenting "*mestizaje* as the inescapable condition and future of a redeemed humanity," he also exhorts U.S. Latina/o theologians to question their own use of *mestizaje* when it comes to issues of otherness, not only in relation to the dominant U.S.

culture but among themselves.[27] In my opinion, this is the path that U.S. Latina/o theologians must take in the near future.

As I have demonstrated, concerns about the uncritical use of *mestizaje* are not absent among U.S. Latina/o theologians. Vásquez is correct in stating that they fail to take seriously their own constructions of *mestizaje* as part of the internal tensions and contradictions in Latina/o theology when compared to the present reality and ethnic composition of the U.S. Latina/o population. But Vásquez's criticism also warrants a deeper exploration of the development of *mestizaje* discourses in Latin America, which is central to dispel idealized understandings of *mestizaje*.

In other words, it is important that Latina/o theologians come to terms with the way *mestizaje* is used, abused, and reused in Latin America by different communities and peoples. There, the reigning versions of *mestizaje* do not connote either a peaceful and mutual coming together of peoples or the inclusion of all peoples as argued by Latina/o theologians. In the Latin American context, where the term was originally used and continues to be used amid violence, rape, and racism, *mestizaje* cannot be reduced to a conceptual category separate from the historical, concrete expressions. There, the concern is not that *mestizaje* represents cultural essentialization (Irvine, Valentín, Rosario-Rodríguez). Rather, the discourse of *mestizaje* represents ethnocultural absolutism.

What, then, are some of the indictments against absolutizing, sexist, classist, racist, cultural marginalizing, and homogenizing notions of *mestizaje* in Latin America that are being articulated by indigenous and African peoples and women? Through these, we will see some of the challenges U.S. Latina/o theologians face in using *mestizaje* as a theological category.

THE MYTH OF *MESTIZAJE* AS INCLUSION: RESISTANCE FROM THE MARGINS

Within the context of Latin America, different thinkers and groups have deployed *mestizaje* in many, and at times contradictory, ways. J. Jorge Klor de Alva indicates that, as national and ethnocultural ideology, people changed the meaning of *mestizaje* depending on the historical context, subjects involved, and the changing interests of the ruling elite to legitimate their positions of power and privilege. For him, this makes the notion of *mestizaje* at once extremely attractive and extremely dangerous.[28]

The notion of *mestizaje* is so attractive that some indigenous and African communities in Latin America have also appropriated the use of the term in order to articulate their own experiences. This helps explain why the term is so profoundly popular, contested, and ambiguous, and why it is impossible to make totalizing claims about it. The appropriation of *mestizaje* by indigenous and African peoples differs from the *mestizos/as-criollos'* culturally monochromatic and assimilationist notions of *mestizaje*. Indigenous and African appropriations of *mestizaje* celebrate their ethnic and cultural distinctiveness, as well as challenge *mestizo/a* notions of a homogeneous Latin American population.

For example, Manuel Zapata Olivella claims *mestizaje* as key for celebrating the presence of African descendants in Colombia. Conceiving *mestizaje* first and foremost means to recognize the fact that each of the African, Spanish, and indigenous peoples was already intermixed. The reality of *mestizaje* preceded the Spanish conquest. For him, then, it is possible to reclaim *mestizaje* as the tri-ethnic intermixture of these already mixed groups that points to the "ecumenical seed of the new man."[29]

Admittedly, he says, *mestizaje* has resulted in governments' policies that have denied the African peoples of Latin America their own cultural particularities, by way of European education and culture. For him, that took place because people understood reality from the perspective of the oppressor. In reality, what took place in the context of Latin America was the interweaving of three already mixed ethnocultures; the indigenous, the Africans, and the Spaniards were all actors in the formation of the Latin American *mestizo/a* culture.[30]

In Zapata Olivella's affirmation of *mestizaje*, therefore, the African roots are highlighted as an element without which Latin America is inconceivable. To speak of Africans in Latin America is not a matter of the past. For him, *mestizaje* is the open recognition that the African people are the oldest root of humanity. They have influenced the rest of the world, and in Latin America they have left a deep cultural impact. In his search for a universally shared humanity that acknowledges ethnic diversity, Zapata Olivella appropriates *mestizaje* to demonstrate the richness of the African ethnocultural contributions to the Latin American sociocultural landscape. For him, *mestizaje* is wrongly understood if used only to talk about the indigenous-Spanish intermixture; the *mestizos/as* are also the mulattos and zambos.[31] Note that Zapata Olivella does not raise questions of power or systemic mechanisms that until now have kept most of the African peoples of Colombia in social and economic disadvantage as well as politically under-represented.

Marisol de la Cadena also mentions the community of indigenous women in the Cuzco marketplace who have adopted the label *mestizas*.[32] She retraces the development of *mestizaje* in Peru, identifying two periods of indigenism deployed by the white elite. In the first period of indigenism (1920s), which sought to promote racial endogamy and purity, *mestizas* were seen as the embodiment of the immoral sexual behavior that led to the degeneration that hybridity represented, and *mestizos* as lazy and abusive men who could not respond to the needs of *mestizas*.[33] In the second wave of indigenism, which began around the 1940s, and which sought to promote *mestizos/as* as embodying the national and ethnic identity of Peru, *mestizaje* was no longer seen as treason or immorality but meant pro-creation, in favor of creating something new.[34]

According to de la Cadena, in reacting against the latter version of *mestizaje* the indigenous women of Cuzco's marketplace are dismissing the dominant version and creatively producing a new regional identity. These women are contradicting the dominant notions of the indigenous peoples as liars, robbers, immoral, ignorant, and uncultured by adopting elements of the dominant culture such as learning to speak, write, and read Spanish. As an expression of their newly found identity these indigenous women have changed the kind of clothes they wear, signifying the passage from one social condition to another. But this does not mean the shedding of "'previous' cultural baggage."[35]

According to de la Cadena, following the dominant anti-indigenous social and cultural constructions by the elite of the region, these women's appropriating the term *mestiza* implies distancing themselves from the "Indian" social condition of servitude, a "de-Indianizing." To "de-Indianize" means to leave such condition; "it does not mean 'disappearing' into a hybrid, gradually homogenizing *mestizo* culture." As she writes, "[De-Indianization] is the process of empowering indigenous identities through economic and educational achievements, *and* displaying this identity in regional events of popular culture that take place ubiquitously in urban and rural stages."[36] For these communities, to be Indian is not seen as a fixed identity. In this complex and ambiguous play of resistance and adoption of elements from the dominant culture, these women turn *mestizaje* into the alternative for engaging the dominant culture without relinquishing their own indigenous identity but rather by celebrating it. By adopting *mestizaje*, the indigenous communities of Cuzco are subverting the dominant understanding of what it is to be Indian, and they are redefining the terms and limits of *mestizaje* and what it is to be a *mestizo/a*.

The two examples of Zapata Olivella and de la Cadena show that there are African and indigenous communities in Latin America that use *mestizaje* to make a sociocultural space without relinquishing their own ethnic and cultural identities. Harsher criticisms of *mestizaje* are also emerging in Latin America among women and the indigenous and African communities. These groups are criticizing the dominant paradigm of *mestizaje* in many Latin American nations. As these communities move to center stage and struggle to become actors in the construction of the Latin American societies, they are unwilling to negotiate with racialized systems that exclude them on the basis of their ethnocultural identity. In the struggle for social inclusion, these communities have taken on the discourse of *mestizaje*, have deconstructed it, and found it wanting.

The Myth of the Ancient Indigenous Communities from the Past

Since the 1960s many things have changed in the sociopolitical landscape of Latin America. The indigenous peoples are taking center stage, reasserting their identities and cultures, and making their voices heard. Many of them are critiquing the dominant versions of *mestizaje*. In Bolivia, for example, Javier Sanjinés tells us that the indigenous peoples were never passive victims in the construction of the Latin American societies. They have participated through their opposition. For him, the elites' proposal of *mestizaje* as the only possible alternative in conceiving national and ethnocultural identity is precisely why there are so many protests, uprisings, and sociopolitical demands for inclusion by indigenous peoples.[37]

In the sociopolitical landscape of Bolivia, writes Sanjinés, the confrontation between the powerful elite and the indigenous majorities is always related to the indigenous people's historical struggle for survival of their communities, languages, cultures, and recovery of their lands. They have become powerful political forces demanding their rightful participation in the construction of the national identities and societies of Latin America, but on their own terms.[38] These communities are questioning the dominant constructions of *mestizaje* for failing to include and reflect the indigenous ethnocultural diversity of Bolivia.

In Nicaragua, Dora María Téllez was the first to unmask the myth of *mestizaje* as a harmonious process of biological and cultural intermixture.[39] In her study of nineteenth- century Nicaragua, she records the manner in which the *Ladino/a (mestizo/a)* elite, following the wars of independence, continued the violent "civilizing" and expansionist impetus of their Spanish ancestors.[40] She writes that, instead of protecting the indigenous peoples as equal citizens, the result of the independence was the annulment of any land claims they had while under colonial rule. She narrates that consequently there were many incidents in which the indigenous peoples of Matagalpa and Jinotega were displaced, robbed of their lands, and discriminated against by the structures of government that claimed that the indigenous lands were unoccupied and unpopulated *(tierras baldías)*.[41]

Téllez argues that often the lands taken from the indigenous communities were offered as incentives to foreign immigrants. In the modern Nicaragua that was being built, and although there were brief moments of indigenous-*Ladino/a* alliances against the filibuster invasion headed by William Walker (1956), there was no room for the indigenous nations. In this *"conquista tardía"* (belated conquest), claims Téllez, the intention was to create "a segregated space [for the indigenous peoples], subordinate, that would serve the ends of the new republic of *mestizos*."[42]

The destructive force of the *mestizo/a* imaginary in the construction of Nicaragua's national identity is also highlighted in the work of Jeffrey Gould. According to him, during the time of the Sandino revolution a unified Nicaragua was envisioned under what he called "*La Raza Indo-Hispana*," which, for all intents and purposes, meant the construction of a *mestizo/a* Nicaragua where all peoples would be "equal."[43] In this national imaginary, says Gould, the indigenous peoples were integrated in the *mestizo/a* national project and at the same time marginalized. Those who insisted on their uniqueness were seen as antipatriotic and antidemocratic. As he sees it, the democratic discourse of equal rights and citizenship effectively suppressed specific indigenous rights to communal land and political autonomy in Nicaragua.[44] It is in this way that Gould debunks the myth that Nicaragua is ethnically and culturally homogeneous, and shows how the discourse of *mestizaje* suppressed cultural differences and rationalized the destruction of indigenous communities.[45]

Similarly, Rafael Polo Bonilla recounts that the indigenous peoples have been effectively removed from the national imaginary of Ecuador.[46] For him, this is evidenced in the invention of the national identity and culture of the country by some elite intellectuals. As he sees it, this was made possible by two related events. First, after the May revolution of 1944 the efforts for developing a more inclusive society were crushed by the powerful oligarchy, which ensured that the lower classes remained outside the political processes. And second, it was the result of the founding of La Casa de la Cultura (1944), the institutional body that quickly became the guardian of the national and ethnic identity of Ecuador.[47] As he asserts, the intellectuals in La Casa de la Cultura invented *mestizaje* as the paradigm for conceiving Ecuador's identity. This was particularly true of Benjamín Carrión, he argues, who is commonly spoken of as the father of Ecuador's culture, and who defined Ecuador as essentially a "mestizo nation."[48]

In the construction of Ecuadorian national and ethnic identity, *mestizaje* was transformed into a metaphor of social order, adds Polo Bonilla. The *mestizaje* metaphor spoke of the (symmetrical) synthesis of the indigenous and Spanish elements reflected in the culture of Ecuador. This notion of *mestizaje*, however, effectively erased the living indigenous peoples from the national imaginary. Even today, he writes, "*mestizaje* functions as a collection of representations, of images, of 'attitudes' that are directed toward homogenizing the population of the country disregarding *ipso facto* the cultural and social diversity of the country." As he suggests, in this complex construction of *mestizaje* the indigenous peoples were first reduced to being farmers *(campesinos)* or proletarian land workers, "ascribing to them a concept of class and disavowing their ethnic realities." Then, they were transformed into objects of anthropological study.[49] In this way the intellectuals responsible for promoting *mestizaje* perpetuated the view of the indigenous communities as "uncivilized," meaning in this case that they lacked the will power and capacity to govern themselves.

In Mexico, Guillermo Bonfil Batalla critiques the notion of *mestizaje* as the expression of the national and ethnic identity of Mexico.[50] His criticism relates to the *mestizos/as* (re)claiming the indigenous cultural background as constituent part of their identity. This form of *indigenismo*, he argues, referred and continues to refer only to the glorious past civilizations that are presumed dead. He makes three claims under this version of indigenism. First, the dominant *mestizo/a* culture presumes the indigenous peoples are entirely or almost entirely exterminated; for the *mestizo/a* the indigenous cultures "can only exist as something dead." Second, in the ideology of *mestizaje* the indigenous cultures are exalted and idealized but only as "our deeper past, the original trunk from which the *mestizo* shall flourish." In claiming the indigenous past as their own, *mestizos/as* see themselves as the next step in the evolution of humanity. Within this ideology of *mestizaje*, the indigenous peoples already fulfilled their mission; their "justification in history was to give birth to the *mestizo/a*." Third, in the affirmation of the indigenous past, *mestizaje* has little to do with the present living indigenous communities. These communities are perceived by *mestizos/as* elite as residues of great civilizations. They are "an anachronistic phantasm that pales and barely remembers what was," without a present and much less a future. More specifically, writes Bonfil Batalla, *mestizo/a* elite perceive the living indigenous as "degraded"; they are devalued before the *mestizo/a* because they "remained Indian and had not 'advanced' toward the superior stage incarnated by the *mestizo*, thanks to the confluence of the European component."[51]

J. Jorge Klor de Alva reports a similar approach among the Mexican Americans in the United States as they appropriated the discourse of *mestizaje*. He recounts that Mexican Americans sought to find a metaphor that would unite them against the dominant Anglo population while at the same time they distanced themselves from the Mexican peoples. They claimed they inhabited the legendary land of Aztlán and asserted their direct connection to the Aztec-Mexica people prior to their encounter with the Spanish.[52] He comments that although Mexican Americans traveled to Mexico to study the Ancient Aztec-Mexica ruins, up until the 1970s they engaged neither the indigenous peoples nor the political situation of Mexico.[53] Thus, Aztlán served the function of a legitimating metaphor for the *mestizo/a* Mexican Americans, but with no connection to the indigenous peoples or other Mexicans inhabiting Mexico today.

Among the similar *mestizo/a* versions of *indigenismo* that were formulated in Latin America, it was not uncommon to think that the indigenous people were "redeemable" if only they would stop being indigenous by adopting methods, practices, and cultures in accordance with the dominant culture and modernity.[54] This was true of intellectuals like Andrés Molina Enríquez, Alcides Arguedas, Justo Sierra, Franz Tamayo, and even José Vasconcelos. It was true even in José Carlos Mariátegui's uncompromising struggle for the indigenous peoples of Peru.[55] The goal was to facilitate the process of cultural *mestizaje* of the indigenous peoples mainly through education. As Tace Hedrick writes, in the case of Mexico the government leaders thought that education was the "only thing which would awaken the Indians to their plight and uplift them from their racial and cultural decay."[56] For Bonfil Batalla, the crux of the issue is that for indigenous people to become Mexicans they need to become *mestizos/as*; they must "abandon being Indian." They did not possess "the seed of redemption."[57]

These types of *indigenism* justified by the construction of a national *mestizo/a* imaginary perpetuated notions of the indigenous peoples as incapable of governing their lives and sociopolitical affairs. The intellectuals of *mestizaje* saw the indigenous peoples as "minors" who needed the help of the *mestizo/a* people, or as faint reminders of great civilizations now being replaced by the *mestizo/a* people, who are the heirs and legitimate guardians of their traditions and cultures.[58]

It is in these ways, and many others, that the indigenous peoples have been effectively removed from the political scene, left without any say about the issues that affect them directly in the societies that claim to be the result of the fusion between indigenous and Spanish ethnocultural elements. In the words of Hale, as promoted by most of the *mestizo/a* intellectuals, the discourse of *mestizaje* falsely promises to open "possibilities for moving beyond the racialized, dichotomous, quasi-colonial ethnic relations in . . . [the] past, *and* signals a dangerous preemptive closure of the discussion on racism and collective [ethnocultural] rights."[59]

Mestizaje and Multiculturalism: The Invisibility of African Descendants

In dealing with *mestizaje* one cannot ignore the African presence in Latin America. While debates about the African–Latin American peoples are better dealt with under the discourse of *mulataje*, I briefly engage this issue here because in many contexts *mestizaje* is articulated as incorporating indigenous *and* African biological and cultural elements. African descendants in Latin America also criticize the dominant ideological, sociopolitical, and cultural constructions of *mestizaje*. Authors, in different places and at different times, have acknowledged the African biological and cultural presence in Latin America, but oftentimes without a deep engagement with the historical violence, exploitation, and racialized discrimination against people of African descent.

Albeit in different versions, the powerful metaphor of *mestizaje* reached all of Latin America. In those places where the indigenous peoples were largely or entirely decimated and were repopulated with masses of African slaves and their descendants, like Cuba, Santo Domingo, Puerto Rico, and Brazil, the discourses of *mulatez* were developed but were subsumed under *mestizaje*. This is clearly illustrated in the work of Nicolás Guillén, who—while remaining staunchly committed to the African presence, and criticizing the pervasive racism in Cuba—preserved the dominant view that Cuba's ethnic identity could not be understood outside of the metaphor of *mestizaje*.[60] Gilberto Freyre's work about Brazil also exemplifies this, as he adopted *mestizaje* to discuss the interrelationship and intermixture that took place primarily between the African slaves and servants and the white Portuguese-European masters.[61] These writers included issues pertinent to the African peoples and their intermixture with Europeans in their discourse of *mestizaje*.

This is the central critique of Luis Duno Gottberg in *Solventando las differencias*.[62] He examines the erroneous notions that the ideology of *mestizaje* in Cuba delivered harmony between cultural and racial differences as articulated by Cuban literary elites. As the essence of national identity, *mestizaje* sometimes subtly and sometimes not so subtly promoted the homogeneity and Eurocentric construction of Cuban culture and identity. Tracing the development of *mestizaje* during three periods in the history of Cuba (1840–95, 1919–40, 1940–59), and examining important literary figures in the construction of Cuban national identity (Severo Sarduy, Fernando Ortíz, José Lezama Lima, Alejo Carpentier, and Benítez Rojo), Duno Gottberg unmasks the discursive tendencies toward ameliorating *(solventando)* racialized cultural differences between blacks and whites in Cuba. This is consistent with José Martí's adamant insistence that Cuban identity stood above and beyond races and racism of any kind. For him, it seemed unpatriotic or even "un-Cuban" to attempt to raise issues of racism in the island. As he wrote, "There is no hatred between the races, because there are no races. . . . The soul emerges, equal and eternal, from the diverse bodies in shape and colour. [He] sins against humanity who foments and propagates the opposition and the hatred of the races."[63]

Duno Gottberg does not see Cuba as white and black; neither does he consider it *mestizo/a*. He uncovers the ethnic and social organization of Cuba around this binary, even when it is commonly accepted that the population is mixed, which explains why the term *mestizaje* is so popular among the elite. Use of the term *mestizaje* to describe national identity denied the African and indigenous elements in Cuban culture and society. So the discourse about *mestizaje*, argues Duno Gottberg, is the myth of reconciling national projects whereby Cuba's population is portrayed as ethnically and culturally homogeneous, as a Europeanized *mestizo/a*. Instead, he argues that Cuba's internal racialized cultural struggles between those who see themselves as whites (the *mestizo/a* light-skinned elite) use *mestizaje* discourse as a façade behind which to hide their privileges over and at the expense of the subaltern black (the *mestizo/a* dark-skinned) communities. To embrace *mestizaje* in Cuba, he concludes, effectively hides the violence of assimilation and abuses exacted upon the African peoples during the conquest and subsequent history of colonial and contemporary societies.[64]

Likewise in Colombia, Elisabeth Cunin argues, the invisibility of African peoples in the political and sociocultural imaginary is directly related to continuing racist notions of the African peoples as primitive and inferior. In *Identidades a flor de piel* she tells us that, compared to the Afro-Colombians, the indigenous people are a reminder of precolonial times, and as a result enjoy a marginal social status as a constituent part of the *mestizo* national identity crystallized in the statue of the India Catalina since 1890. But for the Afro-Colombians such sociopolitical space is simply unavailable.[65] According to her, the 1991 constitutional incorporation of multiculturalism in the Colombian identity functions simply as a mechanism by which the deep-seated racism against Afro-Colombians is effectively disguised by the nation's *mestizo/a* elite.

In reality, *mestizaje* does not impede racism, Cunin declares. Admittedly, the incorporation of multiculturalism in the Constitution of Colombia opened the door for a "positive discrimination" by which people can reclaim their African roots as part of their struggle against assimilation and for their rights as Colombians. But this effectively developed into a dynamic of "avoidance" *(evitamiento)*. Since it is assumed that there is an "anti-racist" government policy of multiculturalism in place, people do not engage questions of racism in the sociopolitical structures of the country. This makes it more difficult for the Afro-Colombians to struggle against systemic racism. As she argues, by taking on the policy of official multiculturalism, the 1991 constitution of Colombia practically removed racist claims from the sociopolitical sphere.[66]

This was clearly seen in 2001 when Vanessa Mendoza, a woman of African descent, became the winner of the national beauty pageant, argues Cunin. The media and the government exploited this incident to promote a Colombia where "racism was a matter of the past." However, she claims, a careful examination of the dominant rhetoric, as well as the social conditions of the peoples of Colombia, particularly Cartagena, where she did her study, reveals a different picture of the racial and sociopolitical dynamics of exclusion at play. In her view, in the dominant government-sponsored monochromatic multicultural discourse the Afro-Colombian communities are referred to using essentialist stereotypical notions of "blackness," reducing their rich diversity to rigid and exotic identity categories. And in the sociopolitical sphere they are kept in the worst conditions of poverty and social chaos. They are made invisible at the levels of culture, politics, society, and ethnonationality.[67]

Afro-Colombians, however, are finding new ways to counter their marginalization, says Cunin. Yes, the context is fraught with racial and social tensions. But as Afro-Colombians see the adoption of elements from the dominant culture as opportunity for social upward mobility, they enter a double process of whitening and of assimilation of the dominant *mestizo/a* culture, and developing new strategies for moving among different social spaces. In this "*mestizo* competition," points out Cunin, Afro-Colombians are challenging rigid identity categories and announcing important changes to racial dynamics.[68]

The Patriarchal, Male-Centered Dimension of *Mestizaje*

Women in Latin America are beginning to criticize the different versions of national and ethnocultural identity articulated in terms of *mestizaje*. Not that women have been passive subjects in the process of intermixture; speaking of the cultural legacy of women in the national *mestizo/a* identity construction of

Paraguay, Clyde Soto tells us that indigenous women were seized to become Spanish concubines (about forty thousand of them, he reports). But he also tells us that during times of war they financed and joined the army to fight during the War of the Triple Alliance (1865–70).[69] Most important, Camilla Townsend tells us that indigenous and African women were pivotal to the development and formation of *mestizaje* in Ecuador. In her study of Guayaquil, she writes of the ways in which these women adopted *mestizaje* as an alternative for survival and as a strategy to avoid paying the taxes imposed by the local governments.[70]

Therefore, the impact of *mestizaje* on women must be part of any analysis of the term. This is why I agree with Breny Mendoza that it is impossible to engage and evaluate *mestizaje* without examining all of the different intersecting dimensions included in the term. She notes that *mestizaje* is not only about issues pertaining to race and ethnoculture, but it is also about questions of gender and sex.[71] And Soto writes that, when it comes to issues of gender, older and newer versions of *mestizaje* reinscribe sexist notions when they portray biological *mestizaje* as a peaceful union, the fulfillment of a romantic saga of love.[72] Women's central critique of *mestizaje* is that it was founded upon the violation of indigenous women's bodies. To romanticize *mestizaje* is to re-victimize the primary victims of the Spanish conquest and invasion. It is to conceal the deep patriarchal overtones, dynamics, and structures of the Latin American societies of today inherited from the colonial times.

There is no question that patriarchalism dominates the national discourses of *mestizaje* in Latin America. Women are entirely excluded from and silenced in the history of the Latin American nations except to legitimize the presence and power of the *mestizos*. For example, while the elite rejected intermixture and promoted the segregation of indigenous and white constituencies of Peru in the 1920s, they used the image of Cori Ocllo to bolster their position. Cori Ocllo was the indigenous woman who was willing to die rather than surrender to the conqueror and be raped by him. Again, in the 1940s, when the elite started promoting *mestizaje*, the image of Isabel Chimpu Ocllo, the mother of Garcilazo de la Vega, became the banner behind the new vision of *mestizaje*.[73]

For his part, Octavio Paz focused primarily on the violence and insult done to the *mestizo/a* children as descendants of the raped indigenous women *(hijos de la Chingada)* epitomized in La Malinche.[74] He insisted that the identity crisis of Mexican people related to having a raped and traitor mother and a rapist and violent father, but he did not specifically condemn the violence perpetrated against the indigenous women-mothers of the *mestizos/as*.[75] According to Rita Cano Alcalá, Paz perpetuated notions of La Malinche as traitor to the Mexica people, but he did not deal with the fact that she was given as a slave to ensure her brother's inheritance.[76] To her, emphasizing the betrayal of La Malinche highlights the "unreliability" and "untrust-worthiness" of women, discourses that effectively removed them from contributing in the construction of the Mexican *mestizo/a* nation and society.[77]

More specifically, there is a connection between the "suffering mother" motif and the identity of women in *mestizo/a* societies. This is closely related to the prominence of Marianism in Latin America. In the history of *mestizaje*, writes Sonia Montecino, the suffering of the woman is expressed in the single mother who bears her children and whose partner carries no domestic commitment and is absent from home, just as the Spanish fathers abandoned the first indigenous women.[78] For Montecino, this kind of behavior both has serious detrimental social effects on women, their children, and the construction of family, and ensures the continuation of the male culture of Latin America. At the same time, adds Milagros Palma, the racial superiority of the Spanish colonizer is preserved in the strict control of women's sexuality and by keeping them in the domestic domain;[79] it is by keeping women suppressed that *mestizos* are racially legitimated.[80] In the legitimation of *mestizos*, then, the female role is manipulated and the violation of the indigenous and African woman ignored.[81] Critiquing the theological work of Elizondo, Palma shows how the *mestizo* male, as an emerging power, is announced under the symbols of the Virgin and Mother, which she considers "supreme symbols that ensure the continuity of the masculine order." In Elizondo, she claims, the *mestizo/a* people are truly proud of their exalted race; they have been born "not from the violated person, but from the pure and immaculate mother."[82]

So, by using Guadalupe as the mother of the *mestizo/a* people, the shame of the violated woman by the conquistador is sanitized, observes Palma. "What had been born in blood and shame, in the battles and consequences of the conquest, was . . . born again in the honor and glory of the sons of the Virgin Mother."[83] For Palma, this also reestablishes the position of superiority of men over women embodied in Guadalupe. Guadalupe responds to the deepest instincts of the *mestizo* men: "the obsession for the legitimacy of their power with the continuity of the image of the [domesticated,] defeated, sacrificed, virginized and maternized woman . . . a people that manages to impose control over their women."[84] In this way what is indigenous is forgotten and replaced by what is *mestizo/a*, and women are provided with an ideal portrait of womanhood.

As shown, the ascent of *mestizos/as* to positions of power and wealth in Latin America has meant the marginalization, impoverishment, exclusion, exploitation, and silencing of women and the indigenous and African communities. And it has also meant the creation of mechanisms to ensure the slow and systematic genocide of the indigenous and African populations. In Latin America the elite *mestizo/a* versions of national identity negate the diversity of the population; *mestizaje* is not a harmonious, mutual "coming together," a symmetrical "fusion" of different peoples constructing a new culture and society where there is room for all. There was a social and ethnic cost attached to the construction of *mestizo/a* societies in Latin America, and it was paid mostly by women and by African and indigenous peoples.

These are the challenges with which U.S. Latina/o theologians must wrestle as they continue the painstaking task of defining themselves and describing the reality of the Latina/o communities. Moreover, in the United States the sociopolitical conditions that initially prompted the use of *mestizaje* in theology have changed. The number of Latinas/os in the United States more than doubled between 1980 and 2000, accounting for 40 percent of the growth in the country's population during that period. The 2003 U.S. Census Bureau designated them the nation's largest minority group—a remarkable event given that in 1980 Latinas/os numbered only slightly more than half the size of the African American population. Many Latina/o groups now have

become powerful social, cultural, and political forces with which
the dominant culture must reckon. Latinas/os have had a profound impact on U.S. society and culture, which can be seen, for
example, in the increasing popularity of Latino/a food, music,
and in the prevalence of Spanish-language signage, advertise-
ments, and media. The business community has also discovered
the economic clout of the Latina/o population.[85] Latinas/os are
considered the fastest-growing consumer group in the nation,
and many banks and financial institution seek to access this
largely untapped market by creating financial resources such as
ahorrando.org. Yet, despite their rapid increase in numbers,
Latinas/os continue to be at the margins of U.S. society and at
the lower end of the economic ladder. According to Marcela
Sánchez, "The share of Hispanics in poverty doubled from 12
percent in 1980 to 25 percent in 2004."[86] This makes necessary
the continuing struggle for recognition of Latinas/os in the U.S.
social and cultural fabric.

With the growing realization of diversity among Latinas/os,
new generations of U.S. Latina/o scholars will have to exercise a
good dose of self-criticism as they come to terms with the uncritical ways in which they and previous generations deployed
mestizaje. This book builds upon the work of these scholars,
highlighting the increasing human cost in the unqualified use of
the category of *mestizaje*. As U.S. Latina/o theologians conjec-
ture about the future course of Latina/o theology, they will have
to engage the different discourses of *mestizaje* in Latin America
because it was there (Mexico) that they found the original inspiration to adopt *mestizaje* in theology. This is also necessary because of the constant flow of emigrants from Mexico and the
rest of Latin America, who bring their own notions of *mestizaje*
from their native countries; because it is becoming increasingly
difficult to make generalizing claims when speaking of the ethnic and cultural composition of the U.S. Latina/o population;
and because their very own history is marked and influenced by
the racialized power struggles between people-groups, which they
intend to describe by using *mestizaje*.

5

THE FUTURE OF U.S. LATINA/O THEOLOGY

Implications

> [The central issue] is not one of merely *acknowledging* difference; rather, the more difficult question concerns the kind of difference that is acknowledged and engaged. Difference seen as benign variation (diversity), for instance, rather than as conflict, struggle, or the threat of disruption, bypasses power as well as history to suggest a harmonious, empty pluralism.
>
> —CHANDRA MOHANTY

The Latina/o communities in the United States have never been a homogeneous group, and as they interact with other ethnocultural communities their sense of identity is changed in profound ways. Moreover, the large masses of immigrants from Latin America are changing the Latina/o ethnocultural fabric. And voices previously absent from national and identity debates are emerging and with vitality carving out their own social and political spaces.

This proliferation of identities among the U.S. Latina/o communities makes any attempt at using airtight globalizing identity markers to describe this diversity problematic. It also raises serious questions as to the desirability of using *mestizaje* to describe this diversity because all groups among Latinas/os do not share the same history. So while one can say that these groups are mixed, for various reasons many of these groups would reject the use of such a label to describe themselves. We must admit that *mestizaje* is not a singularity or an entity, nor is it an experience shared by all people.

Likewise, problematizing the notion of *mestizaje* brings profound implications for previous interpretations of religious symbols and practices using the optic of *mestizaje*. These challenges demand that social, political, religious, and economic power structures be questioned, in order to have a fuller understanding of the true effects of using the notion of *mestizaje*. And they challenge us to create alternative ways for conceiving and articulating the experiences and identities coexisting among the Latina/o communities.

THE AMBIGUOUS WEB
OF *MESTIZAJE* AND THE REALITY
OF HETEROGENEITY

Until now I have strongly criticized the absence of indigenous and African peoples in the Latin American and U.S. Latina/o versions of *mestizaje*. Such analysis is incomplete and simplistic because the debates of *mestizaje* also obscure other internal differences and tensions within Latina/o groups and subcultures. Within the Latina/o population there are seasonal workers, undocumented peoples, newly arrived immigrants, different generations, and urban and rural communities.[1] There are immigrants to the United States from virtually everywhere from South and Central America and the Caribbean whose identity cannot be reduced to their national origin: there are indigenous peoples such as the Guaraní, Quiché, Tzutuhíl, Quechua; and African and indigenous mixed groups like the Garífuna, just to name a few. My analysis is also incomplete because of the absence of other ethnic and cultural groups that inhabit Latin America and that also constitute the U.S. Latina/o population, but who do not trace their ancestry to the Spanish/Portuguese, African, and indigenous peoples.

As we can see from this, these emerging identities are not monolithic and the attempts at describing them using inclusive identity categories point to a complex web of different discursive approaches and directions that also reject the dominant universalizing uses of *mestizaje*. In Honduras, for example, Breny Mendoza engages in a process of "demythologizing" *mestizaje*.[2] According to her, earlier articulations of *mestizaje* in the country contributed to the establishment of racist legislation that had detrimental effects on the indigenous communities in Honduras. Such nationalist versions of *mestizaje* even proclaimed a "mayanización" (understood as commitment to the Mayan identity of the country) that had detrimental effects upon non-Mayan indigenous groups that still live in some regions of Honduras.[3] In the same way, claims Mendoza, the articulation of a global national *mestizaje* prohibited the entry of African peoples, and restricted the immigration of Arabs, Chinese, Turks, and Armenians, and this favored the construction of a national total *mestizo/a* identity. The Honduran intellectuals, she says, discriminated against the African peoples because they understood *mestizaje* as having Spanish and indigenous poles.

As Mendoza describes, the dominant versions and even the official version of *mestizaje* in Honduras are of masculine and heterosexual character. On the one hand, such notions leave out that, as traditionally understood, *mestizaje* has to do with violent heterosexual relations. These versions of *mestizaje* downplay or simply silence the fact that *mestizaje* was built upon the rape of the indigenous women. Not only that, such official constructions of *mestizaje* also assume solely male-female relations, ignoring the homosexual constituency of the country. The *mestizo* male is constructed as a heterosexual, and a heterosexual who inflicts violence against those males who do not fit the heterosexual male script.

Moreover, Mendoza points out that the dominant versions of *mestizaje* in Honduras today must be understood as realignment with the globalizing forces led by the economic power of the United States. The present attempts to use *mestizaje* are led by the interests of the *criollo-mestizo/a* oligarchy that seeks to reap the benefits of the banana plantations with the support of the United States while at the same time seeking to neutralize the growing economic power of Arabic-Palestinian enclaves in the country.

As a result, several sectors of the Honduran population are questioning *mestizaje* with the hope that stronger foundations can be set in place for the construction of an ethnically, culturally, and sexually more inclusive society in Honduras. This, I believe, offers U.S. Latina/o theologians another dimension of evaluation of *mestizaje* discourse, because "sexism, racism, classism are alive and well within the social spaces occupied by [U.S. Latinas/os]" and need to be addressed.[4]

More positively, the discourse of *mestizaje* is being adopted by people of other ethnic and cultural traditions that have made Latin America their home. We see this exemplified by Ricardo Feierstein, who uses the nomenclature of *mestizaje* to name his own experience. In his novel *Mestizo* he portrays identity as a tree, the collection of memories, experiences, and relationships that shape people's perceptions of themselves and contribute to the formation of their identities.[5] This is a crucial task in his novel as he attempts to come to grips with his dual identity as a child of Jewish immigrants in Argentina.

Feierstein wants to show the porous nature of ethnic and cultural identities concretely expressed in immigrant people. As he describes the multicultural character of Argentina, he concludes that there is no such thing as "pure," unmixed identities. He is well aware that *mestizaje* originally was used to describe the biological phenomenon of miscegenation between the Spanish and the indigenous. And he also understands why in places of great indigenous populations *mestizaje* is seen negatively. However, Argentina as "multicultural puzzle" has replaced Argentina as a *crisol de razas* or melting pot, describes new directions for our present conception of identities, which for Feierstein can only be understood as *mestizaje*.[6] He writes:

"Cultural mestizaje" aspires to what is universal without losing its particularity, it heads in the direction of a "national culture," that aspires to preserve the individuality in an expression that is universal. Civilizations do not die,

but are transformed—in the different historical stages—
through a process that synthesizes the contributions of the
past and enriches them with new ones.[7]

There are serious questions concerning Feierstein's "democratic potentiality" in *mestizaje*-intermixture. Why, for example,
does he reject the indigenous roots under the assumption that
these have been exterminated? For him, the construction of a
cohesive Argentinean culture must tap into European immigration since the eighteenth century. But such an assertion carries
the implication that Feierstein identifies Argentinean culture as
European, and vindicates his perception of the present aesthetics
(by which he means that Argentineans look European) of the
population.[8] This is the only way he can conceive of Argentina
developing as a nation.

Feierstein's appropriation of *mestizaje* is yet another example
of the plasticity of *mestizaje* as well as of its contested nature. It
demands that the notion of *mestizaje* be seen in the plural sense,
describing different concrete realities rather than a universal
phenomenon. Moreover, the examples of Mendoza and Feierstein
show how in the ethnically and culturally plural landscape of
Latin America, other ethnic groups are also struggling to carve
out their own social space. Among many others, the Jewish and
Arabic communities are finding in the ideal of *mestizaje* the possibility to name their experiences (Feierstein), or their impedi-
ment toward contributing to the social fabric (Mendoza) of the
different Latin American nations.

In engaging the theological articulations of U.S. Latina/o theologians it has become evident that the discourse(s) of *mestizaje* is
ambiguous, plurivocal, polysemic, and heterogeneous. There is
no one single universal version of *mestizaje*. In the context of
Latina America, where U.S. Latina/o theologians gained their
inspiration for adopting *mestizaje*, and in light of the historical
and contextual changes of the times, different intellectuals articulated different versions of *mestizaje*, and at times these com-
peted against each other. This clearly shows that when we speak
of *mestizaje* we are not talking about a single thing, or about a
single experience or phenomenon shared by all U.S. Latinas/os
or by all people of mixed descent.

Placing Affirmations of *Mestizaje* in Their Social and Historical Context

Examples such as Mendoza's and Feierstein's above shatter the notion that Latin America is culturally and ethnically homogeneous or *mestiza*. They show that besides the indigenous and African peoples there are other voices and stories of violence, intermixture, and power struggle that are part of the ethnic and cultural fabric and history of Latin America. They help explain the sudden explosion and creation of new identities that cannot easily be subsumed under *mestizaje*. And they make the context of Latin America a fertile soil for the cross-fertilization and multiplication of cultures and identities without these being absorbed into one universal homogenizing synthetic *mestizaje*. We cannot underestimate the impact of this proliferation of identities in the U.S. Latina/o population and configuration, as many of these people immigrate into the United States and become a constitutive part of the Latina/o population. Their presence makes it necessary to acknowledge the diversity of the Latina/o population outside of synthetic and universalizing notions.[9]

Part of the difficulties I find in the U.S. Latina/o theological articulations of *mestizaje* relate to the reification of *mestizaje*-intermixture—in the Elizondian version of a double *mestizaje*—as the one thing shared by all of the U.S. Latina/o population. This is what John Francis Burke does when he states that "*mestizaje* . . . concretely illustrates how cultures can combine without any one necessarily becoming dominant or hegemonic."[10] He describes the *mestizo/a* as the "*nueva raza*" that emerged from the intersection of indigenous, African, and Spanish peoples. And he states that "to be Mexican is to be of a culture" constituted by these three ethnic and cultural currents.[11] In my view, Burke's idea of *mestizaje* implies that to be a Mexican cannot be understood outside the framing of *mestizaje*.

With the growing awareness of the living ethnic and cultural diversity within the U.S. Latina/o population and Latin America, such notions are becoming increasingly problematic. The presence of indigenous and African peoples who reject the use of the term in the dominant ethnic nationalistic versions demand that *mestizaje* be delimited. Only a portion, albeit the majority, of the U.S. Latina/o and Latin American peoples, is *mestizo/a*. But not the entire population is. Even when people ascribe to *mestizaje* to define themselves, their experiences of intermixture vary significantly. Thus, any deployment of *mestizaje* cannot be radically separated from its historical moorings, which cannot be universalized. In other words, while it can be said that intermixture is a commonly shared experience by many people in the world, their experience of intermixture is the result of specific historical events that make it impossible to make universal absolutizing claims by using *mestizaje*. This is why I disagree with various other attempts (among them, those of Ángel Rosenblat, Manuel Zapata Olivella, Claudio Esteva Fabregat, and Jacques Audinet[12]) to insist *mestizaje* is one uniform process and reality. *Mestizaje* is a category that must be spoken of in qualifiedly plural terms; there are many versions of intermixture-*mestizaje*, if you will, pointing to multiple intersections among ethnic, cultural, and political subjects, and always colored by power relations.

For example, in order to identify the reality of intermixture or "biracialism," Alice Walker claims that U.S. African Americans are the *mestizos/as* of North America.[13] Zipporah Glass also appropriates the category of *mestizaje* to speak of the mixed nature or racialized diversity within the African American communities.[14] In Canada, *Métis* is the term used to describe the children of First Nations women and French and English men originally part of the Hudson Bay Company and fur trading, and of their struggles as they seek recognition as a people.[15] In Indonesia, *mestizaje* is used to describe the dynamics of intermixture between Indian, Chinese, and Batavian women and Dutch male soldiers as a result of the commercial expansion of the Dutch East Indian Company.[16] And Claudine Bavoux traces the formation in Madagascar of a mixed *métis* cultural tradition by the Sourti indigenous people in the Tamatave who have converted to Sunni Islam.[17] Jean-Loup Amselle also initially chose to speak of *mestizo logics* when describing the tensions between universal right claims and ethnocultural specificity in Africa.[18] (In 2001 he opted instead for the term *branchements* to study the "connections" that occur as people relate, because for him it is less ambiguous.[19]) These examples demonstrate the importance of qualifying and limiting the use of the label *mestizaje* in order to describe a particular experience of intermixture.

I can well imagine that the concept of *mestizaje* is so attractive to people because their experiences of in-betweenness resonate with the ideas of intermixture communicated by the term. As with many other constructed categories, there comes a time when the notions communicated by the term occlude much more than they reveal. Affirming the U.S. Latina/o population as *mestizo/a* silences the rich ethnocultural diversity and conceals the power differential embedded in the social and political structures that guarantee the privileges of the *mestizo/a* elite. Behind the apparent logic of inclusion and harmonious unity, indigenous and African communities and women groups are exposing the underlying racialized, sexist, and, at times, xenophobic exclusion enacted and perpetuated by uncritical or unqualified uses of the term.

The Underside of *Mestizaje*: Interrogating the Power Structures

We have seen that the adoption of *mestizaje* in theology launched U.S. Latina/o scholars on a process of revising and (re)claiming the history they had inherited. They reclaimed the violent invasion and conquest of the Spaniards as enacted in Mexico. They then affirmed a second *mestizaje* resulting from the events that followed the Mexico–United States war (1846–48). And they drew from the Spanish pre-independence colonial experience of discrimination the notion of *mestizo/a* people as illegitimate and applied this experience of discrimination to the context of the United States.[20] Surprisingly, the U.S. Latina/o theologians' historical revisionism and (re)claiming of the history of *mestizaje* failed to engage the ways in which *mestizaje* became the dominant ideology and rallying cry in the Americas during the wars of independence.

During these times it was a few *criollo* and *mestizo/a* elites who cemented their positions of power by continuing with the exploitation and marginalization of the indigenous and African peoples. Téllez documents how in Nicaragua, even after independence, the *mestizos* continued their own type of *conquista tardía* (belated conquest), invading the indigenous peoples in order to expand their territories. She writes that although the indigenous peoples were not sold as slaves, their condition of exploitation and impoverishment was not improved.[21] This resonates with Miguel De La Torre's comment that U.S. Latina/o theologians condemned their oppression by the dominant culture but failed to see how they could also oppress.[22] Any critique of *mestizaje* must begin with a serious analysis of the power relations and racialized structures that the dominant versions of the term support.

This is essential, as we know that the many different national agendas that promoted *mestizaje* did not intend to honor the ethnic and cultural diversity of Latin America, unless these are conceived as a homogenizing assimilatory synthesis. In many places in Latin America *mestizaje* is a real construction of entire societies fed by Eurocentric racialized notions of culture, societies where difference is devalued and denied a proper place in society. The myth of *mestizaje* as national unity was created by patriarchal, homogenizing, and Westernizing cultural tendencies that inhibit the social participation of indigenous and African descendants. It is not only a question of isolated individuals but of national assimilatory agendas and social structuring that have systematically sought to remove the indigenous peoples and African descendants from the mainstream *mestizo/a* national imaginary by means of Spanish (European) education, cultural assimilation, and military force.

The impact of *mestizaje* as a social equalizer deeply affects the psyche of Latin American peoples. For some intellectual elites, *mestizaje* has become the starting point and goal for understanding and constructing the various Latin American ethnocultural and national identities. They understand *mestizaje* as the fusion of indigenous, African, and Spanish biological-cultural elements present in every aspect of Latin American life from architecture and gastronomy, to society, culture, and geography.[23] In the search to define Latin America vis-à-vis Europe, many authors have promoted, defended, and explored the implications of *mestizaje* as the essential and homogeneous identity characteristic of Latin America. This inspired Tinoco Guerra to entertain the possibility of doubting everything except the "fact" that "we are mixed peoples, we are *mestizos*."[24] In the same vein, Armando Zambrana Fonseca celebrates that Latin America is the *mestizo* continent par excellence.[25]

However, no development of intermixture and *mestizaje* has been uncontested or without its own internal contradictions and tensions. It would be a mistake to conclude that the promotion of *mestizaje* as national ethnic and cultural agenda has removed the racialized hierarchies inherited from the colonial societies. While in the United States the dominant racialized discourses are those operating with the black/white binary or the black/white/foreign triad, in Latin America they range between the white/*mestizo*/indigenous and white/*mestizo*/African racialized schemes.[26] The *mestizo/a* population is the dominant cultural force, and the ideology of *mestizaje* is used by ruling elites to ensure their position of privilege, and as a mechanism of social cohesiveness and cultural assimilation.[27]

Economics have played an important role in the whitening process among racialized ethnic groups in Latin America. Since colonial times, people have been able to "whiten" themselves by buying their way into a higher caste.[28] Different phenomena occurred in El Salvador and Guatemala during the promulgation of the *Real Pragmática* in 1776. Mauricio Meléndez Obando tells us that in order to prevent many *mulatos/as* and *mestizos/as* from climbing to the higher echelons of colonial society, the Spanish Crown threatened the Spanish elite with losing their titles of nobility if they married outside their castes.[29] But many other *mulatos/as* and *mestizos/as* who had become wealthy by their own efforts were not prevented from ascending socially. Soon, these groups began to affirm their own whiteness and purity of blood and to deny being mixed.[30]

The poorer groups have also tried to whiten themselves by way of marriage, *para mejorar la raza* (to improve the race), and in order to obtain better opportunities in society. For example, Paul Thomas Lokken tells us that African slaves sought to marry the indigenous peoples because their children would be declared free.[31] While having a socially disruptive role in this context, intermixture was seen as an alternative way to gain upward social mobility. John Gledhill also tells us that in different regions of southern Mexico, for the indigenous to go to non-indigenous

regions offers no advantage in terms of economic or social status because of the pervasive discrimination against indigenous
people. And in the region of Bajío, "remaining an Indian offered
less than becoming a *mestizo*, because there were better opportunities outside the indigenous community and discrimination
against people who looked 'Indian.'"[32] In various and subtle ways,
similar processes and structures of whitening the population are
at work among contemporary Latin American peoples.

Consequently, in Latin America those *who are identified* as
mixed-*mestizos/as*, and those *who identify themselves* as
mestizas/os are two different things.[33] *Mestizaje* is a very fluid,
ambiguous, and porous category. The people most subject to
racism and discrimination are those who display certain sociocultural and phenotypical characteristics by which they are identified as indigenous and/or African descendants, regardless of
the "degree" to which they are mixed. The opposite is also true:
people whose physical features are more European often identify themselves as white and reject any connection to indigenous
or African ancestry, or to *mestizaje*.[34] There are also many others, particularly among the elite, who reject *mestizaje*, claiming
they are direct descendants of the Spanish Europeans and therefore white. They do this to assert or defend their entitlement to
positions of power and privileges, and to preserve the illusion of
their racial purity and superiority. This is clearly illustrated by
the work of Marta Elena Casaús Arzú, who interviewed the
wealthiest families in Guatemala; she claims they are *mestizos/as*,
but they deny having any indigenous ancestry in their genealogy.[35] Similarly, Charles Hale shows how it is these elite groups
that are promoting *mestizaje* as a national agenda in order to
neutralize the demands for cultural rights of the indigenous
peoples of Guatemala and as an "instrument to remove indigenous cultural characteristics."[36]

Many of the most influential articulations of *mestizaje* are
characterized by a racialized cultural self-catharsis that, while
acknowledging implicitly the indigenous and African roots of
Latin America, explicitly denies the rights of the living indigenous and African peoples.[37] In other words, in Latin America
and among the U.S. Latinas/os, *mestizaje*-intermixture has not removed the power differential built into the racialized structures

where people with lighter skin, specific phenotypical character-istics, and particular ethnocultural identities receive more op-portunities in the social sphere. *Mestizaje* does not altogether eliminate the privilege and value assigned to whiteness and white people, even among the *mestizos/as*. This is part and parcel of the inherent tension and ambiguity of the term. In the case of the indigenous and African communities, the general tendency of many of these constructions of *mestizaje* has been to construct a *mestizo/a* national identity by removing these communities, some-times by forced displacement, other times by military persecu-tion, and at still other times simply through education in order to "help" them shed their "primitive" traditions, cultures, and practices.[38]

The most seductive of these versions of *mestizaje* are those which promote a rhetoric of inclusion and anti-racism, with the intention of (re)claiming the indigenous and African roots of the past. These ideologies have served a rhetorical function to legiti-mate the *mestizo/a* ethnocultural and national identity, but with no intention of engaging the living indigenous and African ethnocultural communities of Latin America. While most people in Latin America and Latinas/os in the United States are of mixed descent, there are large masses that do not self-identify as *mesti-zos/as* but as indigenous and African descendants, or as some-thing else. Thus, the dominant versions of *mestizaje* leave no room for these marginal communities and peoples who do not see themselves as *mestizos/as*.

So, for many people in Latin America and for many Latinas/os in the United States, *mestizaje* is not a romantic harmonious and mutual "coming together," a symmetrical fusion of different peoples constructing a new culture and society where there is room for all. The different projects of *mestizaje* have not re-sulted in removing discrimination on the basis of race, ethnoculture, and color. These three can not be separated. And they are the impetus behind the sophisticated hierarchy of col-ors-cultures or *pigmentocracy* (Lipschutz) dominating the racialized landscape of Latin America and the Latina/o commu-nities in the United States.

Looking at *mestizaje* discourses from the intersection of ethnicity, class, and culture, the poorer and most marginalized and discriminated against peoples in Latin America are still the indigenous and the African descendants. While there are masses of impoverished non-indigenous and non-African peoples in Latin America, particularly in the countries such as Argentina, Uruguay, El Salvador, and Chile, in my experience of traveling in some of these countries and of knowing many people from these places, it is striking to note how many comfort themselves by not being indigenous or African. As they would say: *Soy pobre pero no Indio ni Negro* (I am poor but at least I am not Indian or black). Although many times their expressions are more nuanced than this, racialized ideologies and cultural ethos permeate most Latina/o communities.

There is, then, an underside to the dominant versions of *mestizaje*, one that U.S. Latina/o theologians must keep in mind in order not to resolve prematurely the internal tensions (economic, social, ethnic, cultural) within the U.S. Latina/o populations. They need to allow for an internal critique of the presence of racism and structural discrimination in these communities. The present reconfiguration of the U.S. Latina/o population makes it evident that differences among ethnic groups are irreducible and impossible to erase by adopting a superficial universal notion of intermixture-*mestizaje*.

The indigenous and African voices silenced and marginalized by dominant discourses must be allowed to interrogate the totalizing claims and assumptions behind inclusive notions of *mestizaje*. It is not enough to acknowledge the presence of the indigenous and African peoples; we must engage one another in conversation. In interrogating *mestizaje*, the indigenous and African peoples and communities are exposing the historical violence that has existed since the time of the Spanish conquest and invasion, and that continues today at many levels in Latin America. They are rejecting being included from above and are (re)claiming their right to be different and to participate in the very act of inclusion in the construction of the Latin American nations and societies from their own ethnocultural vantage points. By allowing their notions of *mestizaje* to be interrogated by those most affected and silenced, U.S. Latina/o scholars open the door in search of more appropriate labels and nomenclature, ones that do more justice to the rich diversity of the Latina/o communities and that more appropriately provide alternative language for speaking of U.S. Latinas/os without using such general and all-encompassing categories.

As Lourdes Martínez-Echazabal suggests, the dictates of power differentials impede true *mestizaje* from occurring. As she writes, "[To advocate *mestizaje*] without attempting to change the systems and institutions that breed the power differential would simply help to perpetuate the utopian vision that constructs Latin America . . . as the 'continent of hope,'" always in the future, never in the present.[39]

To take seriously the rejection and challenges to *mestizaje* demands reconsidering previous assertions about people's experiences, as well as the rereading of previous interpretation of religious symbols and practices. An attempt at rereading religious symbols without resorting to the notion of *mestizaje* may reveal other aspects not easily detectable because they are obstructed by the optic of *mestizaje*. To illustrate my point, I engage the symbol of Guadalupe to explore other interpretive alternatives.

REREADING OUR LADY OF GUADALUPE: UNMASKING THE VIOLENCE OF *MESTIZAJE*

Sometimes interpreted as Mary, the Jewish mother of Jesus, and at other times as the concrete expression of a syncretistic amalgam of indigenous and Spanish religious elements, Our Lady of Guadalupe remains the most venerated religious symbol in the Mexican and Mexican American communities. Elizondo is correct that Our Lady of Guadalupe is a rich cultural and religious symbol.[40] And I agree with Rodriguez as she shows the various degrees and ways in which Guadalupe inspires and empowers Mexican American women.[41]

Guadalupe is also a particularly contested religious symbol, as she has always been at the forefront of people's movements, even on opposing sides. She was in the vanguard of Mexico's indigenous people's political uprisings during colonial times.[42] And she was the force that inspired the Mexican struggle for independence and later the banner for the Mexican revolution.

She became prominent among Mexican Americans during the United Farm Workers' strikes and other efforts for social justice by these communities.[43] Nowadays, dominant interpretive frames are being challenged because of their potential ideological exclusionary power. Orlando Espín, for example, tells us that reflections about Guadalupe necessitate raising questions of power asymmetry and enculturation of women promoting their submission to men.[44] Carla Trujillo also reinterprets Guadalupe as raising important issues concerning lesbian erotic power and desire.[45] Ross Gandy unmasks some of the ways in which official Catholicism has manipulated and whitened the symbols of Guadalupe and Juan Diego, actions which have detrimental effects for women in Mexico (and elsewhere).[46] Guadalupe's status as mother of the Mexican and Mexican American peoples is also being challenged. In negative ways Octavio Paz had already affirmed Malinalli Tenepal's (La Malinche) right to motherhood.[47] On various fronts women are discovering La Malinche as an example of women's disruptive power against dominant patriarchal cultures.[48] All of this is to say that, in the context of this book, this cannot be an exhaustive study on Guadalupe, and the promises, challenges, and recent reinterpretations associated with her.

In this section I take Virgilio Elizondo's and Gloria Anzaldúa's *mestizo/a* interpretations of the central symbol of Our Lady of Guadalupe to illustrate some of the issues at play in the adoption of *mestizaje* as a central category. A *mestizo/a* reading of Guadalupe disallows the presence of indigenous religious elements; it coopts and subsumes them under the idea of a *mestizo* Christianity, thereby neutralizing them of their disruptive power.

OUR LADY OF GUADALUPE: THE *MESTIZO* SYMBOL OF THE MEXICAN AMERICANS/CHICANOS/AS

No process of intermixture and its articulation is without its own history of violence, conflict, and power struggles. Rafael Pérez-Torrez argues that, more often than not, "the combination of races, ethnicities, and cultures results from an incessant and ruthless history of dispossession [and dislocation]."[49] Similarly, the category of *mestizaje* does not point to de-historicized biological and cultural intermixtures, but refers to racialized historical social forces that conspire together in the creation of the so-called *mestizo/a* societies. More specifically, the category also points to sociopolitical subjects whose interests are expressed in the way *mestizaje* is deployed and made concrete.

This is no less applicable when dealing with important religious symbols such as Our Lady of Guadalupe. Like any other religious symbol, Guadalupe is subject to various interpretations. In the case of Mexican American and Chicano/a scholars, their interpretations are multiple. Elizondo's and Anzaldúa's are two examples that illustrate the multivalence of such an important symbol. For them, Guadalupe is certainly the most central symbol of the *mestizo/a* people (Mexican Americans and Chicanos/as). And they pour much of their creativity into discussing the significance of Guadalupe. Each of these authors engages Guadalupe in creative ways, but they differ greatly in their conclusions, particularly when it comes to discussing *mestizaje*.

Virgilio Elizondo

Elizondo's interpretation of the original *mestizaje* that took place between the Spaniards and the indigenous peoples speaks of the creation of a new race, the *mestizo/a* population, who represent the reconciliation of these disparate peoples. It is the principle of "providential reconciliation" that permeates all of Elizondo's work and is also clearly revealed in his reading of Guadalupe.

Motolinia reported that about nine million conversions of indigenous people took place after the apparition of Guadalupe.[50] In light of the massive conversion of the indigenous peoples, Elizondo names Guadalupe the "evangelizer of the Americas."[51] According to him, the bitter memory of the conquest made it impossible for the people to convert to Catholic Christianity, so the apparition of Guadalupe served as the catalyst for the conversion of the conquered Mexican people. For him, this was a decisive event, as Guadalupe represented the divine alternative to the European-Spanish evangelization.[52] As he claims, one would fail to understand the true significance of Guadalupe if she were interpreted through the categories of Western-European Mariology.[53] Guadalupe is something new and different!

But what is the essence of such newness in Elizondo's interpretation of Guadalupe? For him, Guadalupe was the result of the initial *mestizaje* (mixture) between the indigenous peoples of the land and the Spanish people. This *mestizaje*, he comments, involves biological and cultural aspects as well as religious ones. The biological mixture resulted in a *mestiza/o* progeny, and since these *mestiza/o* children are neither Spanish nor indigenous, they are something new, a "new creation." It follows that since Guadalupe is the religious-cultural result of this first biological *mestizaje* (mixture), a spiritual *mestizaje*, she is therefore the "Mother of the New Creation."[54] Guadalupe is not just the adaptation of the veneration of Mary using indigenous religious symbols. Instead, she is a *mestizo/a* expression of Christianity.[55] She epitomizes the irruption of these new *mestiza/o* people. Through her, "the conquered reclaim the legitimacy, veracity, beauty, and sacredness of the values and traditions of their people."[56]

As to the *mestiza/o* character of Guadalupe, this is expressed in the story narrating her apparition to Juan Diego, which weaves together Nahuatl and Spanish concepts of God.[57] As Teresa Chávez Sauceda puts it, Guadalupe "puts the Nahuatl language for God on the same plane as that of the Spanish missionaries."[58] Guadalupe, affirms Elizondo, is the irruption of the *mestizos/as* because she appeared to a *mestizo* member of the vanquished communities: Juan Diego. At the same time, she appeared in dark *(morena)* complexion, which demonstrates the divine siding for the poor and oppressed *mestizo/a-moreno* (mixed) peoples.[59] In the end, in Elizondo's *mestizaje* scheme the significance of Guadalupe corresponds to the first biological-cultural *mestizaje* that took place and the spiritual *mestizaje* that followed expressed concretely in the devotion to Guadalupe.

This is consistent with Elizondo's reading of *mestizaje* claiming the divine endorsement of the Mexican American *mestizo/a* (mixed) communities in the form of the *mestiza/o* divine symbols of Guadalupe, and the *mestizo* historical Jesus. But the *mestiza/o* reclaiming of the indigenous elements occurs only as part of the Mexican American ancient ancestral heritage. He leaves unaddressed how the indigenous religious symbols embedded in the image of Guadalupe have been coopted by the *mestizo/a* version of the Christian gospel.[60] Indigenous elements have been absorbed by this version of Christianity and stripped of their potentially disruptive (pagan) nature. Elizondo's *mestizo/a* interpretation of Guadalupe amounts to affirming the dual cultural-spiritual ancestry of *mestizos/as* but says nothing of the conditions of oppression of and struggles of resistance by indigenous people at the time of the apparition or in the present.

Moreover, Elizondo's *mestizo/a* scheme is too neat. He emphasizes the *mestizo* identity of Juan Diego without acknowledging his original indigenous name, Quauhtlatoatzin (he who speaks with the snakes), which was changed only after his baptism by a Franciscan priest in order to fit in his appropriation of the apparition of Guadalupe for the *mestizo/a* (mixed) Mexican American communities.[61] In my view, Juan Diego is made a *mestizo* by removing his indigenous background at the time of the encounter, and by some is made to represent the culturally *mestizo/a* population.[62] The implication is that Guadalupe does not mean only liberation and the irruption of a "new" people. For some indigenous peoples, Guadalupe has also functioned as a symbol imposed upon their communities in order to have them abandon their ancient religious symbols and practices. Their religious traditions have been replaced with *mestizo/a* Christianity, and Guadalupe is the perennial reminder of the conquest and eradication of the indigenous religious traditions.

Gloria Anzaldúa

Anzaldúa does not view *mestizaje* as a trump card by which everything is made right by *mixing*. She claims that *mestizaje* is a way of life, a conceptual orientation for interpreting life and constructing identities. In her view, the inconsistencies and tensions in identity building are engaged head on without pretending to ameliorate them or overcoming them by mixture, as if this neutralizes or cures racism. *Mestiza* consciousness is the recognition that Chicanas' racialization is a construction of "otherness," not identical with who they really are. As Yamada writes:

"over my mask/is your mask of me."[63] Anzaldúa appropriates difference and the fluidity of identities as the alternative to the dominant discourse of homogeneous, hermetically sealed identities. Her proposal unsettles, disturbs, breaks from contemporary dominant frames for interpreting reality, cultures, and describing identity, resisting airtight definitions, categories, and iron-cast frames.

Like Elizondo, Anzaldúa's cultural theoretical work tells us that Guadalupe is the "most potent religious, political and cultural image of the Chicano/a and *Mexicano*." In agreement with Elizondo she conceives Guadalupe as a *mestizo/a* symbol: "She like my race is a synthesis of the old world and the new, of the religion and culture of the two races in our psyche, the conquerors and the conquered." There is an interrelation between the indigenous peoples and the *mestizos/as* in Anzaldúa. She claims that to embrace Guadalupe is to (re)claim her indigenous ancestry. "Guadalupe is the symbol of the *mestizo* true to his or her Indian values." In other words, *mestizaje* is the medium through which the authentic indigenous roots are reclaimed. For the people on both sides of the border, Guadalupe is also the symbol of rebellion against the rich and middle class, and against the "subjugation of the poor and the *indio*."[64] Under her favor different races, religions, and languages come together. Thus, Guadalupe is a powerful religious and cultural symbol for Mexicans and Chicanos/as alike.

Unlike Elizondo, Anzaldúa engages Guadalupe and critiques the present state of her portrayal. To her, the present patriarchal version of Guadalupe is the result of the displacement of women from the religious traditions of the people, dating as far back as the great Aztec-México Empire. As she explores the early premilitaristic Aztec-México civilization, she finds that the latter drove earlier indigenous female deities underground and substituted male deities for them.[65] To her, the Aztecs-México became a militaristic state where male predatory "warfare and conquest were based on patrilineal nobility," which established the principle of "opposition between the sexes."[66] The split continued after the conquest, as the Spaniards divided Coatlaxopeuh, the serpent Meso-American fertility earth goddess, from Guadalupe, the holy mother. For Anzaldúa, both are characteristics of the same ancient Nahua deity that kept both the female and male in fine tension. The Spaniards preserved only the side of "Holy Virgin Mother," thus desexualizing Guadalupe.[67] This dichotomy is expressed more emphatically in the juxtaposition of the three mothers of Mexico: "*Guadalupe*, the virgin mother who has abandoned us, *La Chingada (Malinche)*, the raped mother whom we have abandoned, and *La Llorona*, the mother who seeks her lost children and is a combination of the other two."[68]

In Anzaldúa's view, the bifurcation of Guadalupe and Coatlaxopeuh is to blame for dichotomizing women as either saints or whores, which is at the root of all violence against women. This is manifest in the way the legendary image of Malinche (Malinali Tenepal) is communicated. The idea that La Malinche betrayed the Mexican people permeates Mexican cultural ethos and understanding of women. This emerges rather crudely in the work of Paz.[69] Anzaldúa rejects this dichotomy between Guadalupe, the saint and fighter for the people, and La Malinche, the traitor. This dichotomy must be unlearned and people must see Coatlaxopeuh-Coatlicue in the Mother, Guadalupe. Anzaldúa contradicts traditional views that juxtapose the positive role of Guadalupe with La Malinche as "Guadalupe's monstrous double."[70] She states that the Aztec nation fell not because La Malinche (La Chingada) "interpreted for and slept with Cortés," but because the ruling "elite had subverted the solidarity between men and women."[71] La Malinche did not sell her people; they sold her.[72]

What is at stake here is the unmasking of the male-centered patriarchal scheme that caused a rift between the sexes, argues Anzaldúa. They reject the binaries women/men, saint/whore, spirit/body. As Aldama writes, Anzaldúa "(re)centers and unshames desire for sexual and cultural decolonization." She grounds her claims on women's bodies traumatized by poverty and colonial, racial, sexual violence, "to articulate the psychic processes of recovery and decolonization."[73] In other words, elite males have coopted Guadalupe and turned her into a mechanism of oppression for women: the indigenous, the *mestiza*, the Chicana. Just as Espín points out that Guadalupe can be used at once for the oppression or the liberation of women, Anzaldúa insists that Chicana women must be suspicious of the male-centered patriarchal elements inherent in traditional articulations of Guadalupe.[74]

Toward an Alternative Interpretation of Guadalupe

Echoing some of the more radical strands of the Mexican revolution[75] in her emphasis on *mestizaje*, Anzaldúa asserts that in Guadalupe the "Indian, despite extreme despair, suffering and near genocide, has survived."[76] This has great implications for interpreting the cultural, political, and religious significance of Guadalupe. It is clear that for Anzaldúa the indigenous have survived in the *mestizos/as*. Still, she makes the point of siding with the indigenous stating that *la cultura chicana* identified with the indigenous mother rather than with the Spanish father. Thus, for her, Chicana *faith* is "rooted in indigenous attributes, images, symbols, magic and myth."[77] Chicanos/as maintain a deeper connection with the indigenous peoples and their religious symbols. Although Anzaldúa says nothing of the surviving indigenous peoples of today, she leaves the door open for taking the indigenous religious elements in Guadalupe much more seriously than previous interpretations of *mestizaje* have.

I propose that Guadalupe cannot be dealt with appropriately by emphasizing only the evangelization of the indigenous peoples and the chosenness of the *mestizas/os* (Elizondo); nor does she represent only the survival of indigenous religious elements (Anzaldúa). Guadalupe can and must also be interpreted as the concrete symbol of the obstinate resistance and struggle of the indigenous peoples to survive, to the extent of transforming key Christian symbols by bringing them close to their own ancestral religious traditions and practices.

This is something with which Spanish Catholic Christianity in Latin American has been dealing since the encounter and subsequent "evangelization" of the indigenous peoples. From the beginning the Spanish priests perceived the conversion of the indigenous masses to Spanish/European versions of Christianity as suspicious. It was common to find places where people went to church and participated in the Christian mass, but then went to their homes and continued with their religious indigenous practices, symbols, and rites, something still happening today in the indigenous populated areas of Latin America.[78]

The practice of mixing indigenous and Spanish religious elements took place over centuries and was aided by the work of the Spanish missionaries. For example, symbols such as the eagle and the cactus were slowly changed from having indigenous religious significance into *mestizo/a* symbols of national identity. This took place as the priests in Mexico wanted to make the gospel more attractive to the indigenous masses. Solange Alberro tells us that as the Jesuit priests allowed the people to sing songs in their own language using those symbols, they became aware of the incorporation of rites and activities that were part of their indigenous religions.[79] Later, in the efforts to eradicate indigenous "pagan" worship, and in the complex process of identity construction and differentiation of the Spaniards and the indigenous, the growing *mestiza/o* population affirmed these symbols, now with Christian content, as symbols of their *mestizo/a* identity.[80] This unmasks ways in which the dominant *mestizo/a* culture attempted the slow displacement and replacement of indigenous elements in local cultures and later silenced the living indigenous communities through a national agenda of *mestization*. But it also points to a dynamic process of continuing resistance by the indigenous peoples and preservation of their traditions and symbols, even by subverting the Christian ones.

The paranoia over the so-called pagan character of the indigenous religious practices has much to do with the Spanish (mis)construction of the indigenous other. In her discussion of Elizondo's vision of the *mestiza* Guadalupe, Chávez Sauceda tells us that the "good news" of the Guadalupe event was the affirmation of the dignity and legitimacy of the peoples whom the Spanish considered "inferior, superstitious and diabolical." She writes that the Nican Mopogua, the narrative of the apparition of Our Lady of Guadalupe, displays a "creative syncretism that lifts up and synthesizes what is good in two seemingly irreconcilable religious views, and avoiding what is false in both." While Chávez Sauceda readily tells us that the narrative "breaks through the patriarchal, militaristic, judgmental god of the Spaniards," and it also avoids the "blood-thirsty Nahuatl gods who demanded sacrifice," she does not tell us much about how the "sacrificial" death of Jesus might have been perceived by the indigenous peoples.[81] In a civilization driven by sacrifice and shedding of blood, it is conceivable that what happened was not only the evangelization of the indigenous peoples, but the indigenization of Christianity with sacrificial motifs and all, as Rafael Montano Rodríguez suggests.[82]

Reading Guadalupe as *mestiza* impedes seeing her as an indigenous subversive symbol. Recovering the central role of Juan Diego as an indigenous and *not* a *mestizo* is most important here. It was his eyewitness account that Don Antonio Valeriano recorded in the *Huei tlamahuiçoltica* (Nican Mopogua), so his interpretation of Guadalupe is at the heart of this debate. The image of Guadalupe not only contains indigenous elements, but she is depicted as indigenous herself, aspects that function in the most subversive manner in relation to the Spanish-European versions of Mary and understanding of the divine. For this reason I agree with Jeanette Rodriguez's assertion that popular religiosity can be interpreted as a form of resistance.[83]

It is more plausible that Guadalupe's words were interpreted by Juan Diego and those who looked like him as the divine vindication and protection of the indigenous peoples. The narrative's affirmation that she is the mother "of all those who love me, of those who cry to me, of those who search for me, of those who have confidence in me," and that at Tepeyac she "will listen to their cry, to their sadness, so as to curb all their different pains, their miseries and sorrow, to remedy and alleviate their sufferings," applies more appropriately to the indigenous peoples and their struggles against oppression.[84] I propose that the indigenous elements one finds in Guadalupe are not merely expressions of the evangelization of the indigenous, by which the divine "reconciled" the Spanish and the indigenous, but rather are concrete expressions of the indigenous peoples' resilience and resistance to being erased from history.[85]

Stated differently, Juan Diego brings the truth to Bishop Zumárraga; he evangelizes the bishop by bringing a new revelation that stands the Eurocentric version of Christianity on its head by insisting that the divine is revealed in the religious practices, traditions, and symbols of the indigenous peoples.[86] Here I adopt Diego Irarrázaval's notion of syncretism in interpreting Guadalupe and his insistence that the phenomenon of syncretism "constitute[s] a language of the power of the poor [indigenous], of the protagonist role of women, and of an ethics and spirituality that liberate from the roots." He later adds that it "is possible to define syncretism as a conjugation of distinct and uneven socioreligious dynamics, in which subordinate sectors generate symbolic universes." So, while for Irarrázaval it is conceivable that the indigenous peoples were evangelized to a lesser or greater degree, it also remains true that "the Virgin of the Conquest was transformed" into an autochthonous symbol that represents the vanquished indigenous peoples. Along with the other *Patronas* (female patron saints) of Latin America, Irarrázaval makes the connection between Guadalupe and the suffering people, who are the ones who "exalt these icons, that now represent a social project in which all human beings— especially the downtrodden—be appreciated."[87] Contrary to the insistence on *mestizaje* as a fusion of cultures that runs dangerously close to promoting homogeneous expressions of Christianity, popular syncretistic religions demand that we look in positive terms—and in their own rights—at the cultural and religious *plurality* of Latin America.

This is the difference between the Virgin of Guadalupe and Our Lady of Guadalupe. It is the affirmation that Juan Diego was indigenous, and so is Guadalupe. It is to say that regarding Guadalupe as the result of *mestizaje* prevents us from seeing in her the concrete expression of the resistance and survival of the culture and religion of the indigenous peoples.[88] To read Guadalupe through *mestizo/a* eyes alone conceals the systematic *mestiza/o* cooptation that results in the whitening of the indigenous religious elements in her. Guadalupe carries the indigenous collective memory of despoliation and the struggle for survival. In preserving their religious elements, Guadalupe reiterates the indigenous peoples' refusal to be erased from history and the divine siding with those most vulnerable and most affected by the conquest: the indigenous peoples. It is only by historicizing and relativizing our understanding of *mestizaje* that devotion to Guadalupe can also be interpreted as an act of solidarity on the part of the indigenous peoples of today, who continue to be

persecuted, discriminated against, and oppressed. A more complete reading of Guadalupe will have to take seriously the dynamics of social and religious power within which Guadalupe
emerged and became such a central symbol for *(mestizos/as)*
Mexicans, Mexican Americans, and Chicanos/as.

THE DIVERSE ETHNOCULTURAL AND RELIGIOUS IDENTITIES OF THE LATINA/O PEOPLE: *MESTIZAJE* AND INTRA-LATINA/O INTERRELIGIOUS INTERCULTURALISM

In this critical study on *mestizaje* I have emphasized the larger
ethnic and cultural diversity of the U.S. Latina/o population. I
have argued that discussions of *mestizaje* that fail to retrieve the
living indigenous and African presences run the danger of turning *mestizaje* into a weapon of the empire by reproducing the
silences of these peoples. For this reason I insist that U.S. Latina/o
theologians need to enter into conversation with groups and cultural traditions that have, for the most part, been absent from
their debates on *mestizaje*. This means that future U.S. Latina/o
theological debates will have to be characterized by interreligious and intercultural conversations.

So I draw attention to the importance of interrogating the
exclusively Christian imaginary of the U.S. Latina/o versions of
mestizaje. In this I revert to the initial impetus of *mestizaje* when
it was originally articulated by U.S. Latina/o theologians. The
adoption of *mestizaje* launched U.S. Latina/o scholars into a re-
vision of the historical records in order to reclaim and reinter-
pret their history and their identity as people. But their history
and their identity have never been exclusively Christian. In affirming their history and their identity, U.S. Latina/o theologians
must also engage the different non-Christian religious traditions
from which they have come. As González sees it, "Latina/o theology will have to delve more deeply into its own non-Christian
roots, how they have shaped Latino Christianity, and what they
may have to contribute to theology as a whole."[89] It is not enough
to recognize Candomblé, Santería, or Vudú as some of the religious practices of the people without also engaging them in depth

as partners in the discussions in the daring task of articulating the experiences of the people.[90]

In other words, the assumption has been that most Latinas/os are Catholic or mainline Protestants *(evangélicos)*, and that has been the horizon of articulation in theology. That has left out the growing numbers of Latina/o Pentecostals, Adventists, and those converting to Islam. It has also left out those who claim to be Christians but at the same time engage in religious practices that fall outside of the Christian world view. I agree with Irarrázaval's point that, in engaging the indigenous traditions from the Peruvian highlands, and even when Christian symbols are used by the people in their rituals and religious practices, his involvement is already an interreligious one. His participation in these activities, he affirms, is characterized by interactions with indigenous religious traditions that cannot be easily identified as Christian.[91]

I am proposing that we adopt a more extensive recovery of the historical memory of U.S. Latinas/os. And I also propose that we redefine what we understand as interreligious conversations as being more than dialogues with Islam, Judaism, and Buddhism, or with other so-called world religions. For me, the label interreligious is more basic: reclamation and reinterpretation of history by U.S. Latina/o theologians must lead to the appropriation of those indigenous and African histories and traditions that permeate the religious landscape of the different groups that constitute the U.S. Latina/o population. It is to break open traditional strictures on classical-European versions of Christianity by acknowledging the rich and fruitful intersections of different religious universes as people interact at the everyday level, and which demand that we conceive even religious identities and practices as fluid and constantly spilling over their traditional boundaries.

The same is true in the cultural dimension. The task is to create sociopolitical and intellectual spaces where those silenced by dominant discourses of *mestizaje* can speak. As Raúl Fornet-Betancourt insists, this must lead to the creation of intercultural spaces where intersections with other cultural universes lead to polyphony, and to the celebration of multiple points of convergence not dominated by any one cultural tradition.[92] He adds,

"The criticism of colonialism is the development of a hermeneu-
tic of a historical liberation by which the *mute Indian* rediscov-
ers his voice, and the *unknown Black* makes use of the practical
and material conditions to communicate his alterity."[93]

Interculturalism means abandoning any project that promotes
cultural universality or absolutism. We can learn from the "mis-
takes" of *mestizaje* about constructing alternative societies based
upon the celebration of difference and diversity without making
universal, homogenizing claims and without erasing or silencing
the histories and stories of other people-groups by bringing pre-
mature resolution to internal conflicts through superficial unity
that forecloses those conflicts. The creation of intercultural spaces
carries profound theological underpinnings for the U.S. Latina/o
theological understanding of love of neighbor and *convivencia*
(living and sharing together)—which describes people living, interacting, sharing, and clashing with one another's cultural universes. This, I think, is what Fornet-Betancourt refers to when
he affirms that interculturalism seeks to promote interchange
among cultural groups rather than absolutizing.[94]

Postulating interculturalism as an alternative to the reality of
globalization, João Maria André engages the discourse(s) of
mestizaje. He proposes an alternative understanding of *mestizaje*
to the type "underlying the neoliberal globalization." He opposes the "rapacious sense with which the culture of consump-
tion of the great multinationals pretends to *mesticize*" entire
peoples, which he identifies as surface *mestizaje*.[95] Instead, he
proposes a plurality of reciprocal exchanges and interactions—
or *mestizajes*—in different places and at different times.

This is not just the recognition of a surface syncretism of religious, cultural, and ethnic tendencies. Rather, André refers to
constitutive tensions as different peoples relate and to the dyna-
mism characterized by the "creative conflictuality" in which they
operate.[96] As he proposes, if we articulate the history of tension
within which people's identities are generated and formed, then
the notion of one *mestizaje* is problematized and becomes plural. By plural he means not that each individual represents a
mixture of his or her own, but rather, he is speaking of a deep
mestizaje that is a plurality of processes of interaction and conflict that are always "*in fieri*."[97] Thus, there is no such thing as a

finished *mestizaje*, nor one generally agreed upon meaning of *mestizaje*.

André problematizes *mestizaje* stating that when we interrogate what it is "we pretend to say or what we want to signify when we characterize a number of phenomena in contemporary societies with the designator *mestizaje*."[98] He then affirms that the type of dialogue among cultures that he proposes is what some have identified as philosophy or ethics of liberation, or more recently as interculturalism. It is within this qualified understanding of interculturalism that I insist that future U.S. Latina/o theological projects will have to engage as conversational partners the different cultures, traditions, and ethnic groups that constitute the U.S. Latina/o population.

No doubt tensions and differences among Latina/o communities make the task of conversation very difficult. And unquestionably there is need for revisiting the terms and conditions upon which *mestizaje* was originally deployed to define the Latina/o population. As I have demonstrated, the criticisms of *mestizaje* emerging from Latin America attest to an entire tradition as yet untapped by U.S. Latina/o theologians and scholars in general. The exercise of critiquing *mestizaje* creates new challenges for U.S. Latina/o theologians opening new horizons of understanding and for articulating the ambiguous spaces of identity, and for interpreting people's faith experiences.

The criticisms also demonstrate that there is no such thing as a single finished *mestizaje*, as well as the idea of one generally agreed upon meaning of *mestizaje*. Thus, it is impossible to make universalizing and totalizing claims when using *mestizaje*. Its inherent racialized structures occlude the possibilities for interpreting religious symbols and practices in different ways, as acts of resistance and solidarity by those most negatively affected by the dominant ideas surrounding *mestizaje*. The recognition of the plural religious, cultural, and ethnic traditions that constitute the U.S. Latina/o population demands that we view *mestizaje* with suspicion.

In light of that I ask: if U.S. Latina/o theologians are seeking to acknowledge the multiple points of interaction, exchange, and tension, the irreducible differences that manifest as people from different ethnic and cultural traditions coexist, and the celebration of a "multiplicity of consciousness" (Anzaldúa), then, are we talking about *mestizaje* or about another more complex reality that is yet to be named? The immediate reaction would be to feel paralyzed by curtailing the reach of *mestizaje*, but in fact it is an opportunity to talk about finding new ways and language that reflect more appropriately our ethnic composition and cultural diversity. This, I believe, is the direction of intra-Latina/o interreligious interculturalism. This is the type of discourse for which Anzaldúa's label *borderlands* can better evoke her intended decolonizing emphasis marking the intersections of identities, cultures, consciousness, bodies, and peoples.

Conclusion

BROADENING THE HORIZONS OF U.S. LATINA/O THEOLOGY

[The] proposal of *mestizaje* as the future of [Latin Americans and U.S. Latinas/os] unwittingly set[s] the stage for the Europeanization of the *mestizos/as*. . . . *Mestizaje* became a mechanism for whitening the entire population, and for replacing the indigenous peoples with *mestizos/as*. It is in this way that the indigenous people were silenced from the social and political . . . fabric of the vast regions of Latin America for the last five centuries, until very recently. Unlike the utopic dream of . . . bringing the equalization of peoples, *mestizaje* [leaves] the colonial power differential and structures undisturbed and unchallenged.

—Néstor Medina,
"The Religious Psychology of *Mestizaje*"[1]

Few events have changed the course of history as much as Columbus's stumbling upon what later came to be called the American continent. The year 1492 not only marks the explosion of European imperial expansionism, but also the initial contact between Spanish (and Portuguese) Europeans and the indigenous peoples that eventually gave birth to the *mestizos/as*. Many things have changed since, and the discourse of *mestizaje* has undergone profound changes and re-articulations. Today, different communities in the context of Latin America and the rest of the world are reclaiming and reconfiguring *mestizaje* in various ways to describe their reality and identity. Also, among U.S. Latina/o theologians various meanings of *mestizaje* are deployed, so that various versions of *mestizaje* collide with and compete against one another. These various uses complexify the parameters of the debates surrounding *mestizaje*; they create new discursive spaces that contribute to making *mestizaje* richly multivalent but also much more ambiguous and less precise in its capacity to describe people's lives, histories, and experiences.

In the case of U.S. Latina/o theologians, they drew from the literary tradition of Latin America and borrowed the concept of *mestizaje*. But they turned *mestizaje* upside down by using the term to elucidate what it is to be Latina/o in the United States. By using *mestizaje*, these theologians reclaimed their identity and culture, and gave a sense of symbolic coherence to the communities to which they belong. *Mestizaje* became the useful identity category that glued together these diverse communities as they struggled against social and cultural injustice. U.S. Latina/o theologians used *mestizaje* for naming the complex and dynamic reality of cultural intermixture as present among the U.S. Latinas/os' experiences and faith expressions.

In this book I have shown that the use of *mestizaje* has never been without tensions and difficulties among Latin Americans and Latinas/os. Dominant notions of a universal all-encompassing *mestizaje* and/or one generally agreed upon meaning of *mestizaje* have never gone uncontested. Some of the more recent debates among U.S. Latina/o scholars highlight the ways in which they confront the changing sociopolitical, ethnic, and cultural landscape of the United States. And recent criticisms of the dominant versions of *mestizaje* emerging from indigenous, African, and women sectors of the Latin American societies dispel naive assumptions about Latin American (and Latinas/os) as a harmonious and peaceful reality of *mestizaje*. They also unmask the reality that in Latin America and among the U.S. Latina/o population dominant notions of *mestizaje*-intermixture determine not only racial-ethnic and cultural issues, but also economic-class struggles. The dominant versions of *mestizaje* propose the construction of social, political, and economic structures that contribute to the preservation of asymmetrical hierarchies of power with the white at the top of the racialized pyramid. The dominant notions of *mestizaje* as intermixture perpetuate the myth of whiteness, that is, people of lighter skin, being "purer" or less mixed. Ali Ratansi reiterates this in his comment that, despite representing some white races as racially inferior to others, racialized hierarchies "have consistently consigned 'non-white' populations to the lowest rungs of the racial ladder."[2]

As I think about the future of U.S. Latino/a theology, I cannot avoid thinking that the reconfiguration of *mestizaje* becomes all the more necessary. With the present global patterns of migration, conflicts and interactions of masses of peoples are inevitable. These interactions, however, show that what is happening is not the synthesizing of cultural groups in the direction of one global *mestizaje*. Rather, we see a multiplication of syntheses and fusions and the creation of multiple new identities that spill out of rigid, airtight categories. *Mestizaje* is not one thing, or one experience of intermixture shared by all peoples. *Mestizaje* must be seen in the plural sense and qualified in light of the historical contexts from which those plural meanings emerge.

So the debates on intermixture-*mestizaje* bring out into the open the problem of reducing reality into concepts, and they open the door for conceiving the development and construction of identities away from rigid identity labels and paradigms. Such debates propose new parameters for understanding people's identities and render ineffective rigid monocultural essentialist notions. From this perspective we are challenged to take more seriously the work of Anzaldúa and her discussions on *borderlands*, inviting us to create new language and possibilities for conceiving multiple intersecting identities in people. This is the gap on which Manning puts his finger when he stresses the bankruptcy of contemporary identity and race theories in failing to communicate the complex and dynamic web of issues taking place in human social phenomena within the context of identity formation and definition.[3]

The search for creative new language makes revisiting *mestizaje* necessary in order to identify the ways in which U.S. Latina/o theologians have remained within the intellectual frames they inherited from Europe via the colonization of the Americas. The challenge is to ask ourselves how oppressed and marginalized peoples might break away from the cycle of colonialism and Europe's indelible mark of white intellectual frames that govern their reflections. I repeat Gayatri Spivak's provocative question: Can (is it possible for) the subaltern (to) speak? How might Latinas/os speak among ourselves without resorting to the intellectual categories of the "West" (Cómo podremos nosotros/as los/as Latina/os dialogar entre nosotros/as sin pasar por occidente)?[4] In proposing the search for creative language, I am endorsing a de-colonial approach, first, by seeking to describe peoples' realities in ways that dismantle any notion of scientific support for socially classifying into races the different human groups. I am rejecting any idea that "biological differences belie racial and ethnic distinctions";[5] I wish to go beyond ascribing any "biological meaning to the idea of race."[6] And second, I am doing so by abandoning any attempt at discursive harmonization.[7] We have to undergo an intellectual reorientation and abandon the idea that it is possible to describe comprehensively people's realities, identities, and experiences, especially without their participation in the process.

Our search for new language demands that we identify the gaps, fissures, and absences in the U.S. Latina/o dominant discourses of identity and faith experiences using the category of mestizaje. This complicated and self-critical process is necessary in order to engage the indigenous and African Latinas/os as theological dialogue partners. By dialogue I mean mutual conversation, which requires that we learn to value the religious and ethnocultural universes of the indigenous peoples and African Latinas/os, but not as attachments to a larger mestizo/a identity that absorbs their uniqueness. This is a cultural shift of enormous proportions, as we are required to take risks in the process of engaging other Latina/o ethnocultural traditions, discounting any attempts to hide the irreducible differences that make Latinas/os in the United States multicolored, multicultural, and pluri-vocal communities. In my view, it is only in making room for other fellow Latinas/os that we will move in the direction of retrieving their memories from a forgotten past in order to reclaim their unique contributions to U.S. Latina/o societie ___ identities.

As the stories and experiences of indigenous peoples and African Latin Americans are included in the ways we conceive ourselves, U.S. Latina/o theologians will need once again to engage in the painstaking process of historical revising. Not only is this the way in which we can orient ourselves toward the future, but it is also a way in which the victims of our history participate in the rewriting of "Latina/o" historical accounts: "history—the effort to understand and write the past—is at all times a project that extends into the future."[8] The degree to which we may succeed in the task of decolonization depends heavily on the degree to which we learn to understand ourselves as having various intersecting histories and identities.

From the beginning, U.S. Latina/o theologians have insisted that their writings are the formal expressions of their communities' struggles for life and the construction of a better world, and against injustice, marginalization, and the assimilatory forces in the dominant Anglo-European culture of the United States. In my opinion, the plight of most Latinas/os in the United States is endemic to the reality of most of the world's population. In fact, the existence of U.S. Latina/o theology is one way in which oppressed peoples talk back and break away from the forces that stifle them, which is echoed several times over by the rapid proliferation of people groups reclaiming their right to speak. So U.S. Latina/o theology finds resonances in many places in the world, and its contributions carry implications for many groups and communities attempting to name their identities and describe their faith experiences.

In light of this study on *mestizaje*, I want to propose some potential ways in which the revising of *mestizaje* and the engagement of other historical "Latina/o" (the indigenous peoples and Africans) theological partners can broaden the range of issues for which Latina/o theology can contribute to the discipline of theology worldwide. First, given our present reconfiguration of peoples, identities, national borders, and ideas, U.S. Latino/a theological discussions on *mestizaje* have much to offer to larger debates on intermixture and construction of "national," ethnocultural, and religious identities. Latina/o theologians have already gone far in demonstrating the complex and culturally colorful character of the faith experience of Latinas/os in the United States and in so doing have demonstrated that to speak of people's experiences it is necessary to work across disciplinary boundaries. The interdisciplinary character of U.S. Latina/o theology demonstrates the fallacy of disciplinary boundaries when it comes to interpreting life and explaining reality.

More important, in engaging other disciplines U.S. Latina/o theologians resist the fallacy of dominant attempts at keeping religious practices, faith experiences, and expressions in the private sphere of life. In other words, religious life and peoples' faith experiences have profound social, political, and economic repercussions. Religious life and faith expressions are undeniably part of the complex and ambiguous social process of codification of reality and the construction of meaning of human collectives. This is why I am suggesting the adoption of an intra-Latina/o interreligious approach as we recognize the plurality of religious and ethnocultural universes, each of which uniquely interprets reality and interacts with other Latinas/os while at the same time taking a posture of resistance against dominant forces of cultural and religious assimilation.

Second, the critique of *mestizaje* demands that we reappropriate the U.S. Latina/o notion of viewing the faith experiences of the people as a necessary condition for theological reflection; this time it means recognizing the multiple diverse religious experiences. This is not just a cultural shift but an epistemological one as well. Theologically speaking, the challenge to engage ourselves, especially those outside the dominant discourse of *mestizaje*, results in the broadening of our epistemological horizons. It helps us realize the as yet untapped universes of African Latina/o and indigenous cosmologies, cosmogonies, and theogonies that can shed light on the ways we conceive reality, the world, nature, and the mystery of the divine. In a way, then, it is necessary that we go back to "drinking from our own wells," and from that intellectual and theological space rethink our theological articulations. Translation, as articulated by Boaventura de Sousa Santos, will be a key exercise as we navigate the ambiguous universes of knowledge of other Latinas/os toward the construction of truly Latina/o forms of knowledge.[9]

The reclamation of the traditions and wisdom from the diverse groups that make up the Latina/o population exemplify and illuminate Pentecost. On one hand, it is the daring act of naming our reality of ethnocultural and religious diversity, and on the other hand, it is the understanding of this diversity as a plurality of spaces from which the divine is disclosed in fresh new ways and from which different Latinas/os can speak the greatness of the mystery of the divine. Stated differently, our understanding of the divine is always incomplete; only as we interrelate do we come to a fuller understanding of the mystery of the divine. But in the spirit of the event of Pentecost, diversity among Latinas/os ought not to be seen as a weakness; rather, it must be seen as the subversive and disruptive power with which U.S. Latina/os model for the rest of the world the possibilities of constructing a more human reality. As in Pentecost, so also at this time in the history of humanity the Spirit of God can be interpreted to be at work in the efforts toward recognizing the dignity of diverse ethnocultural groups as they coexist with each other.

Third, this study on *mestizaje* also challenges U.S. Latina/o theologians to refine their understanding of divine revelation. These theologians have already advanced our understanding of revelation by affirming that God is present among their diverse communities. This means that the divine is disclosed in multiple ways among different cultural groups. Consequently, the reality and activity of God spills out of our categories and breaks free from our theological frames and paradigms. The epithet "God's disclosure" then refers to a multiform, pluri-vocal, and multicultural reservoir of instances in which the divine is made known to humanity. So for this reason, revelation is not a finished product or a complete process; it cannot be contained in one particular sacred document or by one cultural tradition. The process of divine disclosure continues, and now in richer ways, as we learn to draw from the wisdom and knowledge of other ethnic, cultural, and religious traditions. This is part of the ongoing human attempt to understand reality. In my opinion, this is one of the greatest contributions that U.S. Latina/o theologians can make to the task of doing theology.

Fourth, the discussions on *mestizaje* also raise important questions about our traditional understandings of missions and evangelism. How do we best encounter and enter into conversation with people from different ethno-religious traditions and backgrounds? And when people embrace Christianity, does Christianity remain unchanged? Inevitably, this also leads us to reframe questions about inculturation and interreligious encounters toward providing an understanding of the intricacies of religious experiences, and the role of culture as medium of religious traditions and as locus of divine activity.[10] Here too, the debates of *mestizaje* offer great insights for understanding the power relations and dynamics at play when cultural groups encounter each other under asymmetrical conditions.

Fifth, in my critique of *mestizaje* I have emphasized the importance of engaging the indigenous and African traditions and forms of wisdom and knowledge. In drawing from the wisdom and religious traditions of these communities Latina/o theologians gain a tremendous reservoir of material knowledge for constructing an ecological theology. I venture to say that the lack of recognition of indigenous and African wisdom and knowledge may be linked to the fact that ecology is one of the least developed areas of Latina/o theology. To my knowledge no U.S. Latina/o theologian has attempted to address systematically some of the theological implications of the present environmental crisis we are experiencing.

Nevertheless, I believe that Latinas/os are in the unique position to articulate a theology of creation with profound ecological underpinnings for two fundamental reasons. The first is the issue of environmental racism. Any struggle against racialized forms of discrimination goes hand in hand with issues related to the environment. In the United States the majority of environmentally hazardous material ends up stored in areas populated by African Americans, Latinas/os, and Native Americans. Even worse is the fact that the great polluting corporations of the United States have taken the world as their dump site. So the struggle against the dominant forces of assimilation and racism in the United States are of global proportion, as toxic waste ends up being dumped in countries populated with people of color. In the words of James Cone, "If toxic waste is not safe enough to be dumped in the United States, it is not safe enough to be dumped in Ghana, Liberia, Somalia nor anywhere else in the world."[11]

Thus, U.S. Latina/o theologians should be at the front and center of issues and struggles concerning the environment. As Cone asks, "What good is it to eliminate racism if we are not around to enjoy a racist free environment?"[12] And second, U.S. Latina/o theologians cannot avoid becoming intimately involved in issues related to the environment because of the wisdom and knowledge within the indigenous and African traditions. Drawing from the wisdom and knowledge of these communities can provide Latina/o theologians with key theological insights about how to conceive human existence in relation to the world, nature, and the environment. Attitudes of maintaining balance and coexisting with and depending on nature are not aspects outside of our traditions, and so we can only benefit from engaging our fellow indigenous and African Latinas/os. Notions of domination and exploitation must be considered foreign to the Latina/o imaginary and must therefore be abandoned. All this to say that there is need for U.S. Latina/o theologians to address environmental concerns and to draw from their own reservoir of knowledge to address such concerns.

One final word! It is easy to assume and conclude that North America ends at the northern border of the United States. The recognition of an ethnocultural other is inherent in this study of *mestizaje*, and as U.S. Latina/o theologians reflect on some of these issues they will have to become more aware of the reality of Latinas/os in Canada. It is possible to assume that there are many things these two communities share in common, and that is true. It is also true, however, that there are many other aspects in which these two communities differ, for example, in the ways they participate in society and in how they conceive of and define themselves. There is a great deal that U.S. Latinas/os can offer to Latina/o Canadians, but there are also ways in which Latina/o Canadians can contribute to the struggles against and debates about racialized discrimination, identity definition, social justice, immigration, and so on. Because we do not share the same experiences, it is important that new spaces be made to allow other Latinas/os to the conversational table. New ties and alliances can be established, and new knowledges can be produced when we talk to each other as equal partners in the struggle for justice.

Notes

I. *MESTIZAJE* AS A *LOCUS THEOLOGICUS*

1. According to Orlando Espín, the alliance between Mexican Americans and Cuban Americans dates back to 1988, when a group of Latino/a theologians met at a hacienda in a little town called Ruidoso, New Mexico, to talk about the possibilities of creating an association of Latina/o theologians. Those present were Orlando Espín, Gilberto Romero, Roger Luna, Roberto Goizueta, Arturo Bañuelas, Alan Figueroa Deck, and Virgilio Elizondo (María Pilar Aquino was invited but was unable to attend). There, they began the painstaking work of thinking theologically about the realities and experiences of faith of the Mexican American and Cuban American communities represented among those present. Aware of their differences and of the wrong perceptions they had of each other's communities, they decided to downplay the differences that divided them and instead emphasize the suffering and marginalization they had in common. At that time Virgilio Elizondo had already written about *mestizaje*, and his work figured prominently in these discussions. As a result, *mestizaje* was adopted and soon became a central feature of Latina/o theology (Orlando O. Espín, telephone interview, Toronto, Ontario, 2008).

2. Vatican Council II, *The Basic Sixteen Documents: Constitutions, Decrees, Declarations: A Completely Revised Translation in Inclusive Language*, in *The Basic Sixteen Documents*, gen. ed. Austin Flannery (New York: Costello Publishing House; Dublin: Dominican Publications, 1996).

3. Vatican Council II, *Pastoral Constitution on the Church in the Modern World: Gaudium et Spes*, in Flannery, *The Basic Sixteen Documents*, chap. 2.

4. One important development was the creation of the Ecumenical Association of Third-World Theologians (EATWOT) in Dar-es Salaam in 1976. In the writings of U.S. Latina/o theologians, however, the impact of EATWOT was and remains largely irrelevant.

5. James H. Cone, *Black Theology and Black Power* (Maryknoll, NY: Orbis Books, 1969), vii.

6. Suzanne Oboler, *Ethnic Labels, Latino Lives: Identity and the Politics of (Re)Presentation in the United States* (Minneapolis: University of Minnesota Press, 1995), 39.

7. Ibid., 32.

8. According to Victor Valle and Rodolfo Torres, although it often appears that the official rhetoric of the United States operates under the "black-white" binary, in reality it has always been "white-black-foreigner." They argue that included in the label of foreigners are indigenous persons and Mexican Americans; though they live in the nation, they are not considered part of its sociocultural and political fabric. See "The Idea of *Mestizaje* and the 'Race' Problematic: Racialized Media Discourse in a Post-Fordist Landscape," in *Culture and Difference: Critical Perspectives on the Bicultural Experience in the United States*, ed. Antonia Darder, 139–53 (Westport, CT: Bergin and Garvey, 1995).

9. Juan González, *Harvest of the Empire: A History of Latinos in America* (New York: Penguin Books, 2000), 103.

10. With his novel *The Mestizo*, Bill Parks illustrates the type of negative stereotypes with which Mexican people were viewed by the dominant Anglo population of the Southwest United States. See Bill Parks, *The Mestizo* (New York: Macmillan, 1955).

11. Rodolfo D. Torres and George Katsiaficas, eds., *Latino Social Movements: Historical and Theoretical Perspectives* (New York: Routledge, 1999).

12. According to María Pilar Aquino, U.S. Latina/o theology has been unfairly criticized as having abandoned the "preferential option for the poor and oppressed." She is right in critiquing these views as superficial and unwarranted. As she puts it, anyone familiar with U.S. Latina/o theology quickly encounters the deep commitment to the people. For U.S. Latina/o theologians, the commitment concerns not only the socioeconomic dimension of oppression, but also the critique of racialized and culturized structures of injustice that create the conditions that impede people from leaving poverty. See María Pilar Aquino, "Theological Method in U.S. Latino/a Theology: Toward an Intercultural Theology for the Third Millennium," in *From the Heart of Our People: Latino/a Explorations in Catholic Systematic Theology*, ed. Orlando O. Espín and Miguel H. Díaz (Maryknoll, NY: Orbis Books, 1999), 16.

13. Virgilio Elizondo, "Educación Religiosa para el México-Americano," *Catequesis Latinoamericana* 4, no. 14 (1972): 83–86; Virgilio Elizondo, *Christianity and Culture: An Introduction to Pastoral*

Theology and Ministry for the Bicultural Community (Huntington, IN: Our Sunday Visitor, 1975).

14. Virgilio Elizondo, *Mestizaje: The Dialectic of Cultural Birth and the Gospel* (San Antonio, TX: Mexican American Cultural Center, 1978).

15. According to Elizondo, there are two periods of *mestizaje*. The first *mestizaje* took place when Cortéz invaded the Aztec people and conquered them. The second *mestizaje* began with the invasion of Mexico by the United States; in 1848, at the end of this war, Mexico lost the large territories that make up today's Southwestern United States. In the first *mestizaje* the Spanish people mixed with the indigenous and forced their culture and religion upon them. The second *mestizaje* has been primarily a cultural one, by which Mexican Americans have been introduced to the U.S. dominant culture and English language and expected to shed their own cultural roots, practices, and traditions. For a detailed discussion of Elizondo's double *mestizaje*, see Néstor Medina, "*Mestizaje*, a Theological Reading of Culture and Faith: Reflections on Virgilio Elizondo's Theological Method," *Journal of Hispanic/Latino Theology* (forthcoming).

16. Virgilio Elizondo, *Galilean Journey: The Mexican American Promise* (Maryknoll, NY: Orbis Books, 1983).

17. Andrés G. Guerrero, *A Chicano Theology* (Maryknoll, NY: Orbis Books, 1987).

18. José Vasconcelos, *La raza cósmica: Misión de la raza iberoamericana*, Asociación Nacional de Libreros (Mexico City: Litografía Ediciones Olimpia, S.A., 1983).

19. Espín, telephone interview.

20. Ada María Isasi-Díaz, "'Apuntes' for a Hispanic Women's Theology of Liberation," *Apuntes: Reflexiones Teológicas Desde el Márgen Hispano* 6, no. 3 (1986): 61–71; Ada María Isasi-Díaz and Yolanda Tarango, *Hispanic Women, Prophetic Voice in the Church: Toward a Hispanic Women's Liberation Theology* (New York: Harper and Row, 1988); Ada María Isasi-Díaz, "Mujeristas: A Name of Our Own," in *The Future of Liberation Theology: Essays in Honor of Gustavo Gutiérrez*, ed. Marc H. Ellis and Otto Maduro, 410–19 (Maryknoll, NY: Orbis Books, 1989).

21. John P. Rossing, "*Mestizaje* and Marginality: A Hispanic American Theology," *Theology Today* 45, no. 3 (1988): 293–304.

22. Virgilio Elizondo, "Mestizaje as a Locus of Theological Reflection," in Ellis and Maduro, *The Future of Liberation Theology*, 358–74.

23. Allan Figueroa Deck, "Latino Theology: The Year of the 'Boom,'" *Journal of Hispanic/Latino Theology* 1, no. 2 (1994): 51–63.

24. Roberto S. Goizueta, "U.S. Hispanic Mestizaje and Theological Method," in *Migrants and Refugees (Concilium)*, ed. Dietmar Mieth and Lisa Sowle Cahill, 22–30 (Maryknoll, NY: Orbis Books, 1993).

25. Roberto S. Goizueta, "*La Raza Cósmica?* The Vision of José Vasconcelos," *Journal of Hispanic/Latino Theology* 1, no. 2 (1994): 5–27.

26. María Pilar Aquino, "Doing Theology from the Perspective of Latin America Women," in *We Are a People! Initiatives in Hispanic American Theology*, ed. Roberto S. Goizueta, 79–105 (Minneapolis: Fortress Press, 1992); María Pilar Aquino, "Directions and Foundations of Hispanic/Latino Theology: Towards a *Mestiza* Theology of Liberation," *Journal of Hispanic/Latino Theology* 1, no. 1 (1993): 5–21.

27. Ada María Isasi-Díaz, *En la Lucha/In the Struggle: Elaborating A Mujerista Theology* (Minneapolis: Fortress Press, 1993).

28. Eldín Villafañe, *The Liberating Spirit: Toward an Hispanic American Pentecostal Social Ethic* (Grand Rapids, MI: Eerdmans, 1993), 1–24.

29. Arturo J. Bañuelas, ed., *Mestizo Christianity: Theology from the Latino Perspective* (Maryknoll, NY: Orbis Books, 1995).

30. Alejandro García-Rivera, *St. Martín de Porres: The "Little Stories" and the Semiotics of Culture*, foreword by Virgilio Elizondo, intro. Robert J. Schreiter (Maryknoll, NY: Orbis Books, 1995).

31. Ada María Isasi-Díaz, "Afterwords: Strangers No Longer," in *Hispanic/Latino Theology: Challenge and Promise*, ed. Ada María Isasi-Díaz and Fernando F. Segovia, 367–74 (Minneapolis: Fortress Press, 1996).

32. Miguel H. Díaz, *On Being Human: U.S. Hispanic and Rahnerian Perspectives* (Maryknoll, NY: Orbis Books, 2001).

33. Isasi-Díaz, "Afterwords."

34. Miguel A. De La Torre and Edwin David Aponte, *Introducing Latino/a Theologies* (Maryknoll, NY: Orbis Books, 2001).

35. Teresa Chávez Sauceda, "Community, Mestizaje, and Liberation: Envisioning Racial Justice from a Latino/a Perspective" (Ph.D. dissertation, Graduate Theological Union, 1999).

36. Benjamin Valentín, "Strangers No More: An Introduction to, and Interpretation of, U.S. Hispanic/Latino/a Theology," in *The Ties That Bind: African American and Hispanic American/Latino/a Theologies in Dialogue*, ed. Anthony B. Pinn and Benjamin Valentín, 38–53 (New York: Continuum, 2001).

37. Oscar García Johnson, "The Mestizo/a Community of Mañana: A Latino/a Theology of the Spirit" (Ph.D. dissertation, Fuller Theological Seminary, 2005).

38. Benjamin Valentín, *Mapping Public Theology: Beyond Culture, Identity, and Difference* (New York: Trinity Press International, 2002), 45–58.

39. Virgilio Elizondo, "The New Humanity of the Americas," in *Beyond Borders: Writings of Virgilio Elizondo and Friends*, ed. Timothy Matovina, 272–77 (Maryknoll, NY: Orbis Books, 2000); Virgilio Elizondo, *The Future Is Mestizo: Life Where Cultures Meet* (Boulder, CO: University Press of Colorado, 2000).

40. Jacques Audinet, *The Human Face of Globalization: From Multicultural to Mestizaje*, trans. Frances Dal Chele (New York: Rowman and Littlefield, 2004).

41. Goizueta, "U.S. Hispanic Mestizaje and Theological Method," 22–30.

42. Orlando O. Espín, "*Pasión y respeto*: Elizondo's Contribution to the Study of Popular Catholicism," in Matovina, *Beyond Borders*, 104.

43. Elizondo, "Mestizaje as a Locus of Theological Reflection."

44. Carlos Mendoza-Álvarez, "Vivir en la gratitud: Elizondo's Contribution to Theological Anthropology," trans. Colette Joly Dees, in Matovina, *Beyond Borders*, 192.

45. Elizondo, *The Future Is Mestizo*, 101.

46. Orlando O. Espín, "Grace and Humanness: A Hispanic Perspective," in Goizueta, *We Are a People*, 134, 145.

47. Arturo J. Bañuelas, "Introduction," in Bañuelas, *Mestizo Christianity*, 2.

48. Virgilio Elizondo, "Transformation of Borders: Mestizaje and the Future of Humanity," in Matovina, *Beyond Borders*, 184.

49. Aquino, "Theological Method in US Latino/a Theology," 22–23.

50. Ada María Isasi-Díaz, "The Bible and Mujerista Theology," in *Lift Every Voice: Constructing Christian Theologies from the Underside*, ed. Susan Brooks Thistlewaite and Mary Potter Engel, 267–75 (Maryknoll, NY: Orbis Books, 1990).

51. Aquino, "Theological Method in US Latino/a Theology," 32–39.

52. Elizondo, *Mestizaje*, chaps. 2–3.

53. Aquino, "Theological Method in US Latino/a Theology," 35–37.

54. Alejandro García-Rivera, "Virgilio Elizondo's Place among Theologians of Culture," in Matovina, *Beyond Borders*, 254.

55. Justo L. González, *Mañana: Christian Theology from a Hispanic Perspective* (Nashville, TN: Abingdon Press, 1990), chap. 5.

56. Ibid., 75–77.

57. Ibid., 83–85.

58. Justo L. González, *Santa Biblia*, 81.
59. Ibid., 84–90.
60. Maldonado, "*¿La Conquista?*" 6.
61. Ibid., 13–25.
62. Elizondo, *Galilean Journey*.
63. Maldonado, "*¿La Conquista?*" 12.
64. Elizondo's writings contributed to the creation of romanticized notions of the marginal role of the Mexican American people and simplistic characterizations of U.S. and Latin America relations. Often, U.S. Latina/o scholars write as if all of the members of the U.S. Latina/o population are poor and marginalized, but that is certainly not the case. Writing thirteen years after Elizondo, Maldonado's characterization of the Mexican American people, the United States, and Latin America is a good example of this tendency. He writes: "Rome is to occupied Judea as the U.S. is to Latin America; Jerusalem (as a symbol of establishment Judaism) is to Galilee (as a symbol of border rejects) as Mexicans are to Mexican Americans. Thus, at the same time that Latin America is under the general imperial power of the U.S., there is an internal evaluation separating Mexico from Mexican Americans" (Maldonado, "*¿La Conquista?*" 12). While for Maldonado there are important commonalities to point out, the parallels are not exact. The analogy occludes the complex reality of poor urban and rural Mexican Americans having much more in common with poor U.S. Latina/o, African American, Anglo American, and Latin American people, while the elite Mexican Americans have more in common with the elite U.S. Latina/o, African, Anglo Americans, and Latin Americans.
65. Elizondo, *Galilean Journey*, 124.
66. Espín, "*Pasión y respeto,*" 104.
67. Virgilio Elizondo, "Hispanic Theology and Popular Piety: From Interreligious Encounter to a New Ecumenism," in Matovina, *Beyond Borders*, 282–84.
68. U.S. Latina/o scholars today acknowledge the African presence in Latin America and in the U.S. Latina/o populations. However, the notion of *mestizaje* as first articulated by Elizondo and redefined by subsequent U.S. Latina/o theologians did not include the African component. When U.S. Latina/o theologians originally articulated *mestizaje*, they adopted a type of indigenism—by which they (re)claimed the indigenous traditions and symbols (mostly the ones coming from Mexico), only to legitimate the *mestizo/a* people. It is only later and by very brief mention and superficial engagement of the issues revolving around the African descendants in Latin America that U.S. Latina/o theologians acknowledged the African presence. See De La Torre and Aponte, *Introducing Latino/a Theologies*, 28–40.

69. Elizondo, *Christianity and Culture*, 95–102.

70. Orlando O. Espín, *The Faith of the People: Theological Reflections on Popular Catholicism*, foreword by Roberto S. Goizueta (Maryknoll, NY: Orbis Books, 1997), 64–68.

71. Espín, *"Pasión y respeto,"* 104.

72. Roberto S. Goizueta, *Caminemos con Jesús: Toward a Hispanic/Latino Theology of Accompaniment* (Maryknoll, NY: Orbis Books, 1999), 31.

73. Ibid., 177.

74. Elizondo, "Mestizaje as a Locus of Theological Reflection," 362.

75. Jeanette Rodríguez, "The Common Womb of the Americas: Virgilio Elizondo's Theological Reflection on Our Lady of Guadalupe," in Matovina, *Beyond Borders*, 116.

76. Virgilio Elizondo, *Guadalupe, Mother of the New Creation* (Maryknoll, NY: Orbis Books, 1997), 122.

77. Ibid., 102.

78. Goizueta, *Caminemos con Jesús*, 47–76.

79. See Roberto S. Goizueta, "Fiesta: Life in the Subjunctive," in Espín and Díaz, *From the Heart of Our People*, 84–99. Elizondo lists a number of other celebrations pertinent to this point (see his *Galilean Journey*, 32–43).

80. Elizondo, *Mestizaje*, 401.

2. U.S. LATINO/A THEOLOGY AND THE DISCOURSE(S) OF *MESTIZAJE*

1. Although U.S. Latino/a theologians acknowledge their inspirational indebtedness to Latin American liberation theology, they also go to great lengths to point out the differences between them. For example, Javier Quiñonez-Ortíz argues that for most U.S. Latino/a theologians, "Latin American liberation theology was *the* starting point for [their] Hispanic theological consciousness," but that many aspects of such theology have "been too readily accepted in our midst without being properly criticized" (Javier Quiñonez-Ortíz, "The *Mestizo* Journey: Challenges for Hispanic Theology," *Apuntes: Reflexiones Teológicas Desde el Márgen Hispano* 11, no. 3 [1993]: 63). In the same fashion, Allan Figueroa Deck points out that, contrary to Latin American liberation theology, U.S. Latino/a theology is more culturally contextual, which sets it apart from its Latin American counterpart (see Allan Figueroa Deck, "Latino Theology: The Year of the 'Boom,'" *Journal of Hispanic/Latino Theology* 1, no. 2 [1991]: 55–56).

2. Miguel A. De La Torre and Edwin David Aponte, *Introducing Latino/a Theologies* (Maryknoll, NY: Orbis Books, 2001), 147.

3. Among Protestants, some scholars like Justo González, Luis Pedraja, and Oscar García Johnson illustrate the adoption of the category of *mestizaje*, but it does not carry the powerful cultural overtones among them that are contained among the Catholics. They deserve to be studied in their own right, but such an endeavor goes beyond the scope of this work.

4. Orlando O. Espín, "The State of U.S. Latino/a Theology: An Understanding," *Perspectivas: Hispanic Theological Initiative Occasional Paper Series*, no. 3 (Fall 2000): 21.

5. Mary Doak, "Table Fellowship in a Land of Gated Communities: Virgilio Elizondo as Public Theologian," in *Faith in Public Life* 53, College Theology Society Annual 2007, ed. William J. Collinge, 202–17 (Maryknoll, NY: Orbis Books, 2008).

6. Virgilio Elizondo, *Mestizaje: The Dialectic of Cultural Birth and the Gospel* (San Antonio, TX: Mexican American Cultural Center, 1978), 137. This is an allusion to the *Plaza de las tres culturas* (Plaza of the Three Cultures) in Mexico City, where there is a plaque commemorating the *mestizaje* that took place as a result of the final battle between the Spaniards and the indigenous people of Mexico. The place is of great significance, because it was there that the Spaniards decimated the indigenous people and finally consolidated their power over the Mexican people. Literally, it tells us that what occurred there was "neither a victory nor a defeat, but the painful moment of birth of the Mexico of today, of a race of Mestizos."

7. Ibid., 73–93.

8. Ibid., 136–235.

9. For a further study of Elizondo's theological method, see Néstor Medina, "*Mestizaje*, a Theological Reading of Culture and Faith: Reflections on Virgilio Elizondo's Theological Method," *Journal of Hispanic/Latino Theology* (forthcoming).

10. Elizondo, *Mestizaje*, 229.

11. Virgilio Elizondo, "Our Lady of Guadalupe as a Cultural Symbol," in *Beyond Borders: Writings of Virgilio Elizondo and Friends*, ed. Timothy Matovina, 118–25 (Maryknoll, NY: Orbis Books, 2000).

12. Realizing his condition of ambiguity as neither Mexican nor U.S. Anglo-European, Elizondo tells us how alienating his first school experience was; he went to an Irish-German-run Catholic school that seemed like a "foreign land" to him. He tells us that the educators in the school had done a great job at convincing them [Mexican Americans] they were different, but that they were helping them "be ordinary people," like everyone else. See Virgilio Elizondo, *The Future Is Mestizo: Life Where Cultures Meet* (Boulder, Co: University Press of Colorado, 2000), 15–27.

13. Virgilio Elizondo, *Galilean Journey: The Mexican-American Promise* (Maryknoll, NY: Orbis Books, 1983), 31.

14. I agree here with Isasi-Díaz, who points out that Elizondo makes no explicit reference to Vasconcelos's works. However, it is difficult not to notice how the logic of his arguments, his use of categories such as synthesis to speak about the phenomenon of *mestizaje*, his use of *La raza cósmica* to identify the privileged position of the Mexican American people, and his emphasis on the future "providential" fulfillment of *mestizaje* resonate deeply with Vasconcelos's work (Ada María Isasi-Díaz, "Re-Conceptualizing Difference," in *La Lucha Continues: Mujerista Theology* [Maryknoll, NY: Orbis Books, 2004], 74).

15. Virgilio Elizondo, "Mestizaje as a Locus of Theological Reflection," in *The Future of Liberation Theology: Essays in Honor of Gustavo Gutierrez*, ed. Marc H. Ellis and Otto Maduro (Maryknoll, NY: Orbis Books, 1989), 358–60.

16. This is echoed in Andrés Guerrero's assertion that Chicanos/as bridge communities, and irreconcilable differences are overcome by blending them together. He writes: "*Mestizaje* works. It accomplishes through action what humanists believe in theory. Two different races can marry and make it work provided they see the process of liberation going on. Two cultures can blend to create a new humanity different from the two parents" (Andrés G. Guerrero, *A Chicano Theology* [Maryknoll, NY: Orbis Books, 1987], 130).

17. Elizondo, *Galilean Journey*, 47.

18. Elizondo, "Mestizaje as a Locus of Theological Reflection."

19. Elizondo, *Galilean Journey*, 50.

20. Ibid., 51. Elizondo argues that Galilee *must* have a symbolic significance in the Gospels due to the numerous times it is mentioned. In order to create the parallel with Mexican Americans, he claims that Galilee was a cultural crossroads, and therefore Jesus was culturally mixed *(mestizo)* (50–53). However, he fails to make a convincing argument in connecting Galilee's status as a marginalized region with Jesus' messianic ministry to Jerusalem. Also, there is little to support that Jesus was as culturally mixed as Elizondo makes him out to be. Richard Horsley's work elucidates some of the important elements in this debate (see *Galilee: History, Politics, People* [Valley Forge, PA: Trinity Press International, 1995]). According to Horsley, while there were marked differences and, at times, tension, conflicts, and even antagonism between Jerusalem and Galilee, the sense of independence of both regions and peoples was directed against foreign rulers and not each other; during the time of Jesus that meant the Romans (278–79). Horsley insists that although it is highly dubious to speak of cultural diversity in Galilee, based on the history of the region one can assume local

cultural variations did exist in Galilee, which could be identified more like a "frontier" (241). He then asserts that "the bulk of the Galilean population . . . while not Judean, would likely have been descendants of former Israelites. While sharing certain common Israelite traditions with the Judeans, they would have had traditions of their own and their distinctive versions of the shared Israelite traditions" (243). Galileans differed from Judeans in customs and religious practices, but whether that is sufficient for establishing a parallel with the border history and experience of the *mestizo/a* Mexican American people is a different question altogether.

21. Elizondo, *Galilean Journey*, 55.

22. Ibid., 63–64, 84–85.

23. Ibid., 103.

24. Ibid., 107.

25. Ibid., 124.

26. Elizondo, *Mestizaje*, 240.

27. W. E. B. Du Bois, *The Souls of Black Folk* (New York: Dover Publications 1994 <1903>), 2.

28. Virgilio Elizondo, "Popular Religion as the Core of Cultural Identity: Based on the Mexican American Experience in the United States," in *An Enduring Flame: Studies on Latino Popular Religiosity*, ed. Anthony M. Stevens-Arroyo and Ana María Díaz-Stevens (New York: The Graduate School and University Center of the City University of New York, 1994), 113–32.

29. Virgilio Elizondo, *Christianity and Culture: An Introduction to Pastoral Theology and Ministry for the Bicultural Community* (Huntington, IN: Our Sunday Visitor Press, 1975); Virgilio Elizondo, "Religious Education for Mexican Americans," trans. Colette Joly Dees, in Matovina, *Beyond Borders*, 58–61; Virgilio Elizondo, "Pastoral Opportunities of Pilgrimages," in Matovina, *Beyond Borders*, 133–39.

30. Alejandro García-Rivera, "Virgilio Elizondo's Place among Theologians of Culture," in Matovina, *Beyond Borders*, 250–52.

31. Virgilio Elizondo, "Mestizaje: The Birth of New Life," in *Frontier Violations: The Beginnings of New Identities*, ed. Felix Wilford and Oscar Beozzo (Maryknoll, NY: Orbis Books, 1999), 49.

32. Jacques Audinet, *The Human Face of Globalization: From Multicultural to Mestizaje*, trans. Frances Dal Chele (New York: Rowman and Littlefield, 2004).

33. Virgilio Elizondo, "Transformation of Borders: Mestizaje and the Future of Humanity," in Matovina, *Beyond Borders*, 177.

34. Virgilio Elizondo, "The New Humanity of the Americas," in Matovina, *Beyond Borders*, 276.

35. Ibid., 275; Virgilio Elizondo, "Hispanic Theology and Popular Piety: From Interreligious Encounter to a New Ecumenism," in Matovina, *Beyond Borders*, 278.

36. Guerrero, *A Chicano Theology*, 131–32, 133, 121–22, 125.

37. Ibid., 137.

38. Ibid., 128.

39. Elizondo does tell us that the first *mestizaje* came to an end around the time of the wars of independence, but he seems to argue that the second *mestizaje* is not fully complete. The *mestizaje* that gave birth to the Mexican American people was a cultural clash between the mature "adult-like" Anglo-U.S. culture and the "childlike" culture of the Mexican Americans. At best, this suggests that the second *mestizaje* is still in process, which means that it will only reach its "completeness" in the future. See Elizondo, *Mestizaje*, 368.

40. Elizondo, "Hispanic Theology and Popular Piety," 286.

41. Justo L. González, "América Latina en perspectiva histórica," in *Desde el reverso: Materiales para el estudio de la historia de la iglesia* (Mexico: Publicaciones el Faro, 1993), 138.

42. Elizondo, "Mestizaje," 53.

43. I agree with Marilyn Grace Miller's conclusion concerning the overuse of the term, but disagree with her listing of the terms she considers have become synonyms of *mestizaje*. See her *Rise and Fall of the Cosmic Race: The Cult of* Mestizaje *in Latin America* (Austin: University of Texas Press, 2004), 5.

44. Roberto S. Goizueta, "U.S. Hispanic Mestizaje and Theological Method," in *Migrants and Refugees*, ed. Dietmar Mieth and Lisa Sowle Cahill, Concilium (Maryknoll, NY: Orbis Books, 1993), 27.

45. Roberto S. Goizueta, "United States Hispanic Theology and the Challenge of Pluralism," in *Frontiers of Hispanic Theology in the United States*, ed. Allan Figueroa Deck (Maryknoll, NY: Orbis Books, 1992), 18.

46. Ibid., 17.

47. Goizueta had already hinted at the contextual character of theology in his examination of Enrique Dussel's work. See Roberto S. Goizueta, *Liberation, Method, and Dialogue: Enrique Dussel and North American Theological Discourse*, American Academy of Religion Academy Series (Atlanta: Scholars Press, 1988).

48. "Praxis" here means openness for those oppressed for or discriminated against because of their class, culture, "race," ethnicity, gender, and so forth. As he writes, "The relationship between praxis (human being-human being) and poiesis (human being-nature) thus predicates liberation upon the exteriority of the erotic economy, the

pedagogical economy, the political economy, and the theological economy" (Goizueta, *Liberation, Method, and Dialogue*, 87).

49. Roberto S. Goizueta, "Rediscovering Praxis: The Significance of U.S. Hispanic Experience for Theological Method," in *Mestizo Christianity: Theology from the Latino Perspective*, ed. Arturo J. Bañuelas, 84–103 (Maryknoll, NY: Orbis Books, 1995).

50. Roberto S. Goizueta, "U.S. Hispanic Popular Catholicism as Theopoetics," in *Hispanic/Latino Theology: Challenge and Promise*, ed. Ada María Isasi-Díaz and Fernando F. Segovia (Minneapolis: Fortress Press, 1996), 261–88.

51. Ibid., 270.

52. Goizueta, "U.S. Hispanic Mestizaje and Theological Method," 26.

53. I must point out that although Goizueta explicitly acknowledges that *mestizo/a*-mixed people are children of indigenous, African, and Spanish parents, in his theological articulations he preserves the dual parental ancestry of Spanish and indigenous people and entirely ignores the African presence and cultural influence in U.S. Latino/a—and all of Latin American—people. See Roberto S. Goizueta, "*La Raza Cósmica?* The Vision of José Vasconcelos," *Journal of Hispanic/Latino Theology* 1, no. 2 (1994): 5.

54. Goizueta, "U.S. Hispanic Mestizaje and Theological Method," 26.

55. Goizueta, "*La Raza Cósmica?*" 6, 23.

56. Goizueta, "U.S. Hispanic Mestizaje and Theological Method," 29.

57. Goizueta, "*La Raza Cósmica?*" 24–25. According to Goizueta, Vasconcelos ignored the historical-material character of *mestizaje*, a lacuna that ultimately made it impossible to escape the idealist trap that contributed to his later disillusionment (23).

58. Goizueta, "*La Raza Cósmica?*" 26.

59. Ángel Rosenblat, *El mestizaje y las castas coloniales*, vol. 2 of *La Población Indígena y el Mestizaje en América* (Buenos Aires: Editorial Nova, 1954), 68–69.

60. Goizueta, "*La Raza Cósmica?*" 25.

61. Ibid., 24.

62. Roberto S. Goizueta, "Fiesta: Life in the Subjunctive," in *From the Heart of Our People: Latino/a Explorations in Catholic Systematic Theology*, ed. Orlando O. Espín and Miguel H. Díaz, 84–99 (Maryknoll, NY: Orbis Books, 1999).

63. Goizueta, "*La Raza Cósmica?*" 6.

64. Goizueta, "U.S. Hispanic Mestizaje and Theological Method," 25–27.

65. There is an intimate connection between the manner in which Goizueta articulates and grounds theology and the manner in which he develops his aesthetics. Popular religion is not only the source and grounds of theological knowledge, but also the place and grounds for encountering beauty. This is particularly important when critiquing Vasconcelos's aesthetic *mestizaje*. For Goizueta, the difficulty in Vasconcelos is that the latter remained in the sphere of the abstract, whereas he (Goizueta) wants to base his aesthetics on the experience of the people. See Goizueta, *"La Raza Cósmica?"* 24.

66. The Mayan communities of Jupiter Florida are a good example of people who resist the labels Latinos/as or Hispanics in order to preserve their indigenous ancestral connections and identities. See Timothy J. Steigenga, "Transnationalism and Collective Mobilization among the Maya of Jupiter: Ambiguities of Transnational Identity and Lived Religion," paper presented at the Transnational Religion in Contemporary Latin America and the United States Conference, University of Texas, Austin, January 26–27, 2006. Available online.

67. Goizueta, "U.S. Hispanic Mestizaje and Theological Method," 28.

68. Ibid., 29.

69. Goizueta, *"La Raza Cósmica?"* 6.

70. Goizueta, "U.S. Hispanic Popular Catholicism as Theopoetics," 266.

71. María Pilar Aquino, "La teología feminista: horizontes de esperanza," in *Panorama de la teología Latinoamericana*, ed. Juan-José Tamayo and Juan Bosh, 95–113 (Pamplona, Spain: Editorial Verbo Divino, 2001); idem, "Doing Theology from the Perspective of Latin America Women," in *We Are a People! Initiatives in Hispanic American Theology*, ed. Roberto S. Goizueta, 79–105 (Minneapolis: Fortress Press, 1992).

72. María Pilar Aquino, "The Collective 'Dis-Covery' of Our Own Power: Latina American Feminist Theology," in Isasi-Díaz and Segovia, *Hispanic/Latino Theology*, 240–60.

73. María Pilar Aquino, "Latina Feminist Theology: Central Features," in *A Reader in Latina Feminist Theology: Religion and Justice*, ed. María Pilar Aquino, Daisy L. Machado, and Jeanette Rodríguez, 133–60 (Austin: University of Texas Press, 2002).

74. More than just proposing the rejection of androcentric structures, Aquino adopts Schüssler Fiorenza's term *kyriarchy* to unmask the hierarchical structural and social relations of domination established between masters and servants, within which women are systematically placed as subaltern to their male counterparts. See Elisabeth Schüssler Fiorenza, *Jesus Miriam's Child, Sophia's Prophet: Critical*

Issues in Feminist Christology (New York: Continuum, 1995), 14–17. At the same time, there are clear differences in the ways that such hierarchichal structural and social relations of domination are expressed and articulated among Latinas/os vis-á-vis the dominant white-Anglo culture. Beyond applying the category of kyriarchy, it is imperative that Aquino makes those distinctions clear in order not to project white-Anglo gender concerns onto those of the Latina/o communities.

75. María Pilar Aquino, "Perspectives on a Latina's Feminist Liberation Theology," trans. John W. Diercksmeier, in Deck, *Frontiers of Hispanic Theology in the United States*, 31.

76. Among U.S. Latina/o theologians, the prominent category of *lo cotidiano* as adopted by Aquino was first used by Ada María Isasi-Díaz, whose work I discuss in the following section. It is difficult to trace the intellectual genealogy of the category of *lo cotidiano* in both authors. It seems they borrowed the category from the work of the Hungarian philosopher Ágnes Heller. See Ágnes Heller, *Sociología de la vida cotidiana*, trans. J. F Yvars and E. Pérez Nadal, Historia, Ciencia, Sociedad 144 (Barcelona: Ediciones Península, 1977).

77. María Pilar Aquino, "Theological Method in U.S. Latino/a Theology: Toward an Intercultural Theology for the Third Millennium," in Espín and Díaz, *From the Heart of Our People*, 38–39.

78. Aquino, "Latina Feminist Theology," 134.

79. María Pilar Aquino, "Justice Upholds Peace: A Feminist Approach," trans. Paul Burns, in *The Return of the Just War*, vol. 2, ed. María Pilar Aquino and Mieth Dietmar, Concilium (London: SCM Publishers, 2001), 104.

80. María Pilar Aquino, "Final Reflections: Towards a Culture of Reconciliation: Justice, Rights, Democracy," trans. Paul Burns, in *Reconciliation in a World of Conflicts*, vol. 5, ed. Luis Carlos Susin and María Pilar Aquino, Concilium (London: SCM Press, 2000), 131.

81. María Pilar Aquino, "La reflexión eclesiológica feminista Latinoamericana," in *Teología y género: Selección de textos*, ed. Clara Luz Ajo (Havana: Editorial Caminos, 2002), 372–78.

82. Aquino, "La teología feminista," 106.

83. Aquino, "Doing Theology from the Perspective of Latin America Women," 96, 98. Notice that in identifying herself as *mestiza*, Aquino places herself among the oppressed women with whom she identifies.

84. Aquino, "Theological Method in U.S. Latino/a Theology," 35–37.

85. John Gledhill, "Mestizaje and Indigenous Identities" (1998), available on the www.era.anthropology.ac.uk website; and Lourdes Martínez-Echazabal, "Mestizaje and the Discourse of National/Cultural Identity in Latin America, 1845–1959," *Latin American Perspectives* 25, no. 3 (May 1998): 26–27.

86. Aquino mentions that the most oppressed Latina women in the United States are indigenous, blacks, and *mestizas*. This reveals the internal racialized hierarchies and undeclared racism among the U.S. Latino/a population; white Latina women do not experience the same levels of discrimination. I want to propose that in addition to the internal dynamics of racism among the U.S. Latinas/os, many Latin American immigrants to the United States import their own racialized sentiments against indigenous communities and people of African descent that they learned in their birth countries. This needs to be deconstructed and addressed properly in relation to the use of *mestizaje*, since new migrants bring their own unique understanding of the term that does not necessarily correspond with the goal of inclusion and cultural affirmation as suggested by U.S. Latino/a theologians.

87. I am using here Aquino's own idea of "dis-covery," by which she means the "uncovering" of the truth as a necessary condition for constructing an alternative present and future. Thus, I am "dis-covering" the various ways and dimensions in which the use of *mestizaje* can hide the destructive presence of racism in the Latina/o communities. See Aquino, "The Collective 'Dis-Covery' of Our Own Power."

88. María Pilar Aquino, "Directions and Foundations of Hispanic/Latino Theology: Toward a *Mestiza* Theology of Liberation," in Bañuelas, *Mestizo Christianity*, 197.

89. Dora María Téllez, *¡Muera la gobierna!: Colonización en Matagalpa y Jinotega (1820–1890)* (Managua, Nicaragua: Universidad de las Regiones Autónomas de la Costa Caribe Nicaragüense, 1999), 45–50. See also Armando Zambrana Fonseca, *El ojo mestizo o la herencia cultural* (Managua, Nicaragua: Ediciones PAVSA, 2002). Zambrana Fonseca's work is another example of the manner in which *mestizaje* dominates the national rhetoric. Showing the detrimental role and imposing power of the growing *mestizo* populations during the colony and after independence, he tells us that some indigenous communities in Nicaragua joined the *criollos* in resisting the large *mestizo/a* population, thinking that in this way they would prevent *mestizos/as* from growing in power and taking their lands (35). But the *mestizos/as* grew in power and the present cultural fabric of Nicaragua shows their creativity and vitality. As for the indigenous communities, says Zambrana Fonseca, they have lost the vitality of their ancestors; they have not contributed anything to Nicaragua's cultural fabric. Deifying the spirit of *mestizaje*, he elevates the present *mestizo/a* population of Nicaragua, which has woven a culture with the vestiges of the primitive indigenous and Africans cultures (41–47).

90. Aquino, "La reflexión eclesiológica feminista Latinoamericana," 376–77.

91. Aquino, "Directions and Foundations of Hispanic/Latino Theology," 194. Aquino resonates with Segovia's comment on *mestizaje* in the same volume. According to him, U.S. Latina/o scholars are not only bicultural but multicultural. U.S. Latinas/os are people who feel at home celebrating any of the different cultural aspects coming from their three different ancestral genealogies. See Fernando F. Segovia, "Two Places and No Place on Which to Stand: Mixture and Otherness in Hispanic American Theology," in Bañuelas, *Mestizo Christianity*, 37.

92. Tace Hedrick, *Mestizo Modernism: Race, Nation, and Identity in Latin American Culture, 1900–1940* (Piscataway, NJ: Rutgers University Press, 2003), 5–9.

93. Marco Polo Hernández Cuevas, *African Mexicans and the Discourse on Modern Nation* (Lanham, MD: University Press of America, 2004), 87.

94. Aquino, "Latina Feminist Theology," 153.

95. Zipporah G. Glass, "The Language of *Mestizaje* in a Renewed Rhetoric of Black Theology," *Journal of Hispanic/Latino Theology* 7, no. 2 (November 1999): 35.

96. Ibid., 39.

97. Alice Walker, "In the Closet of the Soul: A Letter to an African-American Friend," *Ms* 15 (November 1986): 32–35.

98. Suzanne Bost, "Transgressing Borders: Puerto Rican and Latina *Mestizaje*," *MELUS* 25, no. 2 (Summer 2000): 187–211.

99. Aquino, "Latina Feminist Theology," 145, 148.

100. Aquino, "Theological Method in U.S. Latino/a Theology," 35.

101. Ibid., 37.

102. Orlando O. Espín, "A Multicultural Church? Theological Reflections from Below," in *The Multicultural Church: A New Landscape in U.S. Theologies*, ed. William Cenkner (Mahwah, NJ: Paulist Press, 1996), 63.

103. Aquino, "Directions and Foundations of Hispanic/Latino Theology," 203.

104. Aquino, "Theological Method in U.S. Latino/a Theology," 37.

105. Ibid.

106. Ada María Isasi-Díaz, "'Apuntes' for a Hispanic Women's Theology of Liberation," *Apuntes: Reflexiones Teológicas Desde el Márgen Hispano* 6, no. 3 (1986): 63.

107. In her first book co-published with Yolanda Tarango, Isasi-Díaz identified her reflections as a Hispanic women's theology of liberation. A year after the publication of that book she appropriated the label of *mujerista* theology instead. But much of what she writes in her first work with Tarango anticipates what later became the content and thrust of *mujerista* theology. See Isasi-Díaz, "'Apuntes' for a Hispanic Women's

Theology of Liberation"; Ada María Isasi-Díaz and Yolanda Tarango, *Hispanic Women, Prophetic Voice in the Church: Toward a Hispanic Women's Liberation Theology* (San Francisco: Harper and Row, 1988); Ada María Isasi-Díaz, "Mujeristas: A Name of Our Own," in Ellis and Maduro, *The Future of Liberation Theology*, 410–19. Indeed, noticeable tensions among U.S. Latina/o women theologians are reflected in the labels they use to define themselves. Some place themselves in the feminist tradition reflected in the recently published collection edited by María Pilar Aquino, Daisy L. Machado, and Jeanette Rodríguez, *A Reader in Latina Feminist Theology: Religion and Justice* (Austin: University of Texas Press, 2002). Isasí-Díaz, however, has opted for the denominative *mujeristas*, but it is difficult to know who she is referring to as there has never been a women's movement, in the church or the greater society, in the United States or Latin America, that has used *mujerismo* or *mujeristas* as a self-identifier.

108. For Isasi-Díaz, *Hispanic* refers exclusively to Mexican American, Puerto Rican, and Cuban women. But although she claims that only the women of these groups are her concern, she constantly refers to "other" Latin American women living in the United States. Here, the label *Hispanic* refers to Isasi-Díaz's own restrictions to the term. Most important, she chooses *Hispanic* because the term is gender inclusive. See "'Apuntes' for a Hispanic Women's Theology of Liberation," 64.

109. Ada María Isasi-Díaz, *En la Lucha/In the Struggle: Elaborating a Mujerista Theology* (Minneapolis: Fortress Press, 1993), 11–28.

110. Ibid., 11.

111. Isasi-Díaz, "Re-Conceptualizing Difference," 84.

112. Ada María Isasi-Díaz, "Afterwords: Strangers No Longer," in Isasi-Díaz and Segovia, *Hispanic/Latino Theology*, 370.

113. Isasi-Díaz, "Re-Conceptualizing Difference," 75.

114. Although much of what Isasi-Díaz appropriates comes from the work of Elizondo, there is no doubt that she also broadens the meaning and usage of the term *mestizaje*. Many of the conclusions at which Isasi-Díaz arrives concerning *mestizaje-mulatez* emerge primarily from her understanding of Elizondo, though she also alludes to Vasconcelos. It is Elizondo's work that, for her, sets the limits, development, and understanding of *mestizaje*. See Isasi-Díaz, "'Apuntes' for a Hispanic Women's Theology of Liberation," 70n17; Isasi-Díaz, *En la Lucha/In the Struggle*, 14n11.

115. While Isasi-Díaz distinguishes between biological *mestizaje* and *mulataje/mulatez*, her early appropriation and endorsement of *mestizaje* erased the distinction. Even lately, when she has incorporated *mulatez*, the general content of the term has not changed, pointing primarily to an amalgam of three radically different peoples, cultures, and religious

traditions, but not recognizing entire indigenous and African communities that exist separate from the dominant *mestizo/a* groups.

116. There is some tension in the way Isasi-Díaz draws from the work of Vasconcelos. In *En la Lucha* she wrongly traces the origin of *La raza* discourse to Vasconcelos and uses his work, however briefly, to articulate some of her views; in *La Lucha Continues* she seems apologetic, denying any connection between Vasconcelos and Elizondo, and arguing that Andrés Guerrero is the theologian who made such direct connections. See Isasi-Díaz, *En la Lucha/In the Struggle*, 15; Isasi-Díaz, "Re-Conceptualizing Difference," 74. In this progression in her thought, Isasi-Díaz does not mention the discourse of *mestizaje/La raza* popularized by the tenure of Porfirio Díaz and his Científicos prior to Vasconcelos's famous essay, which, in my opinion, broadens our understanding of *mestizaje/La raza* discourses and situates Vasconcelos's essay.

117. Isasi-Díaz, *En la Lucha/In the Struggle*, 15.

118. Isasi-Díaz and Tarango, *Hispanic Women, Prophetic Voice in the Church*, 5.

119. Ada María Isasi-Díaz, *Mujerista Theology: A Theology for the Twenty-First Century* (Maryknoll, NY: Orbis Books, 1996), 64.

120. Isasi-Díaz, "'Apuntes' for a Hispanic Women's Theology of Liberation," 66.

121. Isasi-Díaz, *En la Lucha/In the Struggle*, 186.

122. Isasi-Díaz, "'Apuntes' for a Hispanic Women's Theology of Liberation," 66.

123. Ada María Isasi-Díaz, "The Bible and Mujerista Theology," in *Lift Every Voice: Constructing Christian Theologies from the Underside*, ed. Susan Brooks Thistlewaite and Mary Potter Engel (Maryknoll, NY: Orbis Books, 1990), 272.

124. Isasi-Díaz, *Mujerista Theology*, 64–65.

125. Isasi-Díaz, "Afterwords," 370.

126. Ada María Isasi-Díaz, "Un poquito de justicia—A Little Bit of Justice: A Mujerista Account of Justice," in Isasi-Díaz and Segovia, *Hispanic/Latino Theology*, 334.

127. Isasi-Díaz, *Mujerista Theology*, 65.

128. Isasi-Díaz, "Re-Conceptualizing Difference," 84, 87.

129. Isasi-Díaz, *En la Lucha/In the Struggle*, 193.

130. Ibid., 195.

131. Isasi-Díaz, "Re-Conceptualizing Difference," 75.

132. Segovia, "Two Places and No Place in Which to Stand," 30–33.

133. Isasi-Díaz, *En la Lucha/In the Struggle*, 15.

134. Ibid., 15n14.

135. Isasi-Díaz, "Re-Conceptualizing Difference," 75.

136. José Vasconcelos, *La raza cósmica: Misión de la raza iberoamericana*, Asociación Nacional de Libreros (Mexico City: Litografía Ediciones Olimpia, S.A., 1983), 40.

137. Isasi-Díaz, "Re-Conceptualizing Difference," 83–84.

138. Ibid., 83.

139. Segovia arrived at this conclusion. He commented that "there are many and profound differences within the group, the differences which Hispanic American theology must acknowledge and incorporate, if it is to avoid its own version of the 'melting pot' theory" (Segovia, "Two Places and No Place in Which to Stand," 33).

3. *MESTIZAJE* AMONG MEXICAN AMERICAN/CHICANO/A SCHOLARS

1. When I speak of Mexican Americans and Chicanos/as, I am referring to the communities constituted by the descendants of the Mexican masses that saw the U.S. border engulf them after the Mexico-U.S. war that came to an end with the signing of the Guadalupe-Hidalgo Treaty on February 2, 1848. Usually, the term *Chicano/a* is used of militant groups who reclaim their ancestral identity connections to Mexico. Although Latinas/os born in the state of Texas identify themselves as Tex-Mex, and not as Chicanos/as, in this section I refer to the scholars analyzed as Chicanos/as, for that is the descriptive term they use for themselves.

2. Juan González, *Harvest of the Empire: A History of Latinos in America* (New York: Penguin Books, 2000).

3. Adolfo Carlos Vento, *Mestizo: The History, Culture, and Politics of the Mexican and the Chicano: The Emerging Mestizo-Americans* (New York: University Press of America, 1998), 119.

4. Ibid., 91–113, 205–30.

5. J. Jorge Klor de Alva, "Aztlán, Borinquen, and Hispanic Nationalism in the United States," in *Aztlán: Essays on the Chicano Homeland*, ed. Rodolfo A. Anaya and Francisco A. Lomelí (Alburquerque, NM: Academia/El Norte Publications, 1989), 150.

6. Ibid., 149.

7. Klor de Alva comments that Aztlán was a class-based symbol useful to the ruling elite and their founding myth and character of legitimacy. In his view, Aztlán probably generated more interest among those who equated themselves with the U.S. Southwest than for Aztecs at the arrival of the Europeans in the sixteenth century. See ibid., 148.

8. J. Jorge Klor de Alva, "Cipherspace: Latino Identity Past and Present," in *Race, Identity, and Citizenship: A Reader*, ed. Rodolfo D.

Torres, Louis F. Mirón, and Jonathan Xavier Inda (Malden, MA: Blackwell Publishers, 1999), 176.

9. Agustín Benítez Basave, *México Mestizo: Análisis del nacionalismo mexicano en torno a la mestizofilia de Andrés Molina Enríquez* (Mexico: Fondo de Cultura Económica, 2002), 13.

10. Much can be said about the influence of Vasconcelos's work on discourses of *mestizaje* in the rest of Latin America. Vasconcelos's work provided the framing with which to articulate the sentiments of the elite white minorities of Latin America. His *La raza cósmica* (1925) gave many Latin American intellectuals the ammunition and justification for promoting *mestizaje* as the appropriate and desired conceptual expression of the reality of Latin America, although not without serious criticisms. One finds that in a matter of forty years or so after Vasconcelos had published his controversial essay, many writers in Latin America, when dealing with the question of *mestizaje*, adopted similar views as Vasconcelos's *La raza cósmica*. This was the case with Benjamín Carrión, Francisco Beltrán Peña, Luis José González Álvarez, Andrés Molina Enríquez, and Samuel Ramos, all of whom take Vasconcelos as one of their interlocutors. For further discussion, see Marilyn Grace Miller, *Rise and Fall of the Cosmic Race: The Cult of* Mestizaje *in Latin America* (Austin: University of Texas Press, 2004).

11. Juan Reyes Govea, *El mestizo, la nación y el nacionalismo Mexicano* (Chihuahua, Mexico: Ediciones del Gobierno del Estado de Chihuahua, 1992), 171–72. This reform, which was more of a civil war (1857–61), removed the privileges and ownership of great portions of lands from the Catholic Church and introduced a massive process of secularization to Mexico. It was interrupted ever so briefly when Napoleon III invaded Mexico and established the Archduke Ferdinand Maximilian and the Archduchess Maria Charlotte as emperors of Mexico in 1864. But three years later, in 1867, Benito Juárez gathered enough soldiers and retook Mexico. He had Maximilian arrested, tried, and executed. See Ernesto de la Torre Villar and Ramiro Navarro de Anda, *Historia de México II: De la Independencia a la época actual* (Mexico: McGraw-Hill, 1987), 131–80.

12. T. G. Powell, "Mexican Intellectuals and the Indian Question: 1876–1911," *Hispanic American Historical Review* 48, no. 1 (1968): 19–36.

13. Ibid., 22–23. Among Los Científicos, there were some, like Francisco Bulness, who saw the indigenous people simply as the "insuperable obstacle" to the social evolution of Mexico (27–28).

14. The Ateneo de la Juventud was a group of fifty intellectual friends and colleagues of Vasconcelos who believed in the redeeming power of

education; they organized a philosophical war against the ideological and cultural effects of positivism in Mexico.

15. Soraya Saba, "La expresión americana: Americanismo, transculturación y Barroco en el proyecto cultural de José Lezama Lima," *Torre de Papel* 9, no. 2 (Summer 1999): 2.

16. There were other members of the Ateneo who articulated *mestizaje* positively. See Antonio Lomelí Garduño, *Prometeo Mestizo: Estampas de la vida de un mexicano* (Mexico City: B. Costa-Amic editor, 1975). I must mention here that some of the Científicos had also adopted *mestizaje*. For them, *mestizaje*—mixing with people of European origin—was seen as the alternative needed to reverse the negative effects of the intermixture with the indigenous peoples. The positive views of *mestizaje* by the intellectuals of the Ateneo, instead, refer to an attempt to counter such positivist notions by way of reclaiming the indigenous heritage in order to affirm their *mestizo* identity.

17. John H. Haddox, *Vasconcelos of Mexico*, Texas Pan American Series (Austin: University of Texas Press, 1967), 12. In his aesthetic monism Vasconcelos poured much of his energies into countering the social Darwinism of Spencer, the imperialism of the United States, and the epistemological tenets of positivism. The fuller articulation of his system came some years later, after he published *La raza cósmica*, and was developed in his *Indología*. He systematized his thought in five different volumes: *Pitagoras* (1916), *Metafísica* (1929), *Ética* (1931), *Estética* (1935), and *Lógica orgánica* (1945).

18. José Vasconcelos, *Ulises criollo*, vol. 1 of *Obras completas*, Colección Laurel (Mexico: Libreros Mexicanos Unidos, 1957), 507.

19. José Vasconcelos, *Tratado de metafísica*, vol. 3 of *Obras completas*, Colección Laurel (Mexico: Libreros Mexicanos Unidos, 1959), 1119, 1278.

20. Ibid., 1122–23.

21. José Vasconcelos, *Lógica orgánica* (Mexico City: Edición de el Colegio Nacional, 1945), xxx.

22. José Vasconcelos, *Estética*, vol. 3 of *Obras completas*, Colección Laurel (Mexico: Libreros Mexicanos Unidos, 1959), 1275.

23. Vasconcelos, *Tratado de metafísica*, 440. Vasconcelos argued that the divine Trinity as the synthesis of Father, Son, and Holy Spirit, who are different but without whom the reality of the divine cannot be conceived, displayed the principle of trinity and unity in all of creation. To him, since Son and Spirit find their final goal by reverting to the Father, this mirrors the road map for the direction of the world. His proposal of an aesthetic interpreting of the world was like a "paradigm of reality and as an anticipation of the celestial world" (635).

24. Vasconcelos, *Estética*, 16–43.

25. Vasconcelos, *Tratado de metafísica*, 455.

26. José Vasconcelos, *La raza cósmica: Misión de la raza iberoamericana*, Asociación Nacional de Libreros (Mexico City: Litografía Ediciones Olimpia, S.A., 1983). For Vasconcelos, civilization started with the mythological civilization of Atlantis, which prospered but then declined in America, unworthily represented by the Aztecs and Incas, but then civilization moved to Egypt, then to India, and lastly to Greece, where Western civilization was born (13).

27. Ibid., 14.

28. Much later, Vasconcelos engaged the issues concerning the racially purist agenda of the United States—which could only bring chaos and truncate the transcendental mission of intermixture. He criticized the white Anglos of North America for their refusal to mix with and for in fact separating from the black people and the extermination of the indigenous people. For him, it was natural to uphold the "superior" Spanish attempt in Latin America to bring unity to the region by way of *mestizaje*. See José Vasconcelos, *Bolivarismo y Monroismo: Temas Iberoamericanos*, 3d ed. (Santiago de Chile: Ediciones Ercilla, 1937).

29. Vasconcelos, *La raza cósmica*, 24–25.

30. José Vasconcelos, *Breve Historia de México*, vol. 4 of *Obras completas* (Mexico: Universidad Nacional Autónoma de México, 1961), 13–38.

31. As Vasconcelos saw it, the superior groups sought intermixture with the inferior ones because they desired to help them out of their condition of inferiority. Stated this way, even the reality of intermixing was something owed to the "superior" white group: the Spaniards. See José Vasconcelos, *Indología: Una interpretación de la cultura Ibero-Americana* (Barcelona: Agencia Mundial de Librería, 1926), 72, 92–93.

32. Vasconcelos, *La raza cósmica*, 24–25.

33. Luis A. Marentes, *José Vasconcelos and the Writings of the Mexican Revolution*, Twayne's Hispanic Americas Series (New York: Twayne Publishers, 2000), 84.

34. Vasconcelos, *La raza cósmica*, 28, 38–39; Vasconcelos, *Indología*, 90–92.

35. Vasconcelos, *La raza cósmica*, 40, 33. For Vasconcelos, the degree of consciousness of the divine intention toward synthesis could also be seen in the consideration of the contributions the English North American stock could bring into this "cosmic race." As he explained, *mestizaje* would also have its share of the *Sajón*, whose exclusion—just like the exclusion of any other human group—would be tantamount to

mutilation. But the issue is that the degree of the mutilation would be greater than if an "inferior" stock were excluded (ibid., 33).

36. Haddox, *Vasconcelos of Mexico*, 36–37.

37. Vasconcelos, *Indología*, 36.

38. Vasconcelos, *La raza cósmica*, 27.

39. Ibid., 22–26. Tace Hedrick tells us that it was popularly believed among the Mexican elite that the "Indians had suffered for so long under the consequences of the Conquest that their behavior and the state of their culture were effectively innate, and therefore as akin to a racial quality as one might get without actually saying so." From this vantage point, she adds, they thought "education might be the only thing which would awaken the Indians to their plight and uplift them from their racial and cultural decay" (Tace Hedrick, *Mestizo Modernism: Race, Nation, and Identity in Latin American Culture, 1900–1940* [Piscataway, NJ: Rutgers University Press, 2003], 41). This is consistent with Vasconcelos's own policies during his tenure as minister of education. He saw education as the alternative for elevating the indigenous people out of their backwardness. In addition, he also insisted that education served the function of population control. When people educated themselves, he wrote, they ceased to reproduce in such great numbers and this facilitates the process of intermixture. He asserted, "If we are ever going to stop this misery, it is necessary that the superior take pains to educate the inferior and to raise its standards. If we do not wish to be overwhelmed by the wave of the Negro, of the Indian, or of the Asiatic, we shall have to see that the Negro, the Indian, and the Asiatic are raised to the higher standards of life, where reproduction becomes regulated and quality predominates over numbers" (José Vasconcelos and Manuel Gamio, *Aspects of Mexican Civilization* [Chicago: University of Chicago Press, 1926], 100).

40. For Vasconcelos, to revert to the indigenous past was out of the question, because that would mean making Mexico and the rest of Latin America vulnerable to the expansionist attacks of the United States. In a way, this would be like going back to the incident between United States and Mexico during the middle of the nineteenth century. In other words, his proposal of *mestizaje* had what he thought to be the interests of Latin America in mind. See Vasconcelos, *Breve Historia de México*, 1489.

41. José Carlos Mariátegui, "El proceso de la literatura," in 7 *Ensayos de interpretación de la realidad peruana*, vol. 4, *Pensamiento Peruano* (Lima: Editorial Horizonte, 1991), 198–288. Mariátegui criticized Vasconcelos, saying that he stayed in the future, in the tomorrow without the consciousness of today. In Mariátegui's words, "The *mestizaje* that Vasconcelos exalts is not precisely the mixture of the

Spanish, indigenous and African races, which already operate in the continent, but the crucible of fusion and re-fusion, from which the cosmic race . . . shall be born. The *mestizo*, concrete, is not for Vasconcelos the type of a new race, of a new culture, but merely a promise. The speculation of the philosopher, of the utopist, does not know limitation of time or space. Centuries do not count in the ideal construction, no more than moments. The work of the critic, of the historiographer, is of another kind. He has to pay attention to the immediate results and be content with approximating perspectives" (ibid., 280–81).

42. Vento, *Mestizo*, 276.

43. This brought to memory the masses of the mostly *mestizo* Mexican people struggling to be free from the yoke of Spain.

44. John Francis Burke, *Mestizo Democracy: The Politics of Crossing Borders*, Foreword by Virgilio Elizondo (College Station: Texas A&M University Press, 2002).

45. Ibid., 62.

46. Ibid., 82.

47. Andrés G. Guerrero, *A Chicano Theology* (Maryknoll, NY: Orbis Books, 1987), 121–22, 125.

48. Burke is right to conclude that Vasconcelos's notion of biological inheritance echoes the work of Gregor Mendel (see Burke, *Mestizo Democracy*, 38). Yet he is wrong in thinking that Vasconcelos's notion did not draw from the Darwinian and Spencerian positivist school that governed Mexico's (and Latin America's) intellectual landscape during the nineteenth century. Jorge Gracia also states that Vasconcelos displays the influence of Mendel and Toynbee concerning the tendency of races to mingle. What is worth noting, however, is that he adopted and adapted these influences and articulated them using philosophical-theological language. He developed a phenomenology of *mestizaje* similar to Hegel's *Geist* (see Georg Wilhelm Friedrich Hegel, *Reason in History: A General Introduction to the Philosophy of History*, The Library of Liberal Arts [New York: The Liberal Arts Press, 1954]). As Gracia avers, Vasconcelos's "cosmic race" would be "the agent for the creation of the highest possible level" humanity can attain (Jorge J. E. Gracia, *Hispanic/Latino Identity: A Philosophical Perspective* [Malden, MA: Blackwell Publishers 2000], 144).

49. Basave, *México Mestizo*.

50. Burke, *Mestizo Democracy*, 58.

51. Claudio Esteva Fábregat, *El mestizaje en Iberoamérica* (Madrid: Editorial Alhambra, S.A., 1988), 56.

52. Madison Grant, *The Passing of the Great Race or the Racial Basis of European History* (New York: Charles Scribner's Sons, 1916);

Arthur de Gobineau, *The Inequality of Human Races* (London: William Heinemann, 1915).

53. Gobineau, *The Inequality of Human Races*, 74, 93.

54. The logic of this characterization of so-called inferior races is illustrated in the comments by Prescott Webb: "It took more than a little mixture with Spanish blood and mantle of Spanish service to make valiant soldiers of the timid Pueblo Indians." As far as he was concerned, those who were mixed with Spanish blood, the *mestizos/as*, were still Indian. This parallels the popular U.S. notion that "one drop of blood makes one black" (Guerrero, *A Chicano Theology*, 26).

55. Gloria Anzaldúa, *Borderlands*/La Frontera: *The New Mestiza* (San Francisco: Aunt Lute Books, 1987).

56. In acknowledging the richness of Anzaldúa's approach, Aldama tells us that her enunciatory practice "converges radical autobiographical, historiographic, *testimonio*, and theoretical modalities of self-representation" and creates a pluri-genre "radical hermeneutics of antisexist decolonial *autohistoriateoría* (autohistorytheory)" (Arturo J. Aldama, *Disrupting Savagism: Intersecting Chicana/o, Mexican Immigrant, and Native American Struggles for Self-Representation* [Durham, NC: Duke University Press, 2001], 96).

57. Ian Barnard, "Gloria Anzaldúa's Queer Mestizaje," *MELUS* 22, no. 1, *Ethnicities Sexualities* (Spring 1997): 45–46. Barnard writes that as a "literary text, *Borderlands/La Frontera* further shatters any notion of identity as unitary, fixed, stable, or comfortable in its resistance to the categories of genre that inform traditional English courses and the disciplinary demarcation that constitute academic institutions in general. It seems to encompass, for instance, poetry, theory, autobiography, mythology, criticism, narrative, history, and political science, while suggesting the limitations of these delimitations and, ultimately, of delimitation itself" (ibid). Later he adds, "No single reader will be able to 'understand' every addressed identity in the book" (47).

58. Anzaldúa, *Borderlands*/La Frontera, 3, 7.

59. For an early account of the extent to which Chicanos/as are disfigured by using negative ethnocultural stereotypical images and ideas such as criminal, conniving, and lazy, see Bill Parks, *The Mestizo* (New York: Macmillan Publishing Co., 1955). Also, for an account relating the *braceros* to the Chicano/a people and their self-identity as *mestizos/as* and *La raza*, see Pierri Ettore, *Chicanos: El poder mestizo* (Mexico City: Editores Mexicanos Unidos S.A., 1979).

60. Beginning with the Aztecs, Anzaldúa mythologizes a pre-Columbian occupation of Aztlán (commonly believed to be the Southwest region of the United States), which they left in 1168 when

Huitzilopochtli, the God of War, led them to the site where "an eagle with a writhing serpent in its beak perched on a cactus." According to Anzaldúa, they built there the city of Mexico, and there the patriarchal order vanquished the feminine and matriarchal order that had preceded it. This was followed by the Spanish invasion and conquest of the indigenous people, from which mixture emerged the *mestizos/as*. As the conquistadors sought new lands, gold, and the missionaries sought people to evangelize, many *mestizos/as* and indigenous came with them to the U.S. Southwest, a return to Aztlán. Another displacement occurred during the Mexico-U.S. war that divided the Mexican people. As a result, many Mexicans ended up as low-paid and exploited workers, commonly known as *braceros*, working the lands that had been previously theirs. In this history of migration, the present moves of Mexican people into the Southwestern United States continues this return to Aztlán initiated during the 1500s (see Anzaldúa, *Borderlands*/La Frontera, 3–13).

61. Margaret E. Montoya, "Border Crossings," in *The Latino Condition: A Critical Reader*, ed. Richard Delgado and Jean Stefancic (New York: New York University Press, 1998), 641.

62. Anzaldúa, *Borderlands*/La Frontera, 17. I use the masculine (Chicano) to highlight Anzaldúa's point that culture is constructed by those with power, namely, men. "They make the rules and laws and women transmit them" (16).

63. Anzaldúa, *Borderlands*/La Frontera, 17.

64. Ibid., 21.

65. Anzaldúa rejects dominant popular notions that make La Malinche, the indigenous woman who bore Cortéz's children and who helped the Spaniards defeat the indigenous tribes by serving as translator, the traitor of the Mexican people. In fact, she argues, it was not La Malinche who betrayed her people, but rather her people who betrayed her by abandoning her and giving her to the Spaniards (see Anzaldúa, *Borderlands*/La Frontera, 22–23).

66. Anzaldúa rejects the terms *lesbian* and *homosexual*. To her, they emerge from a conceptual world different from her own. *Lesbian*, she argues, is a term that originated as a self-identifying category by U.S. white-Anglo women. *Homosexual*, she also tells us, falls in the category of the deviant counterpart of the heterosexual norm. For this reason, and although she recognizes its dangers for homogenization, she prefers the term *queer*, which to her is more consistent with a politization of her sexuality and identity. See Gloria Anzaldúa, "To(o) Queer the Writer—*Loca, escritora y chicana*," in *Living Chicana Theory*, ed. Carla Trujillo (Berkeley, CA: Third Woman Press, 1998), 264, 266.

67. Anzaldúa's commitment to a greater conceptual paradigmatic revolution is also seen as she admonishes her own Chicana/o people for their divisions, strifes, and failure to see that the U.S. Anglo-European reference points have snuck in and still operate in the manner in which Chicano/a people view certain members of their own community. She proposes that it is time that they resist the "enemy within" their conceptions and finally start using their own frames of reference, those unique to the Chicano/a people. See Gloria Anzaldúa, "En Rapport, in Opposition: *Cobrando cuentas a las nuestras*," in *Making Face, Making Soul*/Haciendo Caras: *Creative and Critical Perspectives by Women of Color*, ed. Gloria Anzaldúa (San Francisco: Aunt Lute Books, 1990), 142–48.

68. Erika Aigner-Varoz, "Metaphors of a Mestiza Consciousness: Anzaldúa's Borderlands/La Frontera," *MELUS* 25, no. 2, *Latino Identities* (Summer 2000): 48.

69. Anzaldúa, *Borderlands*/La Frontera, 20.

70. Ibid., 46.

71. For Anzaldúa, contemporary *mestizas'* capacity to shift among identities destabilizes the dominant culture's drive for using oppositional categories. She finds profound parallels with Nahua mythology, particularly in the deities' capacity to hold opposite elements. She draws from and reconfigures Nahua theogony in order to bolster her claim that female deities and characteristics were systematically excised and replaced by male ones during the pre-Columbian Aztec civilization, and later completed by the post-conquest church. For her, this is precisely the case for the symbol of Guadalupe. She rewrites her origin empowering her as the pre-Columbian Coatlalopeuh, the Meso-American fertility goddess. She connects her with the creator goddess Coatlicue (she of the serpent skirt), the mother of the celestial deities Huitzilopochtli (the war god) and his sister Coyolxauhqui (Golden Bells), goddess of the moon, who was decapitated by her brother. She traces the displacement of female deities and characteristics as far back as the Totonacs. According to Anzaldúa, they renewed their reverence for Tonantsi (Holy Mother), who preferred the sacrifice of small animals and birds, because they were tired of the Aztec human sacrifices to the male god Huitzilopochtli. Later, the male-dominated Azteca-Mexica drove the female deities underground by giving them monstrous attributes and substituting male deities for them. This marks the split between the dark aspects of Coatlicue, Tlazolteolt (earth, sex, childbirth, and a mother goddess), Cichuacoatl (Snake Woman), another of a number of motherhood and fertility goddesses, and her Tonantsi aspects. After the conquest the Spaniards completed the split between Tonantsi/Guadalupe

by desexing her, taking Coatlalopeuh, the serpent/sexuality, out of her; making la Virgen de Guadalupe/Virgen María into chaste virgins and Tlasolteotl/Coatlicue/la Chingada into whores, into the Beauties and the Beasts. In this way, "*Tonantsi* became *Guadalupe*, the chaste protective mother defender of the Mexican people" (Anzaldúa, *Borderlands*/La Frontera, 27–28). However much one challenges Anzaldúa's reconstruction of Nahua theogony and its relation to the symbol of Guadalupe, one cannot deny the powerful disruptive force of turning the Nahua pantheon into a series of subversive female icons. By revising and reclaiming Nahua female deities, Anzaldúa invites *mestizas* to unlearn the masculinist versions of their own history, religion, and myths. See also Silvia Trejo, *Dioses, mitos y ritos del México antiguo* (Mexico: Secreataría de Relaciones Exteriores, 2000); Cecilio A. Robelo, *Diccionario de aztequismos; o sea, jardín de las raíces aztecas, palabras del idioma nahuatl, azteca o mexicano, introducidas al idioma castellano bajo diversas formas* (Mexico: Ediciones Fuente Cultural, 1904); Fray Alonso De Molina, *Vocabulario en lengua castellana y mexicana: reimpreso de la edición hecha en México por Antonio de Spinosa en 1571*, Colección de Incunables Americanos 16 (Madrid: Ediciones Cultura Hispánica, 1944).

72. Anzaldúa, *Borderlands*/La Frontera, 49.

73. Aigner-Varoz, "Metaphors of a Mestiza Consciousness," 55. Anzaldúa identifies rigid conceptual dualistic frames as "serpents that wound." By engaging these "serpents" and cracking them open to unmask and make evident their exclusionary effects, these serpents turn on themselves. That is, they become part of the solution both by being neutralized as their oppressive, exclusionary effects are exposed, and by serving as the platform for the creation of new and more fluid conceptual frames. This summarizes her expression: let "the wound caused by the serpent be cured by the serpent" (Anzaldúa, *Borderlands*/La Frontera, 46).

74. Anzaldúa, *Borderlands*/La Frontera, 43, 48–49; Aigner-Varoz, "Metaphors of a Mestiza Consciousness," 55.

75. Anzaldúa, *Borderlands*/La Frontera, 39, 38.

76. Ibid., 79.

77. Aigner-Varoz, "Metaphors of a Mestiza Consciousness," 59–60.

78. Anzaldúa, *Borderlands*/La Frontera, 79.

79. Claudia Milian, "Breaking into the Borderlands: Double Consciousness, Latina and Latino Misplacements" (Ph.D. dissertation, Brown University, 2001), 33–79; W. E. B. DuBois, *The Souls of Black Folk* (New York: Dover Publications, 1994; originally published in 1903).

80. Aigner-Varoz, "Metaphors of a Mestiza Consciousness," 51.

81. Bernice Zamora, cited in Elizabeth Martínez, "Beyond Black/White: The Racisms of Our Time," in *The Latino Condition: A Critical Reader*, ed. Richard Delgado and Jean Stefancic (New York: New York University Press, 1998), 473.

82. Anzaldúa, *Borderlands/La* Frontera, 79.

83. Notice that *la conciencia de la mestiza* shares the same conceptual disruptive space as Coatlicue, which also symbolizes the presence of "duality in life, a synthesis of duality, and a third perspective—something more than mere duality or a synthesis of duality" (Anzaldúa, *Borderlands/La* Frontera, 47).

84. Anzaldúa, *Borderlands/La* Frontera, 80.

85. Milian, "Breaking into the Borderlands," 42.

86. Aigner-Varoz, "Metaphors of a Mestiza Consciousness," 47.

87. Anzaldúa, *Borderlands/La* Frontera, 81n5. Anzaldúa tells us she borrowed the term *morphogenesis* from the chemist Ilya Prigongine's theory of "dissipative structures." Prigongine, Anzaldúa comments, discovered that "substances interact not in predictable ways as it was taught in science, but in different and fluctuating ways to produce new and more complex structures, a kind of birth he called 'morphogenesis,' which created unpredictable innovations" (97–98).

88. Aldama, *Disrupting Savagism*, 113.

89. Anzaldúa, *Borderlands/La* Frontera, 3.

90. Ibid., 80.

91. Ibid., 46.

92. Aldama engages Anzaldúa at length, but he (along with the other Chicano/a authors he invokes) argues that Anzaldúa reclaims the Meso-American indigenous tradition by drawing from the Aztec world view. He accurately describes the reality of Mexico and Latin America, whereby "internalized colonialism on a national level translates into an internalized colonialism on a personal level." He further claims, "Europeanized mestizos (Ladinos) continue to denigrate and exploit contemporary peoples whose first language is Zapotec, Tzilzil, Yaqui and Nahua, to name just a few" (Aldama, *Disrupting Savagism*, 119). Aldama does not mention that in many places in Latin America it is the very discourse of *mestizaje* that provides the content and social directive to the manner in which such denigration and exploitation take place. (This will be discussed more fully in Chapter 4.) Also, Aldama fails to include the other countries that constitute the Meso-American region; the indigenous communities he mentions are of the southern and northern portions of Mexico. He does not mention other indigenous groupings south of the Mexican-Guatemalan border. In these two counts, Aldama reinscribes what many U.S. scholars do when mentioning Latin America or Meso-America. One, Meso-America refers

only to Mexico, thus effectively displacing the other peoples and countries of the isthmus. And two, in order to engage issues in Latin America, one does not need to go south of Mexico, effectively displacing the rich and complex diversity of Latin *America*. In this way Chicano/a scholars follow the white and imperial racialized dominant biases of U.S. scholarship concerning Latin America.

93. Barnard, "Gloria Anzaldúa's Queer Mestizaje," 47.

94. Anzaldúa, *Borderlands/La* Frontera. Anzaldúa notes that Chicano/a people carry the baggage of the "Indian" mother, the baggage of the Spanish father, and the baggage of the U.S. Anglo-European, but she does not tells us anything about the baggage of the *mestizo/a* Mexican (82).

95. Les Field notes that in the case of Mexico, the particular emphasis on *mestizaje* after the revolution enshrined an *indigenista* glorification and *mestizaje*. *Indigenismo* meant the glorification of the indigenous communities of the *past* (see Les Field, "Blood and Traits: Preliminary Observations on the Analysis of Mestizo and Indigenous Identities in Latin America vs. the U.S," *The Journal of Latin American Anthropology* 7, no. 1 [2002]: 17). In a similar vein, Hedrick traces the impact of modernism in Mexican art and artists. She argues that during the time of the revolution in Mexico there was a move to bring together nation, *mestizaje*, and indigenism. *Indigenism* was the reclaiming of the indigenous roots of the *mestizo/a* people, but it had little to do with the indigenous peoples of Mexico, who were the objects of a systematic literacy (assimilation and deindigenization) program during Vasconcelos's tenure as minister of education. Overall, *mestizo/a* people came to be seen as incarnating Mexican identity; they replaced the indigenous and came to be viewed as the solution to the building of a united modern Mexico (see Hedrick, *Race, Nation, and Identity in Latin American Culture, 1900–1940*).

4. THE SHIFTING SHAPES OF *MESTIZAJE*

1. Spirituality: Roberto L. Gómez, "Mestizo Spirituality: Motifs of Sacrifice, Transformation, Thanksgiving, and Family in Four Mexican American Rituals," *Apuntes: Reflexiones Teológicas Desde el Márgen Hispano* 2, no. 2 (1991): 81–92. Christology: Luis Pedraja, *Jesus Is My Uncle: Christology from a Hispanic Perspective* (Nashville, TN: Abingdon Press, 1999). Anthropology: Miguel H. Díaz, *On Being Human: U.S. Hispanic and Rahnerian Perspectives* (Maryknoll, NY: Orbis Books, 2001). Pneumatology: Oscar García Johnson, "The Mestizo/a Community of Mañana: A Latino/a Theology of the Spirit" (Ph.D. dissertation, Fuller Theological Seminary, 2005). Social ethics: Eldin

Villafañe, *The Liberating Spirit: Toward an Hispanic American Pente-costal Social Ethic* (Grand Rapids, MI: Eerdmans, 1993). Biblical herme-neutics: Robert D. Maldonado, "¿*La Conquista?* Latin American *(Mestizaje)* Reflections on the Biblical Conquest," *Journal of Hispanic/Latino Theology* 2, no. 4 (1995): 5–25.

2. For example, note the manner in which Rubén Rosario Rodríguez carefully downplays the violence of the conquest, despite his strong criticism of *mestizaje*. After listing the five theological uses given to *mestizaje* in Andrew Irvine's interpretive typology, he lists his own multivalent understanding of the term: (1) the historical and biological reality of mixing between two or more human groups, (2) the interac-tion and exchange between two or more cultures, and (3) a distinctly Christian identity grounded in Christ's liberating vision of human rela-tionships of equality distinguished by active resistance to various forms of domination. A careful look at his list shows the absence of any allu-sion to the specific historical violent origins of *mestizaje*. For him, *mestizaje* seems to mean basically any type of intermixture, primarily cultural. This, by itself, drains the term of any potential liberative force. Since anyone would be hard-pressed to claim to have an entirely "pure" culture, this conversely means that if all people-groups have undergone any type of mixture or share parallels with the *mestizo/a* experience of an existential in-between-ness and intermixture, they can be consid-ered *mestizos/as*. While this may open the door to make universalizing claims of *mestizaje*, the issue is that many peoples who are mixed do not consider themselves *mestizos/as* because of the historical specific contexts within which the term was originally applied. To argue for *mestizaje* using these globalizing notions carries the Vasconcelian im-petus of the "fifth cosmic race." See Rubén Rosario Rodríguez, "No Longer Jew nor Greek but *Mestizo?* The Challenge of Ethnocentrism for Theological Reconstruction" (Ph.D. dissertation, Princeton Theo-logical Seminary, 2005), 73–74, 130. This is more explicit in the work of Benjamín Valentín, who states that "because the cultural history of every Latino subgroup has been influenced by the dynamics of His-panic mestizaje either during the Spanish colonial period or in the United States, Elizondo's theorizing of mestizaje is adaptable to every U.S. Latino subculture." In fact, he observes, one might say that "Elizondo's work can be useful to all persons of mixed cultural and racial heritage, whether Latino or not" (Benjamin Valentín, *Mapping Public Theology: Beyond Culture, Identity, and Difference* [New York: Trinity Press International, 2002], 50n20). Valentín's comments lead to turning *mestizaje* into a categorical abstraction, disembodied and dehistorized, that takes the "universal mixed person(s)" as reference point in the analysis. But that is not any different from the abstract Eurocentric universal traditional

theological categories that U.S. Latino/a theologians have criticized so tirelessly. Thus, Irvine's observation that the "new cosmovision" of the mestizo/a future is not an absolute new reality but "one that can never be separated from the colonial violence" confirms my proposal for keeping *mestizaje* grounded in the historical specificity of the people and their experiences, and not just any cultural phenomena of intermixture (see Andrew Irvine, "Mestizaje and the Problem of Authority," *Journal of Hispanic/Latino Theology* 8, no. 1 (2000): 35.

3. Javier Quiñonez-Ortíz, "The *Mestizo* Journey: Challenges for Hispanic Theology," *Apuntes: Reflexiones Teológicas Desde el Márgen Hispano* 11, no. 3 (1993): 65–66.

—— 4. Irvine, "Mestizaje and the Problem of Authority."

5. Ibid., 22.

6. Valentín, *Mapping Public Theology*, 21–34.

7. Roberto S. Goizueta, "*La Raza Cósmica?* The Vision of José Vasconcelos," *Journal of Hispanic/Latino Theology* 1, no. 2 (1994): 6.

8. Ibid.

9. In his summary of U.S. Latina/o theology Valentín makes Vasconcelos responsible for articulating what he calls "lived Latino/a *mestizaje*" into a written discourse, but he says nothing of the debates of *mestizaje* taking place in Latin America before, during, and after Vasconcelos's work. Benjamin Valentín, "Strangers No More: An Introduction to, and Interpretation of, U.S. Hispanic/Latino/a Theology," in *The Ties That Bind: African American and Hispanic American/Latino/a Theologies in Dialogue*, ed. Anthony B. Pinn and Benjamin Valentín (New York: Continuum, 2001), 48.

10. Orlando O. Espín, "The State of U.S. Latino/a Theology: An Understanding," *Perspectivas: Hispanic Theological Initiative Occasional Paper Series*, no. 3 (Fall 2000): 19–55.

11. Ibid., 23–24.

12. Ibid., 24.

13. Loida I. Martell-Otero, "Women Doing Theology: Una Perspectiva Evangélica," *Apuntes: Reflexiones Teológicas Desde el Márgen Hispano* 14, no. 3 (1994): 68.

14. Martell-Otero makes the clarification that the appellative *evangélica* is not synonymous with the English term *evangelical*. She argues that "the latter term implies some very specific political and socioeconomic connotations in the United States, which are not included in the Spanish term." To her, *evangélica* points to those strong Protestant women, especially in the Northeastern United States, mainly of the Baptist tradition, who have held positions of influence and power within the structures of the institutional church. The use of Hispanic *mujeres evangélicas* opens a new dilemma because the Hispanic Protestant

churches where women continue to have strong positions of leadership are by no means homogeneous (Martell-Otero, "Women Doing Theology," 69–74).

15. Loida I. Martell-Otero, "Of Satos and Saints: Salvation from the Periphery," *Perspectivas: Hispanic Theological Initiative Occasional Paper Series*, no. 4 (2001): 8.

16. Ibid.

17. Manuel J. Mejido, "Propaedeutic to the Critique of the Study of U.S. Hispanic Religion," *Journal of Hispanic/Latino Theology* 10, no. 2 (November 2002): 31–63.

18. Ibid., 54n68.

19. Rosario Rodríguez, "No Longer Jew nor Greek but *Mestizo?*" 75.

20. Ibid., 131.

21. Ibid., 138.

22. Rosario Rodríguez does not mention the political issues at stake within the U.S. Latino/a communities. He does not deal with the social and political cost of subsuming the U.S. Latina/o communities under the one general rubric of Hispanic or Latina/o, by way of removing any possibilities for the uniqueness of these communities to emerge in their own rights. This is illustrated in the relation between Mexican Americans and Puerto Ricans and Cubans. Activism among Mexican Americans preceded the articulations by Puerto Rican and Cuban scholars, so the latter adopted the dominant Mexican American concerns, including the discussions of *mestizaje*. Among U.S. Latina/o theologians, issues pertaining to Puerto Rico and Cuba are for the most part left out in discussions of *La raza* and *mestizaje*. Rosario Rodríguez does not pay attention to the fact that the emphasis on Hispanic identity, the use of *La raza*, and *mestizaje* were issues very much at the forefront of Mexican and Mexican American sociopolitical and economic issues, as well as the construction of a national identity. Thus, a careful analysis of the historical and political issues surrounding *mestizaje* among Latinas/os is necessary before one renders any judgment concerning the specific usage of the term.

23. Rosario Rodríguez, "No Longer Jew nor Greek but *Mestizo?*" 138.

24. Ibid., 275.

25. Vásquez uses the label *other Hispanics* to include, for example, people of African descent in Belize, Guatemala, and Honduras (the Garifuna), or of indigenous descent in Guatemala (the K'iches), Ecuador (Quechua), and Bolivia (Aymara). No doubt the use of the term is entirely inadequate. It brings to light, however, the increasingly problematic tendency to speak of the U.S. Latina/o population as homogeneous.

See Manuel A. Vásquez, "Rethinking Mestizaje," in *Rethinking Latino(a) Religion and Identity*, ed. Miguel De La Torre and Gastón Espinosa (Cleveland: The Pilgrim Press, 2006), 131–32.

26. See Jeffrey L. Gould, *To Die in This Way: Nicaraguan Indians and the Myth of Mestizaje* (Durham, NC: Duke University Press, 1998); Charles R. Hale, "Travel Warnings: Elite Appropriations of Hybridity, Mestizaje, Antiracism, Equality, and Other Progressive-Sounding Discourses in Highland Guatemala," *Journal of American Folklore* 112, no. 445 (1999): 297–315.

27. Vásquez, "Rethinking Mestizaje," 152, 149.

28. Klor de Alva defines this characteristic of *mestizaje* as chameleon-like: "Western in the presence of Europeans, indigenous in native villages, and Indian-like in contemporary US barrios" (see J. Jorge Klor de Alva, "Cipherspace: Latino Identity Past and Present," in *Race, Identity, and Citizenship: A Reader*, ed. Rodolfo D. Torres, Louis F. Mirón, and Jonathan Xavier Inda [Malden, MA: Blackwell Publishers, 1999], 177).

29. Manuel Zapata Olivella, *La rebelión de los genes: El mestizaje americano en la sociedad futura* (Bogotá: Ediciones Altamir, 1997), 40.

30. Ibid., 240.

31. Ibid., 73–144, 327–35.

32. Marisol de la Cadena, "The Political Tensions of Representations and Misrepresentations: Intellectuals and *Mestizas* in Cuzco (1919–1990)," *Journal of Latin American Anthropology* 2, no. 1 (1996): 112–47; Marisol de la Cadena, *Indigenous Mestizos: The Politics of Race and Culture in Cuzco, Peru, 1919–1991*, Latin American Otherwise: Languages, Empires, Nations series (Durham, NC: Duke University Press, 2000).

33. De la Cadena, "The Political Tensions of Representations and Misrepresentations," 116.

34. Ibid., 125.

35. Ibid., 133.

36. Ibid., 138.

37. Javier Sanjinés C., *Mestizaje Upside-Down: Aesthetic Politics in Modern Bolivia* (Pittsburgh: University of Pittsburgh Press, 2004), 43–44.

38. Ibid., 164.

39. Dora María Téllez, *¡Muera la gobierna!: Colonización en Matagalpa y Jinotega (1820–1890)* (Managua, Nicaragua: Universidad de las Regiones Autónomas de la Costa Caribe Nicaragüense, 1999).

40. Téllez, *¡Muera la gobierna!* 33, 50–51. The use of the nomenclature *Ladino/a* is peculiar to the context of Central America. While the term is used to identify people of mixed descent, its function is to

distinguish *Ladinos/as* from the indigenous populations. In other words, in practical terms to be *Ladino/a* literally means "not indigenous." The *Léxico del mestizaje* defines *Ladino/a* as the person who has the ability to speak another language besides his or her native tongue. It also says that it is an indigenous person who has adopted speaking Spanish, a *Cholo/a*, which is particularly used in South America. But the lexicon also states that in Guatemala it means "not indigenous but *mestizo*." See Manuel Alvar, *Léxico del mestizaje hispanoamericano* (Madrid: Ediciones Cultura Hispánica, Instituto de Cooperación Iberoamericana, 1987), 151–52.

41. Téllez, *¡Muera la gobierna!* 119–24.

42. Ibid., 104, 31, 91.

43. Jeffrey L. Gould, "Gender, Politics, and the Triumph of *Mestizaje* in Early Twentieth Century Nicaragua," *Journal of Latin American Anthropology* 2, no. 1 (1996): 11; Gould, *To Die in This Way*, 155–61.

44. Gould, "Gender, Politics, and the Triumph of *Mestizaje* in Early Twentieth Century Nicaragua," 12, 6.

45. Gould, *To Die in This Way*, 228–66.

46. Rafael Polo Bonilla, *Los intelectuales y la narrativa mestiza en el Ecuador* (Quito, Ecuador: Universidad andina Simón Bolívar, Ediciones Abya Yala, Corporación editora nacional, 2002).

47. Ibid., 20–26.

48. Ibid., 45.

49. Ibid., 58.

50. Guillermo Bonfil Batalla, "Sobre la ideología del mestizaje (O cómo el Garcilaso Inca anunció, sin saberlo, muchas de nuestras desgracias)," in *Decadencia y auge de las identidades: Cultura nacional, identidad cultural y modernización*, ed. José Manuel Valenzuela Arce (Tijuana, Baja California: El Colegio de la Frontera del Norte, 1992), 35–47.

51. Ibid., 39–44.

52. Klor de Alva, "Cipherspace," 176.

53. J. Jorge Klor de Alva, "Aztlán, Borinquen, and Hispanic Nationalism in the United States," in *Aztlán: Essays on the Chicano Homeland*, ed. Rodolfo A. Anaya and Francisco A. Lomelí (Alburquerque: Academia/El Norte Publications, 1989), 154.

54. Helio Gallardo, "Fenomenología del ladino de mierda," in *500 años: Fenomenología del mestizo (violencia y resistencia)* (San José, Costa Rica: Departamento Ecuménico de Investigaciones, 1993), 163.

55. In addition to the problem of land, Mariátegui arrived at the conclusion that what the indigenous peoples of Peru needed to solve their problems was to integrate into modernity. According to Castro, this indicates that even for Mariátegui the indigenous peoples were in a

state of "underdevelopment." See Juan E. de Castro, *Mestizo Nations: Culture, Race, and Conformity in Latin American Literature* (Tucson: The University of Arizona Press, 2002), chap. 6.

56. Tace Hedrick, *Race, Nation, and Identity in Latin American Culture, 1900–1940* (Piscataway, NJ: Rutgers University Press, 2003), 41.

57. Bonfil Batalla, "Sobre la ideología del mestizaje," 41.

58. Bonilla, *Los intelectuales y la narrativa mestiza en el Ecuador*, 58.

59. Hale, "Travel Warnings," 302.

60. Nancy Morejón, *Nación y mestizaje en Nicolás Guillén* (Havana: Ediciones Unión, 2005), 75–116.

61. Gilberto Freyre, *The Masters and the Slaves (Casa-Grande and Sensala): A Study in the Development of Brazilian Civilization*, 4th ed. (New York: Alfred A. Knopf, 1946).

62. Luis Duno Gottberg, *Solventando las diferencias: La ideología del mestizaje en Cuba* (Madrid: Iberoamericana, 2003).

63. José Martí, "Nuestra América," in *De Colón a Martí: Discurso y Cultura en América Latina*, ed. Olmedo España Calderón, Colección Fundamentos (Guatemala City: Editorial Óscar de León Palacios, 1993), 208.

64. Duno Gottberg, *Solventando las diferencias*, 24–28.

65. Elisabeth Cunin, *Identidades a flor de piel: Lo "negro" entre apariencias y pertenencias: categorías raciales y mestizaje en Cartagena (Colombia)* (Bogotá: Instituto Colombiano de Antropología e Historia; Universidad de Los Andes; Instituto Francés de Estudios Andinos; Observatorio del Caribe Colombiano, 2003), 43, 189–91.

66. Ibid., 52–68, 155–56, 162–67.

67. Ibid., 177–92, 215–70.

68. Ibid., 105–10.

69. Clyde Soto, "Marcas culturales para las mujeres en la sociedad paraguaya," *Acción: Revista Paraguaya de Diálogo y Reflexión*, http://www.uninet.com.py/accion/num_188/mujeres/mujeres1.html (accessed Dec. 15, 2005).

70. Camilla Townsend, "Story without Words: Women and the Creation of a Mestizo People in Guayaquil, 1820–1835," *Latin American Perspectives* 24, no. 4 (July 1997): 50–68.

71. Breny Mendoza, "La desmitologización del mestizaje en Honduras: Evaluando nuevos aportes" (2001).

72. Soto, "Marcas culturales para las mujeres en la sociedad paraguaya."

73. De la Cadena, "The Political Tensions of Representations and Misrepresentations," 119.

74. Octavio Paz, "The Labyrinth of Solitude," in *The Labyrinth of Solitude and Other Writings* (New York: Grove Press, 1985), 7–212.

75. María Himelda Ramírez, "Del drama inicial a la sacralización en los mitos de origen de la sociedad mestiza latinoamericana," in *¿Mestizo yo?: Diferencias, identidad, e inconsciente*, ed. Mario Bernardo Figueroa Muñoz and Pío Eduardo Sanmiguel A. (Colombia: Universidad Nacional de Colombia, Facultad de Ciencias Humanas, Grupo de Psicoanálisis, 2000), 186.

76. Rita Cano Alcalá, "From Chingada to Chingona: La Malinche Redefined or, a Long Line of Hermanas," *Aztlán* 26, no. 2 (Fall 2001): 40.

77. Ibid., 34.

78. Sonia Montecino, "Madres y Huachos: Alegorías del mestizaje chileno," *Tópicos* 90 (October 1990): 106–9. According to María Himelda Ramírez, male culture's portrayal of the man as "the irresponsible youth—his space is the street and neglects any commitment to the domestic life—underlines independence, impulsiveness and physical strength as natural forms of resolving disagreements. The father, centre of authority, is poorly developed as a figure of identification and emblem of masculinity, which encourages in other adult men the perpetuation of the licentious, irresponsible, [and] quarrelsome behaviour. When that boy grows up identifying with a negative or absent paternal image, he will recreate the myth of the irresponsible *macho*" (Ramírez, "Del drama inicial a la sacralización en los mitos de origen de la sociedad mestiza latinoamericana," 194).

79. According to Susan Kellogg, the emphasis on the transference of Spanish superiority to male superiority is reinscribed in caste paintings where men, generally of a higher caste, are portrayed as the ones marrying women of lower castes. The insight of the paintings is that they prescribe specific roles and conduct to the sexes, placing women in positions of subordination to their superior (both by caste and gender) males. See Susan Kellogg, "Depicting Mestizaje: Gendered Images of Ethnorace in Colonial Mexican Texts," *Journal of Women's History* 12, no. 3 (Autumn 2000): 69–92.

80. Milagros Palma, *Nicaragua: Once mil vírgenes: Imaginario mítico-religioso Nicaragüense* (Bogotá: Tercer Mundo Editores, 1988), 246.

81. It is important to note the hierarchy of violence and abuse against the indigenous and African peoples. Benjamín Carrión recounts a very popular adage in Brazil whereby women, depending on their ethnicity, are assigned a social role: "the white woman for marriage, the mulatto woman for sex, the black woman for work." See Benjamín Carrión, "El Mestizaje y lo mestizo," in *América Latina en sus ideas*, ed. Leopoldo

Zea, *América Latina en su Cultura* (Mexico City: Siglo XXI editores, UNESCO, 1986), 387.

82. Palma, *Nicaragua*, 65.

83. Ibid., 67.

84. Ibid., 66.

85. Rogelio Sáenz, "Latinos and the Changing Face of America," *Population Reference Bureau* (August 2004).

86. Marcela Sánchez, "'Poverty Is Relative': Latinos Defy 'Downtrodden' Status, Sending Their Successes Home," *Washingtonpost.com*, Friday, October 20, 2006. Available online.

5. THE FUTURE OF U.S. LATINA/O THEOLOGY

1. Concerning the internal diversity among Mexican Americans, Labarthe asserts that Aztlán was used as a supposed common denominator with claims to the "vatos locos, pochos, pachucos, cholos, and other mestizos" (cited in Rafael Pérez-Torres, *Movements in Chicano Poetry: Against Myths, Against Margins* [New York: Cambridge University Press, 1995], 67). Pérez-Torrez adds that despite the ideological valorization of *mestizaje*, the racism inherent in U.S. and Mexican societies pressured these communities to adopt certain standards of "beauty, identity and aspiration." "In order to belong to larger imagined communities of the nation . . . 'Mexican Americans' were expected to accept antiindigenous discourses as their own" (68).

2. Breny Mendoza, "La desmitologización del mestizaje en Honduras: Evaluando nuevos aportes" (2001).

3. Ibid.

4. Miguel A. De La Torre and Edwin David Aponte, *Introducing Latino/a Theologies* (Maryknoll, NY: Orbis Books, 2001), 147.

5. Ricardo Feierstein, *Mestizo: A Novel* (Albuquerque: University of New Mexico Press, 2000).

6. Ricardo Feierstein, "Todas las culturas, la cultura," in *Contraexilio y Mestizaje: Ser judío en latinoamerica*, Colección Ensayos (Buenos Aires: Editorial Milá, 1996), 123, 129, 131.

7. Ibid., 136.

8. Ibid., 144–48.

9. This is what Manuel Vásquez attempts to acknowledge when he uses the nomenclature *other Hispanics* to speak about the many other ethnic and cultural groups that are part of the U.S. Latina/o population but who do not fit the traditional national labels. See Manuel Vásquez, "Rethinking Mestizaje," in *Rethinking Latino(a) Religion and Identity*, ed. Miguel De La Torre and Gastón Espinosa, 129–57 (Cleveland: The Pilgrim Press, 2006).

10. John Francis Burke, *Mestizo Democracy: The Politics of Crossing Borders*, foreword by Virgilio Elizondo (College Station: Texas A&M University Press, 2002), 9.

11. Ibid., 10.

12. Ángel Rosenblat, *El mestizaje y las castas coloniales*, vol. 2 of *La Población Indígena y el Mestizaje en América* (Buenos Aires: Editorial Nova, 1954); Manuel Zapata Olivella, *La rebelión de los genes: El mestizaje americano en la sociedad futura* (Bogotá: Ediciones Altamir, 1997); Claudio Esteva Fábregat, *El mestizaje en Iberoamérica* (Madrid: Editorial Alhambra, S.A., 1988); Jacques Audinet, *The Human Face of Globalization: From Multicultural to Mestizaje* (New York: Rowman and Littlefield Publishing, 2004).

13. Alice Walker, "In the Closet of the Soul: A Letter to an African-American Friend," *Ms* 15 (November 1986): 32–35.

14. Zipporah G. Glass, "The Language of *Mestizaje* in a Renewed Rhetoric of Black Theology," *Journal of Hispanic/Latino Theology* 7, no. 2 (November 1999): 32–42.

15. Vernon R. Wishart, *What Lies behind the Picture: A Personal Journey into Cree Ancestry*, foreword by Linda Goyette (Canada: Central Alberta Historical Society, 2006).

16. Leonard Blussé, *Strange Company: Chinese Settlers, Mestizo Women, and the Dutch in VOC Batavia* (Holland; Riverton, NJ: Foris Publications, 1986).

17. Claudine Bavoux, *Islam et métissage: des musulmans créolophones à Madagascar: les indiens sunnites sourti des Tamatave* (Paris: L'Harmattan, 1990).

18. Jean-Loup Amselle, *Mestizo Logics: Anthropology of Identity in Africa and Elsewhere* (Stanford, CA: Stanford University Press, 1998).

19. Jean-Loup Amselle, in Elisabeth Cunin, *Identidades a flor de piel: Lo 'negro' entre apariencias y pertenencias: categorías raciales y mestizaje en Cartagena (Colombia)* (Bogotá: Instituto Colombiano de Antropología e Historia; Universidad de Los Andes; Instituto Francés de Estudios Andinos; Observatorio del Caribe Colombiano, 2003), 26.

20. Among Latin American and, more specifically, Mexican intellectuals, no other writer has reflected upon the connection between the rape of the indigenous women by the Spanish males and the Mexican national and ethnic identity as much as Octavio Paz. In his Nobel Prize–winning *The Labyrinth of Solitude* he discusses the connection between the experience of rape and abandonment of La Malinche and the low self-esteem of the Mexican people. While there are some questions about the sexist content of his analysis, it is worth noting that even until the middle of the twentieth century the question of illegitimacy for *mestizos/as*

was at the center of national and ethnic debates in Mexico. See Octavio Paz, "The Labyrinth of Solitude," in *The Labyrinth of Solitude and Other Writings* (New York: Grove Press, 1985), 7–212.

21. Dora María Téllez, *¡Muera la gobierna!: Colonización en Matagalpa y Jinotega (1820–1890)* (Managua, Nicaragua: Universidad de las Regiones Autónomas de la Costa Caribe Nicaragüense, 1999), 40–55.

22. De La Torre and Aponte, *Introducing Latino/a Theologies*, 148.

23. Architecture: Carlos R. Margain, "Materialización arquitectónica del grado de integración del mestizaje indo-español alcanzado en México en el siglo XVIII," in *Identidad y mestizaje*, ed. Gladys M. Sirvent and Jorge González Aragón (Mexico City: Universidad Autónoma Metropolitana, Casa Abierta al Tiempo, 1996), 43–60; Otto Morales Benítez, *Memorias del mestizaje* (Bogotá: Plaza y Janes, Editores-Colombia Ltda., 1984). Gastronomy: Ivonne Mijares, *Mestizaje alimentario: El abasto en la ciudad de México en el siglo XVI* (México: Facultad de Filosofía y Letras, UNAM, 1993). Society and culture: Carolina Prieto Molano, *Hasta la tierra es mestiza*, Historia Colombiana (Bogotá: Colección Bibliográfica Banco de la República, 1994). Geography: Luis Alberto Sánchez, *Examen espectral de América Latina: Civilización y cultura esencia de la tradición, ataque y defensa del mestizo*, 2d ed. (Buenos Aires: Editorial Losada, 1962).

24. Tinoco Guerra, *Latinoamérica profunda: Aproximación a una filosofía de la cultura*, Colección: Ideas y Pensamientos (Maracaibo, Venezuela: Fondo Editorial Esther María Osses, 1996), 27–28.

25. Zambrana Fonseca celebrates the *mestizo/a* creativity of weaving a rich culture from the indigenous, African, and Spanish elements. Downplaying the continuing presence of indigenous peoples and the strong African presence, he writes that the *mestizo* culture is a true reflection of the Nicaraguan cultural reality. See Armando Zambrana Fonseca, *El ojo mestizo o la herencia cultural* (Managua, Nicaragua: Ediciones PAVSA, 2002). See also Benjamín Carrión, *Cartas al Ecuador* (Quito, Ecuador: Banco Central del Ecuador and Corparación Editora Nacional, 1988).

26. The white/*mestizo/a*/African formula became prominent during 1992, the quincentenary of the arrival of the Spanish to the Americas. It became evident that despite the large *mestizo/a* population, there were still large concentrations of African descendants in Latin America, as in the province of Chocó in Colombia, Izabal in Guatemala, Belize, the regions of Esmeralda and Chota-Mira Valley in Ecuador, or more obviously where there has been substantial intermixture between Spanish or Portuguese Europeans and Africans, giving room to the phenomenon of *mulatez* as in Cuba, Puerto Rico, Dominican Republic, and

Brazil. National governments adopted a policy of multiculturalism, as exemplified by the Colombian government's adoption of multiculturalism in the revised constitution of 1991.

27. In providing an example of the powerful force of the assimilationist rhetoric of *mestizaje*, Charles Hale tells us that in Guatemala "the price of achieving an 'antiracist' society is [the] assimilation" of the indigenous people into the dominant *Ladino* (*mestizo/a*) population (Charles Hale, "Travel Warnings: Elite Appropriations of Hybridity, Mestizaje, Antiracism, Equality, and Other Progressive-Sounding Discourses in Highland Guatemala," *Journal of American Folklore* 112, no. 445 [1999]: 308).

28. This was facilitated by the Spanish Royal Edict of January 10, 1795, called *gracias al sacar*. See Rosenblat, *El mestizaje y las castas coloniales*, 180; Magnus Mörner, "El mestizaje en la historia de Ibero-América: Informe sobre el estado de la investigación," in *Coloquio dedicado al mestizaje en la historia de Ibero-América (1960: Estocolmo)* (Mexico City: Instituto Panamericano de Geografía e Historia, Comisión de Historia, 1961), 37.

29. Mauricio Meléndez Obando, "Estratificación socio-racial y matrimonio en la Intendencia de San Salvador y la Alcaldía mayor de Sonsonate," in *Mestizaje, poder y sociedad*, ed. Ana Margarita Gómez and Sajid Alfredo Herrera (San Salvador: FLACSO Programa El Salvador, 2003), 55–60.

30. Ibid., 60–66.

31. Paul Thomas Lokken, "Mulatos, negros y el mestizaje en las Alcaldías mayores de San Salvador y Sonsonate," in Gómez and Herrera, *Mestizaje, poder y sociedad*, 10–12.

32. John Gledhill, "Mestizaje and Indigenous Identities" (1998). Available online.

33. Manuel Espinosa Apolo argues that in Ecuador claiming to be *mestizo/a* entails a denial of indigenous roots and increases the possibilities for more opportunities in society. The self-proclamation of being *mestizos/as* is, for him, a justifiable attitude in a context where social and ethnic stigmatization impedes non-*mestizos/as*' climb up the social ladder, while, at the same time, it displaces them from the social structures. As he puts it, "The self-proclamation as 'mestizos' by the population identified as such is only a partial fact, because it is a self-denomination present only among certain sectors and members of the national ethnos, specially among those social groups for whom such proclamation is a sign of prestige that contributes to guarantee the maintenance of their socioeconomic status, or ensures their social ascent" (Manuel Espinosa Apolo, *Los mestizos ecuatorianos y las señas*

de identidad cultural [Quito, Ecuador: Centro de estudios Felipe Guamán Poma de Ayala, 1995], 78).

34. Marta Elena Casaús Arzú, "La Metamorfosis del racismo en la élite de poder en Guatemala," in *¿Racismo en Guatemala? Abriendo el debate sobre un tema tabú*, ed. Clara Arenas Bianchi, Charles R. Hale, and Gustavo Palma Murga (Guatemala: AVANCSO, 1999), 66–72.

35. Marta Elena Casaús Arzú, *Guatemala: Linaje y Racismo* (Costa Rica: Editorial FLACSO, 1992).

36. Hale, "Travel Warnings," 310.

37. According to Klor de Alva, the *mestizo-criollos* made up the armies that resisted and overthrew the Spanish Empire, and they were also the ones who constructed the Latin American "national identities overwhelmingly out of Euro-American practices, the Spanish language, and Christianity" (J. Jorge Klor de Alva, "Colonialism and Postcolonialism as [Latin] American Mirages," *Colonial Latin American Review* 1, no. 2 [1992]: 3) (title inclusion in original).

38. Néstor Medina, "Hybrid Cultures or Multiculturalism: Navigating the Contested Spaces of *Mestizaje* Discourse," paper presented at the panel entitled Beyond Mestizaje: Revisiting Race, Syncretism, and Hybridity, American Academy of Religion, Religion in Latin America and the Caribbean Group, Washington DC, 2006, 12. See also Victor Perera, *Unfinished Conquest: The Guatemalan Tragedy* (Los Angeles: University of California Press, 1993).

39. Lourdes Martínez-Echazabal, "Mestizaje and the Discourse of National/Cultural Identity in Latin America, 1845–1959," *Latin American Perspectives* 25, no. 3 (May 1998): 37.

40. Virgilio Elizondo, "Our Lady of Guadalupe as a Cultural Symbol," in *Beyond Borders: The Writings of Virgilio Elizondo and Friends*, ed. Timothy Matovina, 118–25 (Maryknoll, NY: Orbis Books, 2000).

41. Jeanette Rodríguez, *Our Lady of Guadalupe: Faith and Empowerment among Mexican American Women* (Austin: University of Texas Press, 1994).

42. According to Diego Irarrázaval, Guadalupe's syncretistic character is not as unique as one might think. There are other instances in which "the Virgin of the Conquest was transformed into a beneficially autochthonous symbol" that eventually served as the inspiration of indigenous protests and uprisings. He comments that throughout Latin America there are numerous examples in which Christian elements mixed with indigenous and African ones to create unique expressions of the people's faith devotion: Caacupé, Virgen del Cobre, Virgen of Zinacatán, Santa Ana, and others. See Diego Irarrázaval, *Cultura y fe latinoamericanas* (Santiago de Chile: Ediciones Rehue Ltda.; Instituto de Estudios Aymaras, 1994), 135–50.

43. Carla Trujillo, "La Virgen de Guadalupe and Her Reconstruction in Chicana Lesbian Desire," in *Living Chicana Theory*, ed. Carla Trujillo (Berkeley, CA: Third Woman Press, 1998), 214–15.

44. Orlando O. Espín, "An Exploration into the Theology of Grace and Sin," in *From the Heart of Our People: Latino/a Explorations in Catholic Systematic Theology*, ed. Orlando O. Espín and Miguel H. Díaz (Maryknoll, NY: Orbis Books, 1999), 139–41.

45. Trujillo, "La Virgen de Guadalupe and Her Reconstruction in Chicana Lesbian Desire."

46. Ross Gandy, "La Movilización de la mujer latinoamericana en la lucha contra la opresión globalizada: El papel de la religión en México (y por implicación, en otras partes de la América Latina Católica)," paper presented at the Mujeres y Globalización Conference (Mexico: Centro para la Justicia Global, 2005). Available online.

47. Paz, "The Labyrinth of Solitude."

48. See Rita Cano Alcalá, "From Chingada to Chingona: La Malinche Redefined or, a Long Line of Hermanas," *Aztlán* 26, no. 2 (Fall 2001): 33–61; Martha E. Sánchez, "La Malinche at the Intersection: Race and Gender in Down These Mean Streets," *PMLA* 113, no. 1 (January 1998): 117–28; Otilia Meza, *Malinalli Tenepal: La gran calumniada* (Mexico: EDAMEX, 1999).

49. Pérez-Torres, *Movements in Chicano Poetry*, 211.

50. Toribio de Benavente was one of the twelve original Franciscan missionaries who arrived to the Americas in 1524 with the intention of evangelizing the indigenous peoples. Motolinia was the nickname he chose from a Nahua term that means "he afflicts himself" or "he is poor."

51. Virgilio Elizondo, *La Morenita, Evangelizer of the Americas* (San Antonio, TX: Mexican American Cultural Center, 1980); Teresa Chávez Sauceda, "Community, Mestizaje, and Liberation: Envisioning Racial Justice from a Latino/a Perspective" (Ph.D. dissertation, Graduate Theological Union, 1999), 195.

52. Néstor Medina, "*Mestizaje*, a Theological Reading of Culture and Faith: Reflections on Virgilio Elizondo's Theological Method," *Journal of Hispanic Latino Theology* (forthcoming).

53. According to Espín, Guadalupe has been traditionally interpreted in at least three ways: (1) the typical colonial Marian devotion, inherited from Spain or developed in the Americas during the colonial period, displaying all the typical structures of colonial-times Marian devotions; (2) the more recent "Romanized" Marian devotion, born during the nineteenth or twentieth century, frequently promoted by Rome, or religious congregations doing missionary work in the Americas, or other groups somehow identified with post–Vatican I Catholicism; and (3) a

syncretic devotion with a Marian side to it, born typically as a colonial devotion but having developed into an intimate, strange, and doctrinally unacceptable relationship with another "holy being" (possibly from a pre-Columbian or African ethnic group), provoking in today's devotees mixture and ambivalence as to "who" is the object of their devotion (Orlando Espín, personal conversation [2006]). But Espín has also added a fourth category of his own, arguing for a pneumatological reading of Guadalupe, in which case she would fall outside of traditional Marian discussions and closer to theological discussion of the divine Trinity culturally manifest in a female form. See Orlando O. Espín, "The Virgin of Guadalupe and the Holy Spirit: A Mexican and Mexican American Understanding of the Divine?" keynote address at Loyola Marymount University, Los Angeles, 2004; Orlando O. Espín, *The Faith of the People: Theological Reflections on Popular Catholicism*, foreword by Roberto S. Goizueta (Maryknoll, NY: Orbis Books, 1997), 7–10.

54. Virgilio Elizondo, *Guadalupe, Mother of the New Creation* (Maryknoll, NY: Orbis Books, 1997).

55. Medina, "*Mestizaje*, a Theological Reading of Culture and Faith," 7.

56. Elizondo, *Guadalupe, Mother of the New Creation*, 110. Elizondo discusses the numerous aspects of Our Lady of Guadalupe that intersect with indigenous religious symbols. To him, it is clear that Guadalupe represents the preservation of indigenous peoples' religious wisdom inscribed in the image of Guadalupe. See Virgilio Elizondo, *Mestizaje: The Dialectic of Cultural Birth and the Gospel* (San Antonio, TX: Mexican American Cultural Center, 1978), 121–35.

57. Elizondo, *Guadalupe, Mother of the New Creation*, 66; Chávez Sauceda, "Community, Mestizaje, and Liberation," 197.

58. According to Chávez Sauceda, from the Christian standpoint this spiritual *mestizaje* (mixture) in the language of Guadalupe creates the possibility of an alternative imagery of the Trinity as Mother, Father, and Child. She adds that for Elizondo, this image can potentially overcome present weaknesses in the patriarchal-hierarchical ways of understanding the Trinity (see Chávez Sauceda, "Community, Mestizaje, and Liberation," 197–98).

59. Medina, "*Mestizaje*, a Theological Reading of Culture and Faith," 8.

60. By way of an example, Chávez Sauceda tells us that in her list of titles La Virgen avoids "the names of those blood-thirsty Nahuatl gods who demanded human sacrifice." But here she preserves the Christian-pagan dichotomy for which indigenous religious images, symbols,

and practices were destroyed and eradicated (see Chávez Sauceda, "Community, Mestizaje, and Liberation," 197).

61. Trujillo, "La Virgen de Guadalupe and Her Reconstruction in Chicana Lesbian Desire," 229n1.

62. This is further evidenced in the way Juan Diego is portrayed by the Catholic establishment in Mexico after his canonization by the Vatican in 2002. He is painted with a beard and lighter skin, features that resemble the dominant *mestizo/a* population and cultural ethos; his indigenous features are removed. This is a form of whitening. For a more developed discussion, see Gandy, "La Movilización de la mujer latinoamericana en la lucha contra la opresión globalizada."

63. Yamada, quoted in Gloria Anzaldúa, "Haciendo caras, una entrada: An Introduction," in *Making Face, Making Soul*/Haciendo Caras: *Creative and Critical Perspectives by Women of Color*, ed. Gloria Anzaldúa (San Francisco: Aunt Lute Foundation, 1990), xv.

64. Gloria Anzaldúa, *Borderlands*/La Frontera: *The New Mestiza* (San Francisco: Aunt Lute Books, 1987), 27–30.

65. According to Anzaldúa, in this way the patriarchal structures of the Aztecs-Méxicas split the female self from the female deities. The religious connection of women to the religious symbols was severed, and the oppressive and bloodthirsty Aztecs created a new myth with male images and symbols (see Anzaldúa, *Borderlands*/La Frontera, 27, 32).

66. Anzaldúa de-romanticizes the Aztec social-religious structures criticizing the male centered–patriarchal characteristics such structures gained as the Aztec Empire and civilization were formed. Nevertheless, by imaginatively reconstructing matriarchal societies, she cannot escape idealizing the female elements in indigenous theogony that, in her opinion, preceded the Aztec Empire. Her problematic proposal is evidenced in the way she speaks of such societies: "Matrilineal descent characterized the Toltecs and perhaps early Aztec society. Women possessed property, and were curers as well as priestesses." She claims, "According to the codices, women in former times had the supreme power in Tula [the central Toltec city], and in the beginning of the Aztec dynasty, the royal blood ran through the female line." In fact, "Although the high posts were occupied by men, the terms referred to females, evidence of the exalted role of women before the Aztec nation became centralized" (Anzaldúa, *Borderlands*/La Frontera, 33).

67. As she puts it, the Spaniards "desexed *Guadalupe*, taking *Coatlalopeuh*, the serpent/sexuality, out of her. They completed the split begun by the Nahuas by making *La Virgen de Guadalupe/Virgen María* into chaste virgins and *Tlazolteotl/Coatlicue/la Chingada* into *Putas*,

into the Beauties and the Beasts. They went even further; they made all Indian deities and religious practices the work of the devil" (Anzaldúa, Borderlands/La Frontera, 27–28).

68. Ibid., 30.

69. Paz, "The Labyrinth of Solitude."

70. According to Aigner-Varoz, Anzaldúa adopts generative discourses to unmask the displacement of female voices, sexuality, and subjectivity. She makes the connection between Eve and La Malinche as the original mothers of humanity and of the *mestizo/a* (Mexican) people, respectively, women who have been displaced by androcentric patriarchal division between the sexes. As Aigner-Varoz puts it, "Like Eve, *La Malinche* is intellectually and sexually dominated by man, and is held up as the prostitute that Chicanas will become if they fail to become nuns or mothers. The politics in this binary system repulse Anzaldúa. Castigated for their voices and sexuality, Eve and *La Malinche*, claims Anzaldúa, are scapegoats for the divisions created by the men/cultures themselves, divisions leading to the fall of those men/cultures" (Erika Aigner-Varoz, "Metaphors of a Mestiza Consciousness: Anzaldúa's Borderlands/La Frontera," *MELUS* 25, no. 2, Latino Identities [Summer 2000]: 58).

71. Anzaldúa, *Borderlands*/La Frontera, 34.

72. Malinali Tenepal or La Malinche is becoming a central figure of female empowerment. She is seen as an example of subjectivity after being sold by her father to another tribe, and as survival strategizing amid the white, Spanish, patriarchal, androcentric culture of the Spanish invaders. See Cano Alcalá, "From Chingada to Chingona"; Martha E. Sánchez, "La Malinche at the Intersection."

73. Arturo J. Aldama, *Disrupting Savagism: Intersecting Chicana/o, Mexican Immigrant, and Native American Struggles for Self-Representation* (Durham, NC: Duke University Press, 2001), 128.

74. See Espín, "An Exploration into the Theology of Grace and Sin."

75. Anzaldúa intends to recover the protagonist role of the indigenous people. The indigenous and poor *mestizo/a* masses were the force behind the Mexican revolution, and they constituted the guerrilla armies led by Emiliano Zapata. Their revolutionary force was particularly expressed in their commitment to agrarian reform and redistribution of lands and was later crystallized in the *Plan ski doesde San Luis Potosí* and *Plan de Ayala*.

76. Anzaldúa, *Borderlands*/La Frontera, 30.

77. Ibid.

78. To illustrate, Rigoberta Menchú describes some of the rites of passage and celebrations the people of her native village in Uspantán,

Guatemala, perform. She comments that these are a constant reminder of ancestral worship and religious activities in which people engage secretly, as they are considered pagan by the Catholic and Protestant churches (and even more so, by evangelicals). See Elizabeth Burgos, *Me llamo Rigoberta Menchú y así me nació la conciencia*, 14th ed. (Coyoacán, Mexico: Siglo Veintiuno Editores, 1997), 65–83.

79. Solange Alberro, "La Iglesia como mediador cultural en la Nueva España, siglos XVI-XVII: La recuperación del complejo simbólico del águila y el nopal," in *Entre dos mundos: Fronteras culturales y agentes mediadores*, ed. Ares Queija B. and S. Gruzinski (Seville: El Adalid Seráfrico S.A., 1997), 408.

80. Ibid., 414.

81. Chávez Sauceda, "Community, Mestizaje, and Liberation," 196–97.

82. In his study of *mestizaje* and *mexicanidad* in José Vasconcelos, Octavio Paz, and Carlos Fuentes, Montano Rodríguez raises very important questions as to the Mexican indigenous cultural substratum pervasive in Mexican culture today. He points out that Fuentes whispers that Christianity became the victim of the Aztecs and not the other way around. With their bloody practices and inflexible structures they could not have used a better religion than Christianity, in which it is the death of the innocent and his shedding of blood that brings about salvation. In this way, he argues, the Aztec religion is preserved, adopting images of Christianity without changing its emphasis on the shedding of blood and without changing the religious nucleus of its bloody beliefs. See Rafael Montano Rodríguez, "De raza a cultura: un acercamiento crítico al concepto de mestizaje y mexicanidad en Vaconcelos, Ramos, Paz y Fuentes" (thesis, McGill University [Montreal], 1994), 49–60.

83. Jeanette Rodríguez, *Our Lady of Guadalupe*, 145.

84. Real Bourque, trans., "Nican Mopohua: Apparitions of Our Lady of Guadalupe," ll. 31–32. Available online.

85. The interrogation of *mestizaje* must take place at every level. Sergei Gruzinski, for example, affirms that the Spanish conquest and invasion inaugurated a process of cultural Westernization of the Americas. He writes that, contrary to other versions of Westernization (French, Dutch, English, and so on), in the Spanish experiment the indigenous peoples were made actors as they helped build the basilicas and paint the frescoes inside those basilicas in Mexico. For him, this was a form of *mestizaje* that took place as the indigenous people reproduced culture, but along the way they changed it, participating in the formation of a new cultural *mestizo* expression. I agree with Gruzinski's provocative notion that *mestizaje* can be understood as an expression of the

expansion of the Western-European racialized ethnocultural ethos. And I also agree that the indigenous peoples were not merely passive victims; sometimes they also contributed to the reproduction of Western culture and Christian religion. However, Gruzinski does not take into consideration that the particular changes and incorporation of indigenous elements in building and painting of those basilicas can also be interpreted as expressions of resistance. The presence of indigenous religious and cultural elements in the basilicas and frescoes does not point merely, or mainly, to ways in which the indigenous peoples "wanted" to enrich the Spanish religious architectural expressions. The presence of such elements is not just a way in which the indigenous appropriated the culture and religion of the Spanish. Rather, they are also concrete examples of how the indigenous people subverted the forceful imposition of Spanish culture and religion. In doing so, the indigenous peoples transformed the European expressions of Christianity to include indigenous symbols and elements that were not always compatible with the European version of Christianity. As can be expected, in doing so, indigenous religious practices and cultures underwent significant changes. See Sergei Gruzinski, *The Mestizo Mind: The Intellectual Dynamics of Colonization and Globalization* (New York: Routledge, 2002), 33, 54, 62.

86. Jeanette Rodríguez, *Our Lady of Guadalupe*, 44, 157.

87. Irarrázaval, *Cultura y fe latinoamericanas*, 135, 137, 143, 148.

88. This is equally true for all other endeavors attempting to interpret the manner in which indigenous elements found their way in church murals and architecture and buildings, labeled as American Baroque. This is inadequately understood through the lens of *mestizaje*, because it disallows any analysis of power differential and dynamics at play, and gives room to notions of a peaceful, voluntary, nonviolent view of *mestizaje*. See Morales Benítez, *Memorias del mestizaje*; Gruzinski, *The Mestizo Mind*.

89. Justo L. González, "Latino/a Theology," in *Handbook of U.S. Theologies of Liberation*, ed. Miguel A. De La Torre (St. Louis: Chalice Press, 2004), 217.

90. Although still in its embryonic stage among U.S. Latina/o theology, it has come to my attention that what I am proposing here has already been started by Espín, as he has come in direct conversation with practitioners of the Lukumí religion. See Orlando O. Espín, *Grace and Humanness: Theological Reflections Because of Culture* (Maryknoll, NY: Orbis Books, 2007), chap. 3. See also Michelle A. González, *Afro-Cuban Theology: Religion, Race, Culture, and Identity* (Gainesville: University Press of Florida, 2006).

91. Diego Irarrázaval, "Re-Foundation of Mission—A Latin American Study," *Missiology: An International Review* 25, no. 1 (January 1997). Avaiable on the www.sedos.org website.

92. Raúl Fornet-Betancourt, *Transformación Intercultural de la Filosofía*, Palimpsesto: Derechos Humanos y Desarrollo (Bilbao, Spain: Desclée de Brouwer, 2001), 29.

93. Raúl Fornet-Betancourt, *Filosofía Intercultural* (Mexico: Universidad Pontífica de México A.C., 1994), 20.

94. Fornet-Betancourt, *Filosofía Intercultural*, 10 In the words of Fornet-Betancourt, "The goal of living and sharing together *(convivencia)* must not be confused at any moment with reconciling *(pacificación)* the (conflicting) controversies [caused by] differences, through gathering these [differences] in a superior totality that appropriates and harmonizes them" (20).

95. João Maria André, *Diálogo intercultural, utopia e mestiçagem em tempos de globalização* (Coimbra: Ariadne Editora, 2005), 132.

96. Ibid., 128.

97. Ibid.

98. Ibid., 125.

CONCLUSION

1. Néstor Medina, "The Religious Psychology of *Mestizaje*: Gómez Suárez de Figueroa or Garcilaso de la Vega," *Pastoral Psychology* 57 (September 2008): 123.

2. Ali Rattansi, "Just Framing: Ethnicities and Racisms in a 'Postmodern' Framework," in *Social Postmodernism*, ed. L. Nicholson and S. Seidman (New York: Cambridge University Press, 1995), 254.

3. Marable Manning, "We Need New and Critical Study of Race and Ethnicity," *The Chronicle of Higher Education* 46, no. 25 (February 25, 2000): B4–7.

4. This provocative question was raised by Raúl Fornet-Betancourt at a symposium concerning intercultural philosophical and theological education in June 2006.

5. Morris W. Foster and Richard R. Sharp, "Race, Ethnicity, and Genomics: Social Classifications as Proxies of Biological Heteregeneity," *Genome Research* 12 (2000): 844.

6. "The Proper Study of Mankind," *The Economist (US)* 356, no. 8177 (July 1, 2002): 11.

7. As I see it, challenging racial differences as self-evident results in challenging racialized hierarchies as immutable part of societies and social and economic life. I agree with Paul Gilroy, who rejects the idea

that the present order of racialized and hierarchized differences "is some-how necessary to the very stability of our conflicted world." Instead, he suggests that the reification of race must be challenged (see Paul Gilroy, *Postcolonial Melancholia* [New York: Columbia University Press, 2005], 151). Moreover, challenging the reification of race in turn requires that we criticize even our notions of whiteness and of white people as a homogeneous group. Rather, we need to understand it as part of specific webs of discourse designed for domination, which has a knowable history, and with profound social and political implications (see John Hartigan, Jr., "Establishing the Fact of Whiteness," *American Anthropologist* 99, no. 3 [September 1997]: 495–505).

. 8. Arif Dirlik, "Whither History? Encounters with Historicism, Postmodernism, Postcolonialism," *Futures: The Journal of Policy, Planning and Futures Studies* 34, no. 1 (2002): 79.

9. Boaventura de Sousa Santos, "The Future of the World Social Forum: The Work of Translation," *Development* 48, no. 2 (2005): 15–22.

10. Orlando Espín has already hinted at new avenues for rethinking issues of inculturation in relation to tradition (see Orlando O. Espín, "Toward the Construction of an Intercultural Theology of Tradition," *Journal of Hispanic/Latino Theology* 9, no. 3 (February 2002): 40.

11. James Cone, "Whose Earth Is It Anyway?" *Cross Current* 50, no. 1–2 (Spring/Summer 2000): 41.

12. Ibid., 42.

Index